Y0-BZF-770

PRAIRIE CITY

PRAIRIE CITY

THE STORY OF AN AMERICAN COMMUNITY

by ANGIE DEBO

COUNCIL OAK BOOKS, LTD.
TULSA, OKLAHOMA

Originally published by Alfred A. Knopf, Inc., 1944
Reprinted by Gordian Press, Inc. 1969
Reprinted by Council Oak Books, Ltd., 1985
By arrangement with Angie Debo

Manufactured in the U.S.A.

ISBN 0-933031-00-9
ISBN 0-933031-01-7 (pbk.)

Library of Congress Catalog Card Number 85-071340

" Here, in this story of a small Oklahoma
community, is America in microcosm. Here
are the hopes, the fears, the dreams for the
future, the development of the civic, social
and economic consciousness of a town . . . "

Alfred A. Knopf
in awarding the 1944
Knopf Fellowship in History
to Angie Debo for Prairie City

TO EDWARD EVERETT DALE

who has taught the children of pioneers
to love the story of their origins

CONTENTS

PREFACE TO THE FIRST EDITION

"EV'RYTHING that iver happened annywhere has happened at Mar-rshall, Oklahoma," says Big Jim Murphy, who still owns the farm he homesteaded on Horse Creek. The keen-witted Irishman has discovered a profound truth.

Fifty-four years ago this region was a virgin prairie. Sturdy old-timers are still living on farms that they brought under the plow by their own hands; and churches and lodges have charter members among their active leaders. The whole epic sweep of American history is compressed into the lifetime of these pioneers. They know from their own experience the throes of settlement at Jamestown; the first harvest, the church, the school of the Pilgrim Fathers; the constitution-making of the Founders of the Republic; the promotion and the railroad-building in the era of Western settlement; oil, and the industrialism of the modern age; and the repercussions of world-shattering events. The one who can understand and interpret their annals knows the history of the United States.

But I have not written the chronicle of Big Jim's home town — and my home town — of Marshall. I have chosen rather to write of a typical, rather than an actual, community, a composite of numerous Oklahoma settlements, of which some are still in existence, and others have long been ghost towns. My "county seat" also is a composite of several county seats in this part of Oklahoma. Frankly, I have used this device because it enabled me to write with greater freedom. It is as essentially true historically; for it is not the actual little town that matters, but its universal significance.

My chronology is exact, and in most cases is that of my own home town; I used these actual dates in order that the historian might see their connection with general movements. My statistics are exact, and are based on much dry research: for rural areas I have used selected townships in the wheat-growing sections of Oklahoma; for the town I have as a matter of convenience used my own town. The events are actual events; even the conversations are recorded or remembered conversations. They all occurred in this part of Oklahoma except that I was not able to resist my mother's Western Kansas story of the homesteader's talking pony, and that my interpretation of a typical bank failure is largely based on my observations in West Texas, where I was living at the time of the Great Depression.

Of my Prairie City inhabitants only Roy Zoellner is a real character; I included his story as a personal tribute to the Marshall boy who died for the way of life of all American communities. Perhaps I should say that "Surprise" and "Gilbert" also are actual characters, the last of those noble horses that carried their riders into the Strip; I do not know that they were ever ridden in a parade, but when they died, "Surprise" in 1911, "Gilbert" at the age of thirty-two in 1916, the home town newspaper carried their obituaries.

All persons mentioned outside the Prairie City community — Dennis Flynn, Roy V. Cashion, J. Y. Callahan — are historic figures; I have taken no liberties with them. And all the surrounding towns and cities mentioned in the text are actual places. The Lions' *Service News* is a literal account of my own town's contribution to the present war effort.

I have carried on exacting research in county records, newspaper files, census statistics, and other documents. More of my history I have found on the headstones of remote country cemeteries. I have interviewed many pioneers, who assisted me with everything they had in family papers and personal reminiscences. I wish I could thank them all. Many of them will recognize their stories: the widow and the daughter of Sylvan Rice, whose experiences I used in my account of the founding of Prairie City; Billy Fox, buffalo hunter, cow puncher, thrifty homesteader, and Mrs. Fox, gracious lady of the frontier, whose personalities have colored my narrative; Mr. and Mrs. George Beeby, who have built so solidly into community institutions; Mr. Albert H. Ellis, builder of government, and Mrs. Ellis, who has presided over the home, whether covered wagon, dug-out, or comfortable farmstead, for sixty years; and many others. And my father and mother were always at hand to answer troublesome questions in forgotten farming and pioneering techniques.

I am deeply indebted to Dr. Peter Nelson, Head of the Depart-

ment of Agricultural Economics of the Oklahoma Agricultural and
Mechanical College, who placed his scholarly resources at my dis-
posal and was kind enough to read and criticize the manuscript. I
am grateful to Mr. Roy E. Heffner of Norman, Oklahoma for his
painstaking care in the reproduction of faded photographs. Most of
all, I wish to thank Mr. Knopf for the Fellowship Award, without
which the book would not have been written.

I hope the people of my community, the finest people I have ever
known, will not be disappointed in this book they have helped me
write.

ANGIE DEBO

Marshall, Oklahoma
October 12, 1943

PREFACE TO THE SECOND EDITION

IT IS A FRUSTRATING experience to an author when his book goes out of print. It is therefore highly gratifying to me that the Gordian Press is bringing out a new printing of *Prairie City*. Incidentally this gives me the opportunity to correct two errors in the original edition.

On page 20, although I expressed my uncertainty in a footnote, I stated that the townships laid out by the territorial governor in 1890 served as election precincts, with his appointed township boards conducting the election. The governor's proclamation of July 23 that year calling this first election is now available in the office of the secretary of state. This shows that the election precincts were not conterminous with the townships, and that the election officials were distinct from the township boards. I still believe that these provisional township boards were largely inactive, except that they functioned as the local relief boards.

On page 89 my misdating of the Free Homes Act on June 17 instead of May 17 is less excusable. I knew as well as any historian that I should consult the original text of the law, but my mind was on the essential fidelity of my Prairie Citians' reactions. An early-day homesteader I knew, who had served as an officer of a Free Homes organization, became in his later years a local historian of some note and wrote a book dating the enactment on the anniversary of Bunker Hill, "another great battle for human freedom." This was so entirely typical of the tendency to make a moral issue out of a profit motive that I gave his sentiments to one of my Prairie Citians. But it could not have been said at the time; it requires the passage of years on old-timers' memories to blur the sequence of events and run dates together. Thus I made one of the most embarrassing errors I ever made in my writing. Getting the date a month off would not have been so bad if I had not fixed it permanently by linking it with Bunker Hill.

I am still convinced that the history of this one small community is the history of the United States in microcosm. This concept must have been old in the fourteenth century when Chaucer wrote. "The proverb saith that many small maken a great." In 1950 Samuel Eliot Morison said in his presidential address to the American Historical Association, "The national field teaches you what to look for in local history; whilst intensive cultivation of grass-roots... teaches you things that you cannot see in the broad national view."

Just at present it is fashionable to refer to contemporary America as "a sick society," and to characterize any study of rural life as a "nostalgic" account of a vanished era of idyllic simplicity. Prairie City knows better. The past was not idyllic, but it was no more "sick" than is the present. It was dynamic, subject to selfishness and greed and violence, but capable of creative achievement, the same spirit that forged a community, far from perfect but a living organism, out of Jamestown or Plymouth—or Prairie City. And not in large abstractions, but in the triumphs and tragedies, the successes and failures of people meeting their problems together—whether in rural village with its continuity of births and deaths and adjustment to change, in new suburb with its emerging group solidarity, even in the closely-knit loyalties of the deprived children of Claude Brown's Harlem—one can see American history unfolding.

It would require another book the size of this one to record the changes in my Prairie City during the last quarter century. As the farms have increased in size and mechanization some of the towns that were its prototype have all but vanished; others have become more completely attuned to the rhythm of seedtime and harvest, the agricultural villages envisioned in my concluding paragraph. Still others have linked themselves to the present industrial development: many of their people commute to outside jobs, but still join in local civic activities; or, as in my own town, the leaders organize in a conscious effort to bring in small industries to supplement the products of the surrounding fields. Thus in its past, its present, and its future Prairie City is an integral part of the larger society. Big Jim's characterization still stands.

ANGIE DEBO

Marshall, Oklahoma
June 12, 1969

INTRODUCTION

ANGIE DEBO:
SEEKER AFTER TRUTH

$\mathbb{A}$NGIE DEBO's *Prairie City* is an appropriate first volume for Council Oak Books. A work halfway between history and fiction, *Prairie City* is the one great book about Oklahoma's settlement. Published initially by Alfred Knopf in 1944, it is a poetic and truthful account of an American community. The author, herself a pioneer, brings together real events in a fictional composite town she has called Prairie City. The result is a widely acclaimed classic which balances the scholar's hard facts with the humanity of a loving memoir.

Angie Debo is herself a child of Prairie City or rather Marshall, Oklahoma, upon which much of the book is based. She is one of those rare souls whose life encompasses much of what she has written about.[1] In her ninety-sixth year she continues to live in Marshall not far from the homestead her parents settled. Born in Beattie, Kansas in 1890, young Angie came to Oklahoma Territory at the age of nine in her parents' covered wagon. In the only identifiable personal note she allows herself in *Prairie City*, she vividly recalls the wagon, the tick mattress, and sleeping alongside the road.

Pioneer life was not always so idyllic. Once settled in the newly opened Oklahoma Territory, Angie attended the early grades of school, waited not so patiently until she could get a teaching certificate at age sixteen, went out to instruct in the rural schools, returned as a young woman to Marshall to attend high school when one was established, and graduated at last at twenty-three years of age. Later she would earn a bachelor's degree from the University of Oklahoma (1918), a master's degree from the University of Chicago (1924), and a doctorate in history from Oklahoma (1933).

Angie Debo's varied career includes high school and university teaching, museum and library curatorship, pastoring a Methodist church, and supervising an Oklahoma WPA historical project. But

Angie Debo is known primarily as a writer. She is Oklahoma's most distinguished historian, having won the John H. Dunning Prize of the American Historical Society for her book *The Rise and Fall of the Choctaw Republic* (1933) and the Alfred A. Knopf Fellowship in History for *Prairie City* (1944). In the more than ninety years since Angie Debo became an Oklahoman she has earned international acclaim.

Dr. Debo is an uncompromising searcher who has tirelessly recorded the frontier experience. In response to a question about her goals and ambitions as a writer, she once suggested, "I suppose I have only one: to discover the truth and publish it." But she modestly added, "When I find all the truth on one side, I have the same obligation to become involved as any other citizen." Dr. Debo has not been an ivory tower scholar. She has selflessly acted to preserve the lands and rights of the Native American whose plight she saw first hand.

Thirteen books and more than a hundred articles list Angie Debo as author or editor.[2] These volumes, written over a period of more than half a century, range from diplomatic history to oral history and biography. In between, Dr. Debo's work includes such diverse tasks as editorship of the Oklahoma volume in the American Guide Series and field work for the Indian Rights Association. Her two tribal histories remain the definitive works on the Choctaws and the Creeks.

And Still the Waters Run is Angie Debo's most important and controversial history. Almost fifty years ago this hard-hitting and meticulously documented study about the theft of Indian lands was scheduled for publication by the University of Oklahoma Press, but Debo withdrew it. Facts she had uncovered about the involvement of prominent Oklahomans caused her to fear that the legislature would dissolve the press if it brought out the book. The press director later resigned and published it as his first book as director of the Princeton University Press. *And Still the Waters Run* remains the premier work about exploitation of Indian lands and is still cited by courts of law as the definitive record of that tragic episode in American history.

Prairie City is not a traditional book of history such as *And Still the Waters Run*. Rather, it is a composite story in which the author has drawn together a great many accurate historical happenings into a synthesis designed to capture the spirit of a time and a place. For while there is no Prairie City there were many Prairie Cities in the settlement of the American west.

Prairie City is as accurate a book as any historian could write; it is also as touching a story as any novelist could pen. Some of it — the names, the places — are creations of Angie Debo's imagination, but most of it — the events, the motivations — are products of Angie Debo's patient research and recollection. Many critics believe this book to be Debo's finest and most enduring achievement.

Prairie City was widely and enthusiastically reviewed when it first appeared.[3] It was a book in which others saw mirrored historical lessons for the modern world. Its publication just as the Second World War was coming to an end coincided with a growing concern for the role of local communities in the creation of post-war economic and social life. Willard Hurst, a young Navy lawyer who would become the most influential legal historian of his generation, saw the *Prairie City* frontier experience as "witness to the tough vitality of community life" and he optimistically suggested that with the "releasing (of) local energies" the nation might be on "the threshold of a new and more fruitful relation of the institution of social control to the life of the people."

Oklahomans saw *Prairie City* as a reaffirmation of the family, religion, and small town virtues, as the model of community. *Prairie City* was generally seen as a study with "implications of tremendous importance on the future of the small town." A reviewer in Fort Worth thought it "as revealing and bitingly true a picture of a small American Community as is Sinclair Lewis' *Main Street*."

Mari Sandoz wrote an enthusiastic review for the *New York Times*. Sandoz affectionately compared Angie Debo to the Indian tribal historians, quoting the Sioux who believed, "A people without history is like the wind on the buffalo grass." *Prairie City*, Sandoz argued, "throws a searching light upon the American community and, through it, upon the small community everywhere." It was, she believed, "a society comparatively transparent," in which "the student can consider modern man." To Mari Sandoz the frontier lessons which could be learned from *Prairie City* included the problems of economic colonial status, the rise of tenancy, the crisis of inadequate schools and taxes, and the exploitation of an unprotected minority.

Debo had written "an historic Middletown," according to Joseph Brandt in the *Chicago Sun*. *Prairie City* recreated "the pattern of village life as it has been lived in our country." "In the time capsule of Oklahoma," Brandt concluded, "Miss Debo has been able to instill the story of pioneer America." Historians who reviewed the book were particularly impressed with the ambition of the undertaking. To them *Prairie City* was "representative enough to serve as a microcosmic recapitulation of American social history."

Most reviewers in Oklahoma, Texas and Kansas saw the book as a personal testimonial to the dignity and achievement of the region's pioneers. The *Tulsa World* called Debo's work full of "honest affection for the people and places," declaring that the author was "no sobby sentimentalist," but rather a "social historian" who "records an important contribution to the history of the American Spirit at work." The *Dallas News* concluded in a similar tone, "The book will be welcome on the shelf of any family which wants to know itself and its country. Through *Prairie City*, Angie Debo (who is called a child of pioneers) is teaching other children of pioneers to love the story of their origins."

Indeed, *Prairie City* is more than history, it is a creative work of the imagination meticulously checked against reams of documents and enlivened by thousands of remembered experiences. In single sentences Debo condenses the most complex of motivations and summarizes epic movements. And through all of this she keeps before our eyes great questions and persistent themes — conquest, challenge, opportunity, individual worth, collective responsibility, generosity, greed, man's resilience, man's vanity, nature's bounty and nature's cruelty. We see settlers in sod houses doing without food, saving their pennies so that the traveling photographer can record their story; we feel the isolation of the immigrant family as they bury a young child beside newly plowed rows; we are present when the first reed organ arrives, when the whole town sings together in celebration, and when the young dance till dawn; we taste the fresh oysters brought in on ice for the picnic; we feel shock when the Lockwoods are murdered; we sense the irony of the service conducted in German so the parents can understand the funeral for their son who enlisted to fight the Kaiser; we share the hope of riches in the oil fields; we sense the fight against bitterness of the unemployed college graduate who declares that the copy book maxims are lies; and we ache with the anxious mother compulsively baking her son's favorite cookies all night after Pearl Harbor.

Although the book ends with the Second World War, *Prairie City* has a continued relevancy which makes this Council Oak reprint even more welcome. At a time when the prairie economy is in the doldrums and high-tech industry is bypassing the wheat belt for the sunbelt silicon centers, *Prairie City* should remind us of why the pragmatic pioneers valued education so greatly. Dr. Debo describes a timeless phenomenon in the impact of education among the young who "found in their tattered books a mystic summons to a realm beyond the boundaries of time and space, and the urge for further schooling became with them a consuming flame."

There is a tragically contemporaneous note when Debo contrasts the stagnation of Prairie City during the depression era with the vitality of those pioneer days. "The community," she notes, "was full of unattached young people fretting their lives away because society had no use for their strength and industry." With regret, rather than bitterness, she recalls, "even college graduates came back home to enforced idleness and dependence. These young people made the sinister discovery that superior skills were disqualifications, that executives were envious and afraid of their attainments."

Prairie City went into print on the heels of the "Dust Bowl" and the greatest exit of citizens the state had ever known. This republication of *Prairie City* comes in the 1980s on the heels of a second great run, in the midst of a great migration into the state. The climate, economic opportunity, and a chance to build a new life draw the 1980s pioneers as they did the immigrants of a century before. And these new urban pioneers are facing many of the same exhilarations and the same disappointments as their pioneer ancestors. There has always been a spirit of challenge and a sense of destiny among those who venture beyond established communities. *Prairie City* appears again at a time when a need for an understanding of the state's historical spirit has never been greater. Angie Debo touches upon the great and enduring themes of human nature, the place of emerging towns, the hopes and dreams of the searchers after opportunity, after wealth, after peace and tranquility, and, in her own case, searchers after truth.

Council Oak Books does the reader a great service in publishing this third printing of *Prairie City*. The book remains in print because it speaks not only of the Oklahoma settlement experience but as Dr. Debo concludes of "the whole sweep of American history [as] compressed in the lifetime of these pioneers." In closing the story of her friends and neighbors Debo quotes Plutarch who wrote: "As for me I live in a small town where I am willing to continue, lest it grow smaller." In the forty years since Alfred Knopf published *Prairie City*, while Angie Debo has remained a citizen of her beloved Marshall, her writings have gone forth to the world. For as she notes of her community in the preface to *Prairie City*, "The one who can understand and interpret their annals knows the history of the United States." And it should be added, knows the human soul, as well.

Tulsa, Oklahoma   RENNARD STRICKLAND
April 3, 1985   *John W. Schleppey Research Professor*
of Law and History,
the University of Tulsa

NOTES

1. Angie Debo's brief biographical statement is found in "Angie Debo: A Biographical Sketch by Herself" which is included along with an extensive listing of her publications in Patrick L. McLaughlin and Steven K. Gragert, *Angie Debo: A Biographical Sketch and a Bibliography of Her Published Works* (Stillwater: Oklahoma State University, Department of History and Edmon Low Library, 1980). Connie Cronley has written three marvelous biographical tributes to Angie Debo. These are: "First Lady of Oklahoma History," *Oklahoma Today*, (Spring 1982), p. 52–53; "Angie Debo: Trail Blazer and Truth Teller," *Tulsa Magazine*, (April 1978), p. 33; "Miss Floy's Disciplinarian," *Oklahoma Monthly Magazine*, (April 1977), p. 40–42.

2. Debo's thirteen books are:
    The Rise and Fall of the Choctaw Republic. The Civilization of the American Indian, vol. 6. Norman: University of Oklahoma Press, 1934; second ed., Norman: University of Oklahoma Press, 1961.
    The Road to Disappearance. The Civilization of the American Indian, vol. 22. Norman: University of Oklahoma Press, 1934.
    And Still the Waters Run. Princeton: Princeton University Press, 1940; reprint ed., New York: Gordian Press, 1966; reprint ed., Princeton: Princeton University Press, 1972; reprint ed., Norman: University of Oklahoma Press, 1984.

Tulsa: From Creek Town to Oil Capital. Norman: University of Oklahoma Press, 1943.

Prairie City, the Story of an American Community. New York: A.A. Knopf, 1944; reprint ed., New York: Gordian Press, 1969; reprint ed., Tulsa: Council Oak Books, 1985.

Oklahoma, Foot-loose and Fancy-free. Norman: University of Oklahoma Press, 1949.

The Five Civilized Tribes of Oklahoma; Report on Social and Economic Conditions. Philadelphia: Indian Rights Association, 1959.

A History of the Indians of the United States. The Civilization of the American Indian, vol. 106. Norman: University of Oklahoma Press, 1970.

Geronimo: The Man, His Time, His Place. The Civilization of the American Indian, vol. 142. Norman: University of Oklahoma Press, 1976.

Writer's Program. Oklahoma. *Oklahoma; a Guide to the Sooner State.* American Guide Series. Compiled by Workers of the Writers' Program of the Work Projects Administration in the State of Oklahoma. Edited by Angie Debo and John M. Oskison. Sponsored by the University of Oklahoma. Norman: University of Oklahoma Press, 1941; second ed., Norman: University of Oklahoma Press, 1945; reprint ed., Norman: University of Oklahoma Press, 1947.

Nelson, Oliver. *The Cowman's Southwest; being the reminiscences of Oliver Nelson, Freighter, Camp Cook, Cowboy, Frontiersman in Kansas, Indian Territory, Texas, and Oklahoma, 1878–1893. The Western Frontiersmen,* vol. 4. Edited by Angie Debo. Glendale, Calif.: A.H. Clark Co., 1953.

Cushman, Horatio B. *History of the Choctaw, Chickasaw, and Natchez Indians.* Edited by Angie Debo. Stillwater, Okla.: Redlands Press, 1962.

Rippy, James Fred and Debo, Angie. *The Historical Background of the American Policy of Isolation.* Smith College, Studies in History, vol. 9, Nos. 3–4, (April–July 1924), pp. 71–165. Northampton, Mass.: Department of History of Smith College, 1924.

3. Reviews cited here include:
Willard Hurst, "The Uses of Law in Four 'Colonial' States of the American Union," *Wisconsin Law Review,* 1945, pp. 579–592.

Hugh Cowdin, "Oklahoma Has Telescoped Time in Settling the Last Frontier," *Fort Worth Star Telegram,* June 4, 1944.

Mari Sandoz, "The Oklahoma Story," *The New York Times Book Review,* May 21, 1944, pp. 3, 26. Compare with the equally favorable Stanley Walker, "Out on the Plains of Oklahoma," *New York Herald Tribune,* May 21, 1944.

Joseph Brandt, "The Waxing and Waning of an Oklahoma Small Town," *The Chicago Sun,* May 3, 1944.

"Review of Books," *Pacific Historical Review,* XIV, No. 1 (March 1945), pp. 11–12.

"Prairie City," *Wichita Eagle,* May 28, 1944; Lewis Gannett, "Books and Things," Gannett News Service, May 23, 1944.

Alice M. Allen, "Angie Debo Traces History of an Oklahoma Community," *Tulsa Daily World,* June 18, 1944.

Mrs. T.V. Reeves, "Prairie City Seen," *Dallas News,* June 11, 1944.

I
STAKING THE CLAIM

A FEW seconds past noon of April 22, 1889 two riders drew rein and looked upon a scene that telescoped nine generations of American frontier settlement into one flashing moment.

The "Oklahoma Lands" lay before them, a level plain pitted with the wallows of the vanished buffalo and broken in the distance by irregular green lines of timber that marked the courses of the streams. Across the grassy swell of the prairie scattered horsemen were racing, each striving to find in the unknown waste ahead one hundred and sixty acres of rich land, which before the sun should set that night would be his home.

"I'm going to stop here," said Arthur Goodwin, the younger of the two men, to his companion.

"Don't you suppose we'd better try for bottom land?" asked Frank Colby, his father-in-law.

Goodwin looked across the green sweep of the prairie. The figures of the other riders were already merging into the distance; their shouts and the sound of galloping hoofs came back faintly on the spring air. The land lay once more in empty solitude. The new grass was bright with flowers under the April sun.

"This claim is good enough for me," he said dismounting. "I'm going to drive my stake right here."

Colby followed his example and staked the adjoining claim. Thus the town of Prairie "City" was born.

II
THE LITTLE STORE IN THE WILDERNESS

Early in May Arthur Goodwin looked again upon the now familiar contours of plain and winding streams. This time he brought his wife and little daughter, and two neighbor men had come along to try their fortunes in the new land; his family rode in a surrey and two covered wagons followed with clothing, bedding, and household furniture. Colby and his wife with their goods followed close behind.

From Caldwell on the Kansas line the two families had come sixty miles across the immense pastures of the "Cherokee Strip" — at that time leased by the Indians to cattlemen — following a dim trail from ranch to ranch, passing great herds of longhorns, spending the night in a lonely cow camp.

As they came through the last gate of the Circle Ranch, Goodwin pointed to the vacant prairie.

"Right there," he cried. "Right there on that rise we will build our house." He tried to hold his voice steady, but it broke into exultation with the question, "How do you like our new home?"

"Oh, Arthur, it looks so bleak! Do you suppose trees will ever grow there? And will we ever have any neighbors?"

But the child had sprung from the surrey, and ran to pick a handful of the unfamiliar flowers.

That night they made their camp on the nearest creek, half a mile beyond the surveyor's corner stone that marked the boundary of their claim. Here they lived while the two men who had come with them dug a well at the place Colby had chosen as his building site. A dug-out was hastily constructed — a crude dwelling, partly underground, partly walled up with sod, with an earthen floor and a roof of overlapping sod. Here the two families lived and cooked and boarded their helpers, but the Goodwins observed the provisions of the homestead law by sleeping in a tent on their side of the line. Colby's claim was a fractional strip one hundred rods wide lying along the border, while Goodwin's hundred and sixty acres joined it on the south.

Goodwin had been a merchant before he left the old home in Iowa, and he had come to the new country with the intention of establishing a crossroads store. He returned almost immediately to Caldwell for a load of lumber, and began to erect a building on the corner of his claim — a long, low, narrow structure with the inevitable false front. The work went slowly. The hauling was a serious problem. The Santa Fe Railroad had built a north-south line across the "Oklahoma Lands" before the Opening, but the nearest station — Orlando — lay fifteen miles to the east across a trackless jungle of black-jacks, twisting streams, and sandy hills. It was easier to take the two days' journey to Kansas across the great reaches of ranch country that comprised the Strip.

As they worked, the grass grew taller around their tiny island of settlement. The wind moved it in majestic waves or stirred it into whirlpools, the same wind that made the canvas of their tent flap and crack. They went to sleep to this mighty rhythm of wind and grass, and the lonesome howl of the coyote; they woke to the booming and cackling of the prairie chickens and the clear song of the meadow larks. Once a deer came fleeting by, but it was swallowed in the green waves of prairie before a man could grasp a gun.

The "Oklahoma Lands" lay almost idle that first summer. Some of the men who had staked claims that wild day of the "Run" never returned to make proof of settlement. Others had plowed a few furrows to fulfill the legal requirement of "improvements" and returned to civilization to grow a crop, accumulate a little capital, and prepare to remove their families. But there was a constant movement of travelers up and down the trail.

Men rode down on horseback, belated homeseekers who came in search of land that had not been taken in the Run, or had been abandoned by the original claimant. There were others in covered wagons, who came to dig a well, build a crude shelter, possibly to plant a few turnips on the sod, to make ready for their families. And as the summer wore on, an increasing number brought their women and children and household goods in their covered wagons, possibly a crate of chickens, a dog, and a trailing cow.

All stopped at "Goodwin's Corner," where they heard the sound of hammering and caught the shine of new lumber in the waste of grass. They were always welcome to camp overnight in the yard, to water their tired horses at the well, to join the family in an evening of neighborly visiting. The men exchanged names and claim locations ("I staked the Northwest Quarter of Section 14," and "Mine is the Northeast Quarter of Section 20"), and compared notes on farming practices in the widely separated states from which they came. The women were especially welcome. Mrs. Goodwin and "Mother" Colby exclaimed over the babies and took them in their arms. The little Goodwin girl led the children to the playhouse she had hollowed nestlike in the tall grass; and the air was filled with shrill shouts as these youngest of Oklahomans on imaginary steeds reenacted the exploits of their fathers in the Run.

By midsummer the store building was ready for occupancy. A small stock of groceries, dry goods, and hardware was hauled over a new trail from Orlando, and placed on the shelves. The first sale was made July 25. Even to the present day Arthur Goodwin keeps the record of this transaction. He decided on *Prairie City* as the name of his little station in the wilderness — the "Prairie" eloquent of his own love for the clean, wild land he had settled, the "City" expressing the boundless optimism of the frontier.

In his Iowa newspaper — strange loyalty of pioneers to the old state — Goodwin read that at Guthrie, a station southeast on the railroad, a tented town had sprung up like magic the day of the Run, and that farther south Oklahoma "City" was rising through the same feverish promotion. He was only remotely interested; he did not trouble even to subscribe to one of the ambitious newspapers of these bustling settlements. He had chosen to own a prairie farm, to run a country store. The "City" would come later. He put up hitching racks along the side and front of his building, and waited for more families to settle on their claims.

As soon as the store was completed, the men began to build a substantial house on Colby's claim. By fall the two families were installed there in comfortable quarters, though the Goodwins fulfilled residence requirements by sleeping in the back part of their store. The new dwelling loomed up strangely in that wilderness of grass, through which trails were beginning to branch off to the lonely dug-outs in the creek banks or the one-room "soddies" on the prairie where the homesteaders were now establishing their families.

Everybody who came to the store talked about the height and

richness of the blue-stem grass. By fall after it had gone to seed it covered the whole country in a dense reddish-brown blanket. In the bottoms along the creeks it hid all but the tops of the covered wagons, and settlers amused themselves by braiding the tasseled heads above the backs of their horses along the trail. People began to plow fireguards around their claims, to burn off the area around their crude dwellings. Occasionally a prairie fire raced across the country, and the air was filled with smoke, and the night sky glowed with flame. Many stories were told of hairbreadth escapes, but everybody understood the technique of back-firing, and no lives were lost.

By the spring of 1890 only sections 16 and 36 in the six-mile-square surveyor's township stood vacant; this land had been withheld from settlement to be used as an endowment for education. Every other "quarter" was occupied by a homesteader; the Federal census of that year gave a population of 454. Most of the settlers were young married people with small children, but a considerable number of young unmarried men — even a few young unmarried women — maintained an ephemeral residence by "batching" at intervals on their claims. There were a few more mature couples with grown or almost grown families (whose daughters were in great demand by the bachelor homesteaders and the cowboys of the Cherokee Strip), but no old people. Most of the mature men were Union veterans of the Civil War. These "Old Soldiers" were allowed to deduct the term of their military service from the five years' residence required of other homesteaders to obtain patent to their claims.

The community now had a postoffice, railed off in one corner of the store. It was established March 1, 1890. The Washington officials refused to recognize the future of the settlement, hence it received the official name of "Prairie." It might have comforted the pioneer merchant if he had known that for many years the builders of Oklahoma "City" were to suffer the same grievance. Mail was directed to "Prairie, Indian Territory," for the "Oklahoma Lands" still formed only a small patch of white settlement in the center of the Indian country.

The homesteaders soon had daily mail service from alternate directions. Another railroad — the Rock Island — was building from Kansas to Texas along the great cattle thoroughfare even then famous in song and story as the Chisholm Trail; and it established

a station named "Hennessey" twenty miles to the southwest. The
sixteen-year-old son of a homesteader made the drive one day from
Hennessey to Orlando, the next from Orlando to Hennessey, stopping to deliver the mail at Goodwin's Corner and changing horses
at his father's claim.

Everybody came to "the Corner" for mail and groceries. Children came riding bare-back, sliding off at the hitching post to do
their parents' errands, and pulling themselves back in place, climbing with bare toes up the legs of their mount. Men and women
came in farm wagons, or even walked while their underfed, tired
horses grazed at home on the lariat after a day of breaking the
tough sod. A few even drove oxen. And trim cow ponies with their
reins dangling stood at the hitching rack, as the line riders of the
Circle Ranch came to buy flour and coffee and beans and slabs of
bacon. The settlers eyed these slim young men of the teetering gait
and dragging spurs and gun-at-hip with interest and admiration.
Every half-grown boy aspired to imitate them — affecting a broad-
brimmed hat and riding with a rope coiled at his saddle horn. But
the most interesting customers of the frontier store were bands
of Indians — Cheyennes from the west, Poncas from the east who
rode across the "Oklahoma Lands" to visit each other. Several hundred strong, they formed a mile-long caravan, a few riding in covered wagons, the rest jogging along on their tough little many-
colored ponies, the women hunched over, babies on back, the men
erect and — somehow — fluttering. Whenever they appeared, they
were greeted by "Howdy, John" and other guttural grunts from
the settlers, but they looked straight ahead and disdained to
answer.

One night the Daltons stopped. They came riding swiftly from
the scene of their bank robberies and train hold-ups in the region
to the northeast, to visit their mother who lived on an Oklahoma
claim thirty miles to the southwest. They woke the merchant and
asked him to open the store. Quickly and courteously they made
their purchases, paid their bill, apologized for their intrusion, and
vanished into the night. Nobody in the settlement feared outlaws
— the universal poverty furnished a sure protection — but the news
of their visit spread through the countryside.

The store was a clearing house of neighborhood gossip. The talk
was of the dance on the earthen floor of John Clark's new soddy,
of the preaching at Joe Scott's dug-out, of the charivari when the

bachelor "on the Northwest Quarter of Section 35" married Fred Peters' girl ("but they wasn't married soon enough"), of the serious illness of the little O'Hagan boy.

There was no physician in the community. People depended mainly on home remedies and an uncritical use of the patent nostrums Goodwin carried in stock. In cases of childbirth and other emergencies they sent a neighbor boy on horseback to call a doctor who lived with a Negro wife on a claim ten miles south. Neighbors nursed the sick and buried the dead. Coffins were home-made of material purchased at the store, a pine box covered with black velvet and lined with a padding of cotton and muslin and an edging of lace. The hitchracks were deserted during a funeral; the whole countryside gathered in sympathy at the home of the bereaved, where the body was laid away in a grave on the claim, with a few songs and a prayer led by one of the neighbors.

Every claim had a small acreage planted that second spring. A special kind of plow called a "Grasshopper" was a favorite for breaking the land; in place of a mold-board it had curved rods, which turned the sod over in strips as rich and smooth as red ribbons. While the men plowed, the women thrust in hills of corn with a hand planter, a spade, or a home-made wooden spud. And everybody planted a few acres to kaffir corn or cane, and sowed a patch of turnips.

The season was not as favorable as it had been the year of the Run, when the rich grass grew so exuberantly. Drought and hot winds damaged the corn crop. The kaffir, however, grew tall and rank — "like timber," said the settlers. ("The Lord must have made that crop to help poor folks in a new country.") Potatoes planted on the sod were the size of marbles, but the turnips reached an enormous size and sweetness. Some of the cane was made into sorghum, and a few settlers raised peanuts.

Most of the homesteaders had a cow or two, which they kept on lariat, and a few chickens. Many ran out of flour and had no money to buy more; they substituted turnips and clabber, or turnip kraut and boiled kaffir corn, or they ground the kaffir in their coffee mill and used the coarse flour to make pancakes. Fortunately game was plentiful: rabbits and prairie chickens were easily shot if one could procure the ammunition, there were a few wild turkeys in the timber, and some hunters were lucky enough to kill deer or antelope. The women gathered wild plums and grapes along the creeks, and some even experimented with pies of sheep sorrel or redbud blossoms.

Some men obtained a little money by working for wages in the surrounding states, leaving their families to hold the claim; others carried on an illegal trade — against Federal laws protecting the game of the Indian country — shipping prairie chickens from the railroad towns to outside cities; still others camped out in the Cherokee Strip gathering up the bones of cattle that had died in the terrible winter of 1884–85, hauling them to the railroad to be shipped east and used in sugar refining. Most of this money went into the purchase of meagre necessities at Goodwin's store. The pioneer merchant supplemented this cash by a judicious extension of credit; in a few cases he actually loaned five dollars or ten dollars to a customer who had to meet some obligation. Some of these bills were never paid, but in general people lived too strait and hard a life to be careless about their debts. Once Mr. Goodwin caught a woman stealing some groceries. When accused, she paled and trembled. Then she spoke defiantly,

"Yes, I stold. My childern hain't got a thing to eat but boiled kaffir. If you don't want me to steal, you'd better watch me, for I'm agoin' to steal every time I git a chance."

The kind-hearted merchant loaded her arms with groceries, and she walked away to her dug-out three miles across the prairie.

A dreadful story circulated through the crowd that gathered one day to wait for the mail. People repeated it avidly, fascinated by its horror. Nobody vouched for its truth, but it happened, they said, about twenty miles west, over on the other side of the railroad. A woman had brooded over hard times and scanty food until she had lost her reason. One day she called out to a passer-by, "Look here! We're goin' to have some fried chicken. I'm dressin' it now." *And she held up the dismembered body of her infant. . . .*

The story of what happened to Jim Cobb was less tragic, and the sympathy of the community was tinged with laughter. Jim had brought a horse-power cane mill from Missouri, and set it up to make his own and his neighbors' sorghum. The sorghum was black and strong from drought-scorched cane, but he was thankful to have a whole barrel of it for his family. He kept it in a rude corn-crib covered with a tightly stretched cloth. One Sunday two or three families were visiting the Cobbs in the friendly frontier way, the women filling the house, the men grouped on the sunny side of the crib. Several dogs were making exploratory advances to each other. Nobody ever knew how it happened, but there was a sudden yelp, and Jim's dog lighted on top of the barrel; the covering gave way and she sank in a sitting position in the midst of the molasses. Jim grasped the scruff of her neck and lifted her out, while she yelped and kicked and the sticky mass streamed from her body.

The men shouted with laughter. But all accepted Jim's sheepish conclusion: "I don't guess it hurt the molasses in the barrel; all that touched her is still stickin' to her." Certainly nobody would have said that a man should destroy a year's supply of food because of an accident. The visitors sat down to dinner and ate heartily of the sorghum, and all agreed that it gave zest to the flatness of the boiled kaffir. But Jim Cobb never outlived the incident. At the store the men told the story with embellishments — "Nothing goes to waste on Jim's claim. He washed the 'lasses off of that dog and made a barrel of vinegar out of the water." "Don't you fellows wish you had some of that vinegar on your turnips?" countered Jim.

For in spite of hardships it was a happy people that came to Goodwin's Corner to claim their mail and swap experiences. There was an ever-present sense of living through great days, an exuberant faith in the future. The homesteader looked at his square of virgin prairie, with its stark habitation and its tethered team and cow, and saw a stately house deep in orchards, great barns bursting with plenty, blooded live stock knee deep in pasture, and tilled fields rich with grain. And if this vision was mostly materialistic, there was also a sense of founding a stable, ordered society in a savage land, of starting out afresh to build a civilization. For the most part the settlers were inarticulate — "Hell, this land lays pretty," "This country is the last place a poor man'll have a chance," and "I'm keepin' that horse as long as he lives; I rode him in the Run" were their utmost in expression — but every humble task was keyed to joy.

This light-hearted acceptance of poverty expressed itself in a sort of indigenous irony. A bachelor homesteader spent many hours teaching his pony a trick to ridicule the scarcity of provender. At the store when there was a crowd around him, he would address the animal,

"What would you like to eat? Do you want a nice feed of oats?"

The pony would shake her head slowly and sadly.

"What! No oats? What about corn then? Big, yellow ears of corn?"

The pony would shake her head again in deeper dejection, while the crowd broke into delighted laughter.

"No corn or oats? But think how hard you work breaking prairie. You need something to keep up your strength. Don't you want *any kind of grain?*"

By this time the pony's refusal was downright miserable.

"What *will* I feed you then? Do you want to be tied out on a lariat where you can have all the good old grass you can eat?"

At some hidden signal which the crowd could never catch, the animal's ears would jerk forward, her expression would become alert, and she would nod her head vigorously.

"I've been feedin' that horse too heavy," the young man would explain seriously to the by-standers. "She's plum tired of corn and oats. All I can get her to eat is prairie grass." But he always managed to slip her a piece of candy at the close of the dialogue.

Never for a minute did the settlers feel that in giving them a farm the Government was bestowing a bounty upon *them.* They felt rather that *they* were conferring a benefit upon their country by establishing a new commonwealth. And as soon as they had attended to the most elemental requirements of shelter and subsistence, they entered with zest into the creation of political institutions.

III
BUILDING A GOVERNMENT

FOR more than a year after the Run the settlers were without legal government. They felt little inconvenience. There was no serious crime in the community; true, it was soon evident that Bill Weaver, the shiftless appearing homesteader "on the Northeast Quarter of 28" was a sneak thief — John Clark missed part of the load of corn he had hauled from Kansas and other settlers lost a few hens — but laws and courts would scarcely have helped the matter. As for schools and roads, they would have to wait on the breaking of sod and the building of dug-outs. But by the summer of 1890 the people were ready to turn their attention to permanent political institutions.

Congress by this time had passed the Organic Act — May 2, 1890 — creating the Territory of Oklahoma for the settlers and for others who might enter subsequent tracts to be purchased from the Indians. For temporary purposes it established seven counties with designated county seats, selected Guthrie as the capital, and placed portions of the Nebraska statutes into effect as a legal code. President Harrison then appointed a governor and the necessary judges and court officials. The governor — George W. Steele of Indiana — arrived at Guthrie May 22. He fixed the county boundaries, named and organized the townships, and appointed temporary county and township officers; and he provided for the election of a legislature, apportioning the members among the counties, and setting August 5 as the date of the election.

All this had repercussions in Prairie City. The people spent more time than ever at "the Corner" that second summer, for there was now a blacksmith shop beside the store — a little frame shack where Dave Hodge, newly arrived from Kentucky, worked all day sharpening plow "lays." Here farmers waiting for their work to be done discussed the need of rain, politics, and the prospects of statehood.

Charles Lester was the most active of the local politicians. Born in Indiana, starved out in Western Kansas, he had made a fresh start in Oklahoma. Originally a Republican he had been converted by hot winds and grasshoppers into a Democrat with People's Party leanings. He had little formal education, but he had read widely and superficially, and without grace of bar examination had become a shrewd country lawyer. Tall, fine-looking in a gaunt Lincolnesque way, with a resonant voice and a flamboyant eloquence, he was equally effective in talking to a neighbor or addressing an audience. The settlers had found him honest in fundamentals, deadly in a horse trade — the exact combination of integrity and sharp dealing that inspired their confidence.

Even before the Organic Act was passed, Lester had called a meeting in his dug-out and organized a local Democratic club. Later he traveled over the county and organized clubs in other neighborhoods. Thus he attracted the notice of the leading Democrats in the ambitious little year-old city thirty miles to the southeast that had been designated as the county seat; and he received the nomination to one of the four places to which the county was entitled in the lower house of the legislature.

Meanwhile the Republicans made their party organization in the unaccustomed comfort of "Dad" Colby's frame house. The People's Party met in a grove along the creek on Joe Spragg's claim, bringing rough cottonwood boards from a small sawmill Joe had, and placing seats under the trees; and Fred Peters called the people, both men and women, to a meeting in his dug-out, where they formed a Farmers' Alliance to work up party enthusiasm. By this time politics had blotted out the weather as the topic of conversation at "the Corner."

Dad Colby was the most dogmatic of Old Soldier Republicans. To him pensions, patronage, and patriotism were all synonymous. "I haven't got a bit of use for a Rebel or a Democrat," he asserted. "The Grand Old Republican Party saved this Union and she's going to keep it running. Look at Harrison's appointments; he fought in the war himself, and every job goes to an Old Soldier or an Old Soldier's son. And look what Cleveland did — gave jobs to Rebels. And if the Democrats get in, where will our pensions be? I tell you boys I fought for the old flag, and I'm going to stand by it."

Fred Peters was an Old Soldier, too, but in the ferment of

Kansas politics he had become an apostate. His approach was philosophical. "The trouble with you, comrade, is that you haven't had a new idea since you cast your first vote for Lincoln. The People's Party aims to free the common people from the money trust just like Lincoln freed the slaves. Now you can go back to ancient Persia — "

A vehement voice cut across his exposition. It was George Hadley, a hot-headed settler with a shrewish wife, who lived in the south end of the township. His voice cracked and his thin face was contorted with hate as he shouted, "The farmers demand relief and it must come by the ballot or the bayonet. You mark my words: we're either goin' to have relief or they'll be a war within ten years. It's bound to come. The Farmers' Alliance will have a heap of stren'th in the national election. We're goin' to have our rights."

Jim Cobb was temperate. "You People's Party fellows are too radical. They ain't no need to be a calamity howler. The Democrats will clean out the protectionists and the blasted monopolistic Republicans. We're goin' to sweep the country next fall." And Joe Scott added with some heat, "The Democrats is a white man's party. Right now in this county the Republicans is running a nigger for the legislature. In Texas where I come from we know how to keep the niggers in their place. I've got just as much use for a nigger as for a damned nigger-loving Republican."

"Your two old parties is just alike," ranted Hadley; "the Democrats makes slaves of the niggers, and the Republicans makes slaves of the farmers. We're goin' to git rid of both. I tell you — "

And thus they argued. Dave Hodge steadily hammered the plow shares to a thin edge — "This ground gits so hard you can't drive a nail in it," he grumbled. It would have been difficult for him to explain why he was a Democrat. And Arthur Goodwin, steady Republican that he was, went about his business of waiting on customers. He liked to have the men gather in his store; he always kept a barrel of unroasted peanuts handy for them to shell and eat as they talked. He knew it was nothing but talk. As citizens of a territory they had no voice in national policy, and any legislature they would elect would be occupied with matters of local sectionalism.

The election was held in Dad Colby's house. When the votes were counted, it was found that the township was strongly Peo-

ple's Party. But the county went Republican; the ambitious city
builders at the county seat and a Negro settlement in "the jacks" —
a belt of post oaks, black-jacks, and sand that lay along the north
side of the Cimarron River — had outvoted the prairie sections.
Similar conditions prevailed throughout the territory, and thus the
Republicans obtained a slight majority in the legislature.

Prairie City voted again at the regular Congressional election
in November, when the territory was privileged to elect a delegate
to sit in the House of Representatives. Local People's Party members and Democrats joined in denouncing the iniquitous McKinley
Tariff, which had been passed by Congress the previous month,
but they were not wise enough to join forces. Their separate candidates were defeated by the Republican, David A. Harvey of Oklahoma City, who was elected for the short term of the following
winter, and for the regular term beginning March 4. But Democrats and People's Party were jubilant over victories in their home
states. "After all," they reminded the Republicans, "a territorial
delegate can't vote in Congress; by next election we'll have statehood, and then we'll vote for President."

Meanwhile the legislature had convened in Guthrie August 27
for a four months' session. Most of the four months was taken up in
jockeying among the representatives of rival towns for the permanent location of the capital and other territorial institutions —
a subject in which Prairie City was only remotely interested. Even
so, the establishment of an organized government had one immediate result; for the first time official notice was taken of the settlers' destitute circumstances.

By the fall of 1890 the sod that had been planted to spring
crops had softened so that it could be "back-set" (a deeper plowing
cutting across the ribbons of sod) or disced, and sowed to wheat;
but how to purchase the seed? Governor Steele appealed to the
two railroads, and each shipped in ten thousand dollars' worth of
seed wheat and distributed it from the stations to settlers who
agreed to pay for it after the next year's harvest. This was sufficient
to plant about one-fifth the wheat sowed in Oklahoma that year.
The railway officials of course were interested only in the increased
hauling from a developing country; yet for a time even the People's Party modified its fulminations against the "soulless corporations."

The governor also appealed to the Federal Government for

food; Congress responded — September 1, 1890 — by a small appropriation, and the legislature created machinery for the distribution. A territorial board of relief purchased commodities and apportioned them among the counties; a board in each township passed on individual cases, and a county board distributed commodities in accordance with these recommendations.

The township west of Prairie City refused to accept aid; its people came through on turnips and kaffir and wild game, while the most destitute were assisted by their neighbors. But the Prairie City community was not so proud; most of the relief went to families with sickness or other misfortunes, but some able-bodied settlers accepted help simply because they were hungry. By the first of October they began making trips to the county seat, traveling together and pooling rides, and coming back with supplies — for each family a twenty-five pound sack of flour, the same amount of corn meal, five or ten pounds of bacon, five pounds of beans, five pounds of salt. And for many, this meagre subsistence during their hardest winter was the extra lift that enabled them to hold on.

In one other respect the settlers received aid from the Federal Government — a grant of $50,000 in the Organic Act for the use of the public schools. The legislature, however, was too busy with the capital fight to pass a school law until the end of the session. Prairie City did not wait for permission.

As soon as the wheat was sowed, Fred Peters influenced his neighbors to build a sod schoolhouse. They made most of their plans at the meeting of the Farmers' Alliance. Thomas Lockwood, who lived on the creek, volunteered to furnish a cottonwood ridge log. Another promised to bring poles. Joe Spragg agreed to saw the necessary lumber. Peters promised to give an acre of land, under a provision of the homestead law permitting a settler "to transfer by warranty deed against his own acts" any tract needed for public purposes. Later a committee waited on Arthur Goodwin and got his consent to furnish the windows.

The site selected was a mile south of Goodwin's store. The men all worked together, while the women set out a basket dinner each day at the Peters home. Before they set a plow in the sod, they carefully burned off the grass so that the tiers in the finished wall would pack closely. They plowed to an even depth of two inches — "If you plow too deep, you'll get below the roots and have nothing but dirt" — and cut the sod into convenient lengths with their spades. Then they laid the walls, placing the sod grass-side-down, setting in rude cottonwood frames for windows and door. Opposite each other inside the walls, two straight posts with crotches were planted to hold the weight of the ridge log, which formed the peak of the roof. "Don't put it too high," warned John Clark, wise from Western Kansas experience; "if you pitch a sod roof too steep, the rain'll wash it off." Next they laid closely spaced rafters of poles, with one end nailed to the ridge log and the other resting on the sod wall and projecting slightly beyond to form the eaves. They covered this framework first with a thatch of long prairie hay, and then with two layers of sod lapped like shingles. Then with their spades they trimmed the inside of the walls smooth and plastered them with "gyp" (gypsum) from a nearby gully. They brought clay from the same gully and packed it down to form the floor. When the building was done, it fitted as naturally into the level landscape as a prairie-dog mound.

"What shall be call our school?" they asked, stepping back to view their work.

Fred Peters threw a spadeful of clay on the roof and patted it down where he thought he detected a weakness in the sod. He looked around at that poorly clad group of men from many states who had cast their lot together to build a civilization. "Let's call it 'Union,'" he said; "in union there is strength." And so the school received its name.

Before the building was finished, Pat O'Hagan, the younger of the two O'Hagan brothers, had received permission to open a subscription school there. His term started October 27. Tuition was one dollar a month payable in cash, wood, breaking prairie, pigs, credit — any commodity but turnips. There were twenty-five children in irregular attendance for two months; then the term closed because it was impossible to finance it further.

The people used the schoolhouse with exuberant appreciation for a place of community meeting. Within a month they were using it three times a week — for Sunday school, "literary," and Farmers' Alliance. By this time the country was dotted with such schoolhouses — some of sod like Union, some mere dug-outs in the creek banks, some substantially built of hewn oak logs brought from "the jacks." The area around each became a social unit called by the name of its school. The names reflected the character and loyalties of a people to whom pioneering was an exhilarating experience: "Sunnyside," "Fairview," "Pleasant Ridge," showing their love for the land; "Liberty," "Columbia," declaring their exultant patriotism; "Antioch," "Bethel," voicing their religious aspirations; "College Corners," "Science Hall," revealing their extravagant hopes for the future; and "Possum Hollow," "Frog Pond," "Hard Scrabble," expressing their unquenchable humor.

Early in 1891 the public schools were organized under the act passed by the legislature. A territorial superintendent and county superintendents took charge of the administration, teachers were examined and certificated, and the money appropriated by Congress was expended. Local authority was placed in the hands of a township board — a system displaced two years later by a separate organization of each school district.

Thus the Union school became a public school. Pat O'Hagan obtained a certificate and applied for the teaching position. But the people refused to employ him — "Since my children went to subscription school, they talk with such a brogue I can't understand them," said John Clark. They hired instead Old Bareheaded Jenkins, who lived in a ramshackle cabin somewhere in "the jacks." Eccentric in appearance, mighty in spelling and ciphering, given to long sleeps at noon, he enforced obedience by sudden rages and sporadic bursts of energy.

The teacher's salary was $27.50 a month, the term three and a half months, from April to July. Seventeen boys and twenty-one girls were enrolled, with an average attendance of six boys and eight girls. It was a shabbily dressed but sturdy group of young people with a strange blending of self-confidence and diffidence who walked bare-footed across the prairie to the sod schoolhouse carrying books from many different states. Most of them failed to overcome the handicaps of unskilled teaching and inadequate equipment; they never learned to read except haltingly, or to write except with painful concentration. But two or three found in their tattered books a mystic summons to a realm beyond the boundaries of time and space, and the urge for further schooling became with them a consuming flame.

In the spring of 1891 Congress authorized the governor to lease the "school land" set apart for the endowment of education. Bidding was not very brisk, for the settlers had not yet had time to place all their own claims under cultivation; but the eight quarters in the township were taken eventually at an average annual rental of thirty dollars a quarter. The lessees were men debarred from homesteading because they had already exhausted their right in Western Kansas, or ambitious homesteaders who needed additional pasturage for their cattle. The money went into a territorial fund, which was distributed among the schools according to scholastic population. Only districts maintaining a three months' term were entitled to share — a rule which had the practical effect of setting a minimum term.

Besides establishing a school system, the legislature had provided during the closing days of its session for permanent county and township governments. This election was held early in 1891, Prairie City voting at the Union schoolhouse.

In the county election the Democrats and the People's Party put aside their mutual animosities to unite against the Republicans. They held conventions and made separate nominations for a full complement of officers; then just before the election each party withdrew half its candidates, leaving a clear field to its ally. The Republicans largely nominated the old officers who had been serving by appointment of the governor. The voters, angry at the legislature, which had just closed its inglorious session, swept the fusion candidates into office.

Larry O'Hagan of Prairie City was elected as one of the three county commissioners. The other successful candidates were Democratic or People's Party farmers from other parts of the county. When they assumed their official duties, they continued to live on their claims, spending such time at the county seat as was needed to transact the public business.

When the governor had organized a municipal township [1] coinciding with the thirty-six sections numbered by the surveyor, he had given it the name of Prairie, and had appointed local settlers for the officers named by the Nebraska statutes. This provisional government had been largely inactive, but the township had served as an election precinct, with the township board conducting the elections. The same officials had also received appointment as the local relief board, which recommended the distribution of commodities.[1] Now the Democrats and the People's Party

---

[1] Because of the loss of territorial records it is apparently impossible to reconstruct these provisional township governments with absolute certainty. The Organic

met in caucus at the Union schoolhouse to agree on a fusion ticket and to dicker for road grading and bridges. After balancing the claims of creek against creek and "that steep hill by my farm" against "that bad place on the Orlando road," they finally nominated Fred Peters as township trustee — the office charged with assessing the property for taxation and with general direction of the road work. The other two members of the township board were nominated without opposition: Jim Cobb as treasurer — "Treasurer of what?" asked Jim — and John Clark as clerk. Little interest was shown in the offices of constable and justice of the peace — two of each — but the places were filled in order. Peters' judgment was followed somewhat in the choice of the four road overseers, each in charge of a three-mile-square district; Pat O'Hagan, Joe Scott, George Hadley, and Tom Lockwood were finally nominated. The Republicans also held a caucus and made nominations, but their candidates received few votes in this People's Party stronghold.

Peters went to work at once to assess the property for taxation. Nothing was exempt except food and fuel; improvements on claims, furniture, farm implements, even money owed by solvent debtors — all were taxed. The usual assessment, based on about half the actual valuation, ran from thirty to one hundred dollars. The levy was 45½ mills distributed as follows: territorial 4 mills, county 31½ mills, township 10 mills. Payment was not made until the end of the year. Meanwhile the township board issued warrants to pay for a minimum of materials and labor and Peters began to improve the roads.

The longer bridges were built by county funds under the direction of the county commissioners, but a disproportionate share of this money was used on roads close to the county seat. Prairie Township was largely dependent on its own efforts. Most of the labor came from the "poll tax" required of every able-bodied man: four dollars worth of work at the rate of a dollar a day for a man with a shovel, two dollars for a man and team. Many donated

Act authorized the governor to organize and name the townships, and an early newspaper reference implies that he carried out this duty. It is the impression of Mr. Fred L. Wenner, distinguished Eighty-Niner of Guthrie, that the appointed township officers served as election officials on August 5; and relief applications still in existence indicate that the township board served as the local relief board in the fall of 1890. But Mr. W. H. Matthews of Mulhall, who was elected justice of the peace at the first election, is very certain that he had no predecessor. It seems probable, therefore, that the provisional township governments were largely inactive.

extra days, improving the roads along their own claims. Peters purchased oak planks from a sawmill in "the jacks," and hired men to build bridges on the most important crossings.

Thus the settlers established political institutions to carry out their collective will. To them the democratic process was not an abstraction, but a necessary course of action. It was based on an almost literal equality of economic opportunity. This economic equality also expressed itself in the energy and vigor, the spontaneous democracy of their social life.

IV
A SOCIETY IN THE MAKING

LIVING was never quiet or static at Prairie City; it was as restless and fluid as the population. The independent, the ardent, the young in spirit who had left the settled ways of older states entered with zest into every social activity.

They gathered at each other's homes in crowds for Sunday visiting, feasting on light bread and venison, or eating turnips and clabber with laughter and appreciation in a comradeship too real for false pride. They spent long evenings together, talking, popping kaffir corn, pulling taffy. Everywhere they met they sang, and when they returned late at night with two or three families packed in a lumber wagon they sang the whole way home. They liked religious songs, not deeply spiritual, but gay and tuneful; popular ballads they had brought from the old home; and light-hearted ditties of their own that were already springing up from the fresh Oklahoma soil. Best of all they liked humorous parodies of familiar songs, depicting the incidents of the Run or the trials of pioneering. A feeling deeper than laughter underlay their appreciation.

Always they felt the white light of history converging upon their everyday acts. Consciously they adopted Oklahoma slang, Oklahoma folk sayings, Oklahoma ways of doing things as an esoteric ritual showing that they were the initiate, they knew the password. If a traveling photographer came through the country, they denied themselves food to buy pictures of their dug-outs or their sod schoolhouses, confident that these photographs belonged to the unrolling ages. And they gathered in houses and groves to celebrate the anniversary of that tumultuous twenty-second of April when they had entered into possession of their land.

They never tired of dancing. The host furnished a house; the guests did everything else. The unmarried young men would make a trip to Orlando for oysters and crackers, somebody would bring a violin, all would help to take down the beds and move the furniture outdoors. Here bachelors holding down claims, cowboys from the Strip, half-grown farm boys, did their courting, swinging the daughters of homesteaders. And married couples made bunks along the wall for their sleeping children and danced the whole night through. When the east was grey with dawn, they brought in the table and served the oyster stew; then they moved the furniture back in place and returned without resting to morning chores and a day of farm work.

The dance steps were varied — polka, schottische, waltz, two-step. Sometimes instead of dancing they "played party games," where the couples dipped and whirled in intricate figures to singing and clapping of hands. The more modest touched hands only; in these groups if a man would "swing a girl waist swing" it was an insult to her and *casus belli* to her escort.

A few austere souls frowned on the dancing, but all joined in the literary at the sod schoolhouse. It was vaguely felt to be educational; certainly it furnished courting facilities, intellectual stimulus, and hilarious entertainment. Even today old-timers remember their shocked disapproval when Perry Eaton — a bachelor homesteader given to dime novels — tried to carry out a Wild West tradition by shooting out the lights. This was the only disorderly incident.

Children "spoke pieces" in sing-song tones, with conscious strutting, while their parents watched in pride. The Peters girls in clear, sharp voices sang dismal ballads of tragedy and unrequited love. Pat O'Hagan brought down the house by his "funny songs" and witty impersonations. People stamped and cheered and shouted with laughter when Mrs. Clark read a burlesque newspaper with barbed references to neighborhood happenings and personalities:

"Jim Cobb's molasses is said to have a peculiar flavor.

"Wonder why Professor Jenkins never tips his hat to the ladies.

"Lost — A triangular piece of pants cloth, last seen on the teeth of a bulldog belonging to Mabel Peters' pa. Finder return to Hugh Channing."

Children egged on by adults recited labored parodies of familiar lines:

"Hugh stood on the burning deck
With his arms around his Mabel's neck.

Her father cussed; he would not go,
Because he loved his Mabel so."

And men made careful preparation — sometimes even writing and memorizing their speeches — and debated philosophical questions or current political issues. Even the most frivolous listened respectfully as they argued:

"Resolved: That moral causes have greater influence than physical in the formation of national character.

"Resolved: That the right of suffrage should be extended to women.

"Resolved: That all the laws enacted by Congress for the past thirty years have been in favor of the money trust.

"Resolved: That man will do more for love of woman than for love of money."

It was an un-self-conscious crowd that gathered at Union schoolhouse — and other schoolhouses — laughing gustily at crude witticisms or moved to tears by sentimental songs. Everyone knew that Mrs. Lockwood had only one dress — of hickory shirting — which she washed at night and ironed in the morning, clad in her petticoat and her husband's shirt. The children wore cast-down garments of every shape and hue. The men's clothes were loaded with patches, and two or three went barefooted and unashamed. "These clothes have got to last till harvest," they said; "then I'll dress like a dude."

For the wheat grew green and rank during the winter of 1890–91. It furnished pasture for the cows, and the cows converted it into cream and yellow butter for the settlers. All the wild new land lay in disciplined beauty that third spring — dark corn growing, sturdy kaffir on fresh sod, stiff oats, and dimpling, waving fields of wheat. Nobody had ever seen such wheat.

But harvesting was a perplexing problem. The acreage was still small — twenty to forty acres of wheat to a farm, and a smaller patch of oats — but a binder cost one hundred and forty dollars. ("All on account of that blasted Republican tariff," said Jim Cobb; "they ship binders across the ocean and sell them cheaper than they do right here.") A few of the older farmers were fortunate enough to have machines, which they had brought from the old home. Others on the strength of their prospects managed to borrow money from a grain buyer or make the purchase on credit from an implement dealer in one of the railroad towns. To some the cost was prohibitive; they had to rely on hiring their neighbors to cut their fields.

There was the additional problem of storage. The previous winter most of the farmers had built crude stables — a framework of poles holding thick walls of hay and supporting a roof of hay — but the scanty store of corn and kaffir had been piled in the open. Now granaries would have to be built to hold the wheat until it could be hauled fifteen or twenty miles to market at Hennessey. More credit, and more expedients.

Dick Martin has never forgotten who staked him to a granary. Dick had punched cattle all the way from Texas to Montana; he knew the rutted trails of half a continent and all the ins and outs of a trade where a man's life might depend on his nerve and skill. Now he was married and settled on a claim. He was a steady farmer — the men said he was "broke to harness" — but some of the grubby ways of homesteading irked his spirit. Struggling against an embarrassment that colored his tan and almost choked his speech, he went to a lumber dealer in a railroad town and asked for credit. The man asked too many questions about his circumstances and prospects. Dick's head went up and his manner became lofty.

"My mistake," he apologized. "I thought you had your lumber there to sell. It does look pretty, all stacked, and I wouldn't think of messin' it up. I'll find another place, where they aim to *sell* their lumber." And he walked out, stepping lightly, managing in spite of broken work shoes to convey an illusion of jingling spurs.

Dad Colby had also gone to town that day to cash a pension check. He had heard part of the dialogue and guessed the rest. He found Dick on the street, nerving himself up to try the bank.

"You wanted that lumber pretty bad, didn't you?" he asked.

"I sure did," said Dick; "but that stuck-up son-of-a-gun made me so blamed mad I didn't care. I don't know what I'm goin' to do with my wheat."

"Spring this on him," said Dad. "I didn't figure on using it for awhile. I heard you wanted to sell your saddle. We might make a deal on it. If not, you can pay me back after harvest."

There was sixty dollars in the roll he handed over. Not a word was said about interest or security. When Dick went back to the lumber-yard, there was a confidence plainer than any jingle of spurs in his walk.

Thus each homesteader struggled with his individual difficulty. And as the wheat ripened, all was merged into the stress
and toil, the zest and excitement of that first harvest. As one long
day of perfect weather followed another, the grain fell evenly
before the sickle and was piled into smooth golden shocks. For
the first time in all the brooding ages the prairie landscape
stretched field after field to the horizon bearing this crown of
ordered beauty.

Something of this feeling of mystery and wonder came to the
people as they worked. Characteristically they planned a celebration; nothing else would express their thankfulness for the harvest,
their pride in the new land they had tamed, their joy in the work
of their hands.

They could not wait until the crop was garnered and sold. There
were few threshing machines in the country. Joe Spragg managed
somehow to purchase a separator; he already had the engine that
had done service at his sawmill. Other outfits were shipped in,
crew and all, from Kansas — one even came from Illinois — for an
early run before the Northern grain was ready. And many of the
farmers stacked their wheat while they waited their turn. Meanwhile nearly all the older boys and bachelor homesteaders and a
good many of the married men went to Kansas to work in the harvest (current wage, one dollar a day) during the slack season that
followed the cutting of their own crops.

As soon as their first fields were threshed, stories began to circulate of the marvelous yield — of Tom Lockwood's twenty acres
turning out thirty-seven bushels to the acre, of Pat O'Hagan's
thirty-acre field producing at the rate of forty-three bushels, of
John Clark's four hundred and sixty bushels from eleven acres, of
an average yield of twenty bushels. And the oats, it was said, were
threshing out sixty bushels to the acre. If the people suspected ex-
aggeration in these accounts, they appreciated them the more; it
showed faith in the country.

Hauling a load to Hennessey was a hard day's work for the
half-starved, skinny horses; most of the wheat would be left in
the granaries until winter. But everybody hauled a few loads soon
after threshing. The price was good that year — 65 cents or more
a bushel. Families bloomed out in new clothes, farmers bought
needed machinery, people no longer did without necessary groceries. The larger purchases were made at Hennessey, but Good-

win's store also bulged with new stock — pretty lawns and India linens on the shelves, boxes of dress shoes lining the wall, horse collars hanging from the ceiling. And in the midst of these blessings the settlers planned their harvest festival.

They decided to do it in style. A group of substantial farmers met one evening in Goodwin's store, formed a company, and subscribed to stock of the "First Annual Harvest Picnic." They went to the county seat and had posters printed, to be placed in all the stores and blacksmith shops and country postoffices in the county. The young people cleaned and trimmed the grove on Joe Spragg's farm, cutting out the matted briar vines and underbrush; they built a platform, decorating it with flags and bunting; and they placed seats under the trees. A program committee arranged for songs and recitations and speeches, and a silver cornet band was engaged to come from the county seat to furnish music.

The date set for the festival was Saturday, August 8. It was a bright, clear day, not too hot for comfort in the shade. By nine o'clock people began to arrive, unhitching, tying their teams to their parked wagons. Within an hour the grove was packed with humanity; fully a thousand people were gathering in knots to talk or drifting over to the seats in front of the speakers' stand.

The program began at eleven. The band played. The people sang "America," looking out on the fresh land they had settled, finding new meaning in the familiar words. "Let music swell the breeze . . ." How cleanly the wind swept across the stubble! "And ring from all the trees . . ." The brave, precious trees of a prairie country! "Long may our land be bright . . ." How bright it seemed! How bright its future! "Great God our King." They ended on a note of prayer.

Dad Colby read a lesson from the Bible. Again familiar words had a strange significance.

"For the Lord thy God bringeth thee into a good land, a land of brooks of water . . .

"A land of wheat, and barley, and vines . . .

"A land wherein thou shalt eat bread without scarceness, thou shalt not lack any thing in it . . .

"When thou hast eaten and art full, then thou shalt bless the Lord thy God for the good land which he hath given thee . . .

"Lest when thou hast eaten and art full, and hast built goodly houses, and dwelt therein:

"And when thy herds and thy flocks multiply, and thy silver and thy gold is multiplied, and all that thou hast is multiplied;

"Then thine heart be lifted up, and thou forget the Lord thy God . . .

"And thou say in thine heart, My power, and the might of mine hand hath gotten me this wealth.

"But thou shalt remember the Lord thy God: for it is he that giveth thee power to get wealth, that he may establish his covenant, which he sware unto thy fathers."

The youngest Lockwood child, relaxed on his mother's lap, looked up wonderingly as a tear dropped on his face.

Arthur Goodwin introduced Charles Lester as the speaker of the occasion. It was understood that a truce should be declared on politics — a limitation that did not handicap Lester's style. This was his opportunity, and he made the most of it. He began with the discovery of America, paid tributes to Pilgrim and Cavalier, lauded the deeds of "this glorious republic," and finally reached "the settlement of our beloved Oklahoma, the crowning feat of American genius. This fairest of all lands, where the sun shines brightest, peopled by the strongest and finest of our race. When this new state is admitted to the glorious sisterhood there will be such a big star on the American flag it will splash the blue out to the bounds of infinite space." Bombastic, of course, and uncritical, but he — and his audience — believed every word he said.

After the program came the dinner. The whole grove was one vast dining hall. Could these people have been actually starving less than a year ago? Here were products of bountiful gardens: tomatoes ("Have some of this green tomato pie"), pickles, melons, enormous potatoes. ("My husband says he is goin' to plant potatoes again next week; they's no reason why we shouldn't grow two crops a year in this country.") And there was fried chicken, cake, ice cream, lemonade. . . . Even the horses at the wagons munched Oklahoma's first oats with the relish of long abstinence. Tom Lockwood proudly exhibited two peaches and five plums carefully preserved in alcohol. "How's this for Oklahoma fruit? I raised them from that nursery stock I brought from Kansas. I'm prepared to take orders for the same kind. How about setting out an orchard this fall?"

After dinner the crowd gathered again before the speakers' stand to listen to songs and recitations by the children and music by the band, and to effect a permanent organization. A brief constitution was adopted. The date of the "Farmers' Annual Harvest Picnic" was set as "the Saturday on or before the first full moon in August." Officers were elected: Arthur Goodwin, president; Fred Peters, vice president; John Clark, secretary-treasurer. Before the business was finished, the children were wandering off through the grove, and the young people were casting impatient looks at the band.

When the meeting adjourned, the platform was cleared, the band tuned up, and the dance started. Most of the married couples soon gathered up their children and their empty dishpans and platters, and went home to chores and family responsibilities. But the young people danced until the early August dawn; it was their job later to come back and clear the wreckage of Prairie City's first — and happiest — community gathering.

V

THE OLD-TIME RELIGION

THE RELIGIOUS spirit manifest in the Harvest Picnic was deep in the character of the settlers. Some were devout; more were profane, disorderly, consciously sinful; but all were profoundly susceptible to religious meanings. Even Jim Cobb, the community "infidel," expounded his heretical views with self-conscious defiance, implying that religion was important, and that his own importance was enhanced by opposing it.

During the first months of settlement there were no organized church services, but any visiting preacher was sure of a community turn-out in some homesteader's sod house. The first Sunday school was started largely through the quiet insistence of Mrs. Lockwood, who talked for it every time she met her neighbors at the store or in their homes. It was organized in Spragg's Grove in the summer of 1890.

Dad Colby was elected as superintendent, John Clark was chosen to teach the adults, and Mrs. Lockwood volunteered to teach the children. The people sat on boards brought from the sawmill. With Fred Peters up in front beating time they sang bright songs of a beautiful country ("Beulah Land," "Shall We Gather at the River?"), songs full of the familiar sights of the farm ("Bringing in the Sheaves"), and — strange affinity of prairie dwellers — songs of the sea ("Pull for the Shore, Sailor," "Let the Lower Lights be Burning"). They used tattered song books brought from many places, and they had no lesson helps.

Everybody came. Young men rode their ponies; farmers came from a distance bringing several families in a lumber wagon; those who lived closest walked. Jim Cobb was a regular attendant. He liked to throw confusion into the ranks of the righteous by such questions as: "Where did Cain get his wife? How could he build a city when there wasn't any people?" and "Here the Bible says the men with Saul 'heard a voice, but saw no man,' and here it says

they 'saw the light, but heard not the voice of him that spake';
which story is true? And how do you know either one is true?"

But an outdoor meeting place was not satisfactory even in summer; and when fall came the Sunday school was disbanded. It was
reorganized as soon as the Union schoolhouse was completed. A
year later regular preaching services were established there.

The preacher was "Brother" Hopkins of the "Campbellite" persuasion. An energetic young man with pleasing manners and an
active mind, he had recently come from Nebraska to throw in his
lot with the Oklahoma settlers. Penniless but undaunted, he had
landed at one of the railroad towns and made rapid inquiries as
to neighborhoods in need of a minister. Picking up rides or traveling incredible distances on foot, he had gone over the country
holding a meeting, baptizing his converts, organizing a church,
going on to another place. Dad Colby heard him preach at a schoolhouse ten miles south, and invited him to hold a "protracted
meetin'" at Prairie City. He accepted gladly, and for two weeks
preached nightly to a congregation assembled at the Union schoolhouse.

There were a number of Campbellites in the community. Their
tenets were particularly fitted to frontier thinking. Democratic in
organization, making a ritual out of the absence of ritual, dogmatic
in doctrine — their sermons were arguments, their prayers were
propositions. And although they condemned "man-made creeds"
and asserted that "The Bible is our only rule of faith and conduct,"
their beliefs and words followed a pattern as exact and rigid as
though they had all graduated from the same Jesuit seminary.

Brother Hopkins' sermons fell into the familiar design. The sod
schoolhouse by this time had a blackboard, which he covered with
diagrams and notations. He showed how the "denominations" bore
names of human origin — "Baptist," "Methodist," "Presbyterian" —
whereas his group carried only the name of Christian — "for there
is none other name under heaven given among men whereby ye
must be saved." He condemned these "sects" for disunity, and
urged his hearers to "obey the New Testament" and join "the true
Church of Christ." Whenever two people of this faith came together, he asserted, no matter how many "denominations" were
established in the community, it was the sacred duty of these two
to start a church "That they all may be one."

He offered to defend his thesis in a formal debate against all

comers. Nobody accepted his challenge. Few of these homesteaders, so unlettered, so naïve, and yet so open-minded to reason,
could resist his logic. Twenty-nine persons expressed their readiness to form a church organization: several families of Campbellites — the Colbys, the Goodwins, the Hodges, the Clarks — who
came in by statement; seven "converts from sectarianism" — Methodists and Baptists — convinced by his arguments; and the re-
mainer, new converts — married couples, three or four bachelor
homesteaders, and a few of the older children. At intervals during
the meeting new converts and such of the former "sectarians" as
had not been immersed were baptized at a deep place in the creek
on Joe Spragg's claim.

The church was organized on Sunday morning at the close of
the meeting. The date, November 1, 1891, after the lapse of more
than half a century is still held in sacred remembrance. It was a
simple service there in the bare sod schoolhouse, the mere essen-
tials of enrolling names and electing officers. But the people were
deeply stirred. They shook hands exultingly after the meeting was
over. "This will go down through the ages," said Dad Colby. "I
have prayed for this day," said Mrs. Clark. "Now my children will
always have church privileges."

The members employed Brother Hopkins to preach for them
one Sunday a month. In the bountiful measure of that time, this
meant three services: Saturday evening, Sunday morning, and
Sunday evening. They arranged for him to live in the vacant dug-
out of Mike McGraw, a bachelor who was away working in the
coal mines of the Choctaw Nation, and his young wife came and
joined him there. From this place he continued his travels to distant fields. But he held meetings in neighboring schoolhouses, enrolling his converts in the Prairie City Christian Church; and almost every time he preached at the Union schoolhouse there were
more additions. Thus the membership increased.

He made a precarious living. The settlers were no longer entirely destitute, but the money from their first harvest had long
been spent. In April the Prairie City congregation gave him a
young horse, which they purchased for fifty dollars on six months'
time from one of their members. This was the first compensation
of any kind he had ever received from them; he wrote in his diary,
"They could not have suited me any better than to get me a horse
at this time for I needed one badly." The same week the men

turned out and broke five acres of sod on the claim where he was living; this he planted by hand to corn, kaffir, and melons. The same spring another of his churches gave him a cow. Others took up small cash collections, and made donations of flour, corn, and home canned goods. When harvest came, he worked as a hand in the field; later he took a job with a thresher. In the fall, he cut his wood from a creek on the claim of one of his members. During the winter at the close of a successful "protracted meetin'" at the Union schoolhouse, he received $4.45 in cash, and some meat, flour, and potatoes. Thus like the other settlers, he made out to live.

The formation of this church had no effect on the community Sunday school meeting in the same building. By this time the school was using lesson helps, but they were purchased from a private firm in the East, unconnected with any church. Dad Colby continued as superintendent, and "sectarians" who had not been convinced of their error served as before in various offices. All turned out to hear Brother Hopkins preach; everyone liked and respected him, and preaching of any kind was too precious to ignore.

Early in the spring of 1893 another preacher came to the sod schoolhouse. Harry Hayman, a serious-minded young homesteader, had decided that he was "called to preach." When the Baptists organized a church in a little inland village eight miles southwest of Prairie City, he and his family joined them, and there he was ordained to the ministry. But he was diffident about beginning. Once in Goodwin's store he confessed his perplexities to Dick Martin.

"Why don't you try out on us?" asked Dick. "We ought to be good to practice on; we're plenty ignorant. And I don't think anybody needs it any worse than we do."

Harry agreed. Dick spread the word around, and everybody came out to hear him. He spoke with some hesitation, but his discourse was full of homely lessons drawn from the labor of the fields. The people urged him to hold a "protracted meetin'." During this meeting he organized a Baptist Church.

True to Baptist convictions against transacting business on Sunday, the founders met at the Union schoolhouse on Saturday afternoon — February 25, 1893, another date held in sacred memory. A territorial missionary was present, with three men from the neighboring village church. From the Bible he read the familiar story of another race of pioneers who settled a Promised Land, and he preached with Baptist fervor from the text, "Speak unto the children of Israel that they go forward." Then with an ease born of generations of practice they fell into the same parliamentary forms that had taught their ancestors how to unite in founding the Republic.

Harry Hayman, his three fellow members of the village church, and the visiting minister organized themselves into a "presbytery," with a chairman and a secretary. Six Prairie City couples then presented letters from Baptist churches in widely separated states; they were formally admitted and given "the right hand of fellowship." The meeting then adopted with some revision "the articles of faith and church covenant as given by Pendleton"; decided on the name, "Missionary Baptist Church of Prairie City"; set the time for the monthly Saturday business meeting; elected Harry Hayman as pastor; voted to have the preaching services immediately after Sunday school on the second and fourth Sundays of each month; and took up a collection of seventy-seven cents for "incidental expenses." All this went down in the secretary's minutes. Trivial in its details but mighty in its influence; for in such proceedings was the very essence of frontier democracy at work.

Half a dozen young people presented themselves for membership during the following week; they were immersed in the same "babtizin' hole" used by Brother Hopkins, and enrolled with the other charter members. One of these accessions was a young man of Baptist background who had joined the Campbellites. Brother Hopkins was greatly chagrined when the Baptists proceeded to immerse him again.

"Brother Harry" never preached on denominational differences or attempted to answer the Campbellite arguments. But he soon overcame his diffidence. He learned to fit his theology into a "plan of salvation," and to attack sin and the devil and the neighborhood dances with good Baptist enthusiasm.

A few families — mostly Methodists — still remained outside, unmoved by Campbellite logic or Baptist zeal. But they were so active in supporting the Baptist organization that the Baptists became sympathetic. Joe Scott went to Brother Harry about it.

"They haven't got no church of their own," he said. "Can't you just take them in temporary, and forget about babtizin'?"

But Brother Harry said that was against Baptist rules. Joe then talked to Tom Lockwood.

"Why don't you just be babtized and come into the church, Tom?" he asked. "You take more interest in it now than most of the members. But you can't take communion and you can't hold office. And we need you bad. I wouldn't ask you if they was a Methodist Church here."

"I can't be babtized again when I don't believe in it," said Lockwood; "that'd be makin' a mock of religion. But I'll help the Baptists every way I can. The Lord knows we need churches in this country."

But at a "protracted meetin' " Brother Harry held that summer the oldest Lockwood boy tore himself from his place and plunged forward to present himself for membership. One glance at his young face — flushed, set in desperate resolve — was enough for Mrs. Lockwood. Quick as thought she passed her baby to a friend and hurried up the aisle to stand beside him. Tom Lockwood stood in his place and looked distressed. He still looked distressed a few days later when he collected the younger children and stood with the rest of the crowd at the "babtizin' hole" to watch his wife and the boy go down into the stagnant water. But he never relaxed his support of the church he could not join.

Other settlers unable to fit into the two organized churches found religious affiliations outside the neighborhood. The two O'Hagan families and a few others drove fifteen or twenty miles to Hennessey for infrequent attendance on mass. The neighbors knew very little about their beliefs, but they respected their religion as a stabilizing influence. The Weavers, scorning the meetings at the Union schoolhouse, joined a strange sect of "Comeouters" in the black-jack-covered hills that lay along the east of the township. Here a group of fanatics worked themselves up to an emotional frenzy, consigned all others to hell, and broke out in noisy quarrels among themselves. Apparently it was good for the Weavers. Weaver was still shiftless and his wife was a slattern, but they began to nurse the sick and to share with the unfortunate, and as long as their religion lasted, the neighbors' poultry was undisturbed.

Prairie City soon had another kind of religious excitement. In the summer of 1893 Mormon missionaries began to travel, two by two, through the country. People invited them to meals and kept them overnight with the open-hearted hospitality they extended to all strangers; then impressed with the pleasing manners of the visitors they read the tracts they distributed. One pair announced a meeting at the Union schoolhouse, and as usual the whole neighborhood turned out to hear them preach.

The Campbellites with their glorification of argument had no defenses. The Mormons spoke with a skill, a logic, a persuasive charm that proved every point. And they were sure of so many things — not mundane matters like modes of baptism and names and church unity, but the whole cosmos: the beginning, the end, revelation, prophecy, the sweep of infinity. Several of the Campbellites became interested and began to invite the visitors to their homes for private instruction. The upshot was that five families and two young daughters of another settler withdrew from their church and embraced the new faith. These converts were not molested, but the community regarded them with a certain suspicion. Within a year they left the country and settled in Utah.

Except for this incident the people were not disturbed by their religious differences. The two separate church organizations used the same building without friction. They grabbed each other's converts, but their competition was tempered with neighborliness; they assisted each other financially and joined in each other's services.

The union Sunday school dominated the programs and special days that joined recreation with religious activity. Christmas was not publicly observed during the first hard years, but from 1892 on it furnished the greatest occasion of celebration; the schoolhouse was packed with people who came to enjoy the candle-lighted tree, the alluring presents, the humorous gifts (a doll baby for a bachelor, a mustache cup for a fuzzy-lipped boy), the jokes of Santa Claus — rites only slightly Christian but wholly entertaining. And there were summer picnics in the grove, and conventions with neighboring Sunday schools, and Easter, and Children's Day. Always there was "speaking pieces" and above all, singing.

The two pastors often appeared together on these occasions of doctrinal truce. And they assisted each other or deferred to each other in conducting funerals.

There were a good many funerals. Men died of typhoid, leaving their widows to rear the children and carry on the homesteading alone. Babies died of cholera infantum. Women and young

girls drooped from "chronic debility." Malaria was a constant ener-
vating influence; and quinine and chill tonics were the most popular remedies sold at Goodwin's store. There was no general diphtheria epidemic, but half a dozen deaths in the summer of 1892
struck the hearts of all the mothers cold with fear. By this time a
homesteader had given an acre of ground for a cemetery just across
the road from the Union schoolhouse, and a few straggling monu-
ments and starveling shrubs began to show through the tall grass.

Thus Prairie City lived and died and played and labored. There
was the bountiful season of '92 and the good harvest of '93 — if
only the price of wheat had not been so low: 48 to 50 cents the
first year, 32 to 40 the second. There was the excitement when
some of the young men rode over to join the Run into the Sac and
Fox and the Pottawatomie lands in the fall of '91, and the Cheyenne and Arapaho Opening in the spring of '92. There was the
election year of '92, when the Union schoolhouse was filled with
rallies and caucuses, and the political enthusiasm even overflowed
into the harvest festival; that year the country elected Grover
Cleveland and a Democratic Congress, but Oklahoma elected a
legislature with a precarious Republican majority, and a Republican, Dennis Flynn of Guthrie, won by a slight plurality over his
Democratic and Populist opponents for the office of territorial
delegate. The next spring there was the organization of an Industrial Legion at the Union schoolhouse — a new society designed to
take the place of the Alliance and the labor unions, welding farmers and workers into one group.

Thus by 1893 a settled community was firmly rooted in the
new soil of Oklahoma. The land had been brought under cultivation or fenced for pasture, and the grass was tamed to a measured
growth. Small unpainted shacks of finished lumber, comfortable
dwellings of hewn logs hauled from "the jacks," or well-built sod
houses had replaced the first crude dug-outs; pink and yellow
roses, brought from the old homes, bloomed in the yards; young
orchards were coming into fruitage. The few cows brought behind
the covered wagons had become the progenitors of growing herds.
The roads now followed the section lines in orderly checkerboard-
ings, and rude bridges spanned the creeks. The hardest years were
over.

Goodwin's Corner with its store and blacksmith shop had become an increasingly busy place. Arthur Goodwin's family now

lived in their own house — an attractive new dwelling on a knoll a few rods from the store and just across the road from the residence of Dad Colby. Young trees were beginning to shade it, and a hedge of tamarisks fringed the drive.

Thus the community grew into ordered progress. Then its quiet was dramatically shattered and its tempo was suddenly increased by the greatest of all land rushes — the opening of the Cherokee Strip.

VI

THE RUN INTO THE CHEROKEE STRIP

Sixty miles wide and two hundred miles long, the Cherokee Strip lay along the north edge of the settlement, one hundred rods from Goodwin's store. The year after the opening of "Old Oklahoma" the Government had forced the cattlemen to vacate, but it had taken three more years to persuade the Cherokees to part with their title. A deepening trail led across it from Prairie City to the Kansas border.

The settlers stripped it of everything movable. They rounded up the strays overlooked by the ranchmen, and converted them into beef or started herds of their own. They rolled up the wire that had enclosed the great pastures, hid it along the creeks, and fetched it by night to their claims to build their fences. Braving the penalty against "stealing from Indian land," they cut their firewood from the timber along the streams. As their farms came under cultivation, they drove their growing herds of cattle to graze on the vacant prairies, setting their children on ponies to watch them. And some of them surreptitiously burned off the grass, starting the fires by dragging blazing ropes soaked in kerosene behind their saddles; this practice was supposed to prevent a possible return of the cattlemen, but most of all it satisfied an impulse as old as the American frontier — the urge to lay strong hands on a virgin land and tame it into submission.

They were eager to see the land opened for settlement. They all wrote to their friends and relatives at the old home urging them to try their fortune. And while the Cherokee negotiations dragged on, homeseekers came to the community and waited — breaking sod for the privilege of planting a crop, working a few days in harvest, making a living as best they could. They made temporary dug-outs along the roadside, in the banks of creeks, or on the claims of their friends.

Dave Hodge, the blacksmith, was among this number. He had

waited ever since the summer of 1890. And Brother Hopkins had decided to try his hand at homesteading. The men of his church built him a shack of cottonwood lumber, set temporarily at Goodwin's Corner, but designed to be taken apart and moved to his claim. Several prospective business men were camped close to "the Corner." They intended to take claims and live on them enough to satisfy the homestead law, but their real ambitions lay in the future of the town. Young Dr. C. D. Lindsey built a little frame shack on Dad Colby's land just across the road from the store and the blacksmith shop, brought in a small stock of drugs, and opened an office. Antoine Le Rossignol, a French Canadian of guarded reticences and strange enthusiasms, hauled a few loads of lumber from Orlando and opened a lumber-yard beside the drug store; he planned to be ready for trade when the first shacks should be built in the Strip. Prairie City was beginning to look like a town, with buildings facing each other across a street.

The interest mounted in the summer of '93, when the Government began to prepare for the opening. The land had been surveyed in the 1870's, but now it was divided into counties, sites were platted for the county seats, and land-offices were erected. On August 19 President Cleveland issued the long-awaited proclamation declaring the land open at noon of September 16, and warning all who should enter before that time that they would be disqualified from filing. Soldiers were stationed inside the country to patrol it and keep it clear of intruders. Booths were set up on the line north of Hennessey and Orlando for the registration of prospective settlers.

This proclamation was the signal for greater throngs of homeseekers to gather along the border. These newcomers now made up more than half the crowd that waited for the mail or gathered for gossip at Goodwin's Corner. They joined in the church services and swelled the throng at the Harvest Picnic. The settlers gave them much friendly advice.

"I wouldn't pay no fifty dollars for the use of a race horse. Ponies have got more sense, and they're not afraid. And they're more sure footed."

"You'd better take a compass so you won't git turned around. You can borry mine, and sent it back when you git settled. I wanta keep it because it helped me git my claim."

"You must gitcha a good saddle."

"Now, I don't agree with that. Ride with just a pad and a sur-
cingle. I seen too many fall in the Old Oklahoma Run when a horse
stepped in a prairie-dog hole. If you don't have a saddle, you'll
be throwed clear, and you won't git hurt."

Forbidden to enter, they spent much time looking across the
border trying to figure out the lay of the land. They studied "Homeseekers' Guides," prepared by an enterprising printer at the county
seat, giving a map of the country, explaining the homestead laws,
showing how to read the surveyors' hieroglyphics on the corner
stones. Many of the former cowboys of the Strip were among the
homeseekers. They were in a favored position; knowing every
spring and stream and every foot of ground, they had mentally
picked their claims and the shortest way to reach them.

During the last week the "Strippers" drove to Hennessey or
Orlando to register. They returned with stories of immense throngs
before the booths, of terrible heat and dust, of incredible suffering
from thirst and standing in line. But they bore certificates authorizing them to file on land. Even yet they hold it as a grievance that
these hard-won slips of paper were never called for.

As Saturday, September 16, approached, the "Strippers"
moved up closer to the border. The last night about half the throng
camped on the line. In order to protect the fields of the settlers,
they were allowed to occupy a strip one hundred feet wide just
beyond the boundary. As far as the eye could see to the east and
west stretched the long encampment — family groups around the
wagons, men talking in knots or lying apart with their heads pil-
lowed on their saddles. The vast plain before them was lighted
with prairie fires. Everybody believed the soldiers had set them;
some said so the corner stones could be located, others said to
drive out intruders.

All were aware that while they waited many had slipped into
the forbidden land and were even then hiding on choice quarter
sections. Honest homeseekers reserved a special brand of scorn
for these "sooners"; it was the irony of history that this term of
reproach would in time become a title of honor to be carried by
all the people of a state not yet born. They resolved to yield them
nothing, to drive them off by threats, to contest their right to file
at the land-office.

No one ever forgot the morning of September 16. It was a day
of terrible heat, the culmination of a severe drought, and a fierce,

dry wind was blowing from the southwest. Back of the line of camps were the four bare buildings of Prairie City and the farms that stopped so dramatically at the boundary. Ahead was emptiness — huge tracts blackened by fire, lines of flame still eating into patches of brown, sun-scorched grass.

About the middle of the forenoon, "Strippers" who had camped at farmhouses began to arrive and take up positions. Those who were to take part in the race were out in front. Most of them planned to ride horseback. Two or three had made curious carts by fastening a makeshift seat on a pair of wagon wheels. A few had buckboards. The only woman sat tense and determined in a light spring wagon; beside her was a sixteen-year-old farm boy she had employed to drive her team.

Covered wagons — and a few other vehicles — in charge of friends and relatives were lined up in the rear, some ready to follow the men, others parked, with the horses unhitched and feeding. Here the women tried to gather up their broods, but children popped in and out of the wagons or dashed about the camp almost frantic with excitement. A serious-looking homeseeker spoke to a little girl balancing on the wheel of a parked buggy — "Remember this as long as you live. This is history."

The whole population of Old Oklahoma had driven up to watch, sympathetic spectators of even a wilder race than they had engaged in four years before. Goodwin's Corner was closed and deserted. The adult Goodwins and Dad and Mother Colby were standing out in the field watching. Bertha Goodwin, now a long-legged youngster, had ridden up to the line on her white pony; a fat three-year-old brother sat behind her, his hands grasping her sides, his short legs sticking almost straight out from the pony's back. Brother Hopkins was riding the horse his people had given him, while John Clark prepared to follow in a wagon with provisions and a barrel of water. Dave Hodge, Dr. Lindsey, and Le Rossignol had saddled their horses and joined the homeseekers. The last two were deep in conference with S. W. Brown, an implement dealer from Hennessey, who had come to take a claim and start a hardware store.

The men were making final preparations: seeing to their horses, sharpening long, slender stakes, filling their pockets with food and their canteens with water. Some had dressed conspicuously so they could be easily identified. A young brother-in-law of Jim Cobb named Will Sadler wore a blue and red jockey jacket, a derby hat, and chin whiskers. Two strangers who gave the name of Alexander wore white shirts with red sashes tied over their shoulders. A tall, sun-burned Kansan held a stake bearing a floursack flag with the words lettered in blueing, "This claim taken by A. T. Strickland." Friendships were formed that morning during that chance meeting that have endured for fifty years.

Few were making the venture alone; but a German, strange to frontier ways, was taking tearful leave of his wife and children, plainly expecting to be scalped by Indians, and a Negro stood apart, conscious of hostile glances. Other hostile glances were directed toward three horsemen who boasted that they had taken claims in every Run. They belonged to a rather numerous class of professional "homeseekers," who filed on land purely for speculation, holding it only until they could relinquish at a profit.

Once or twice a blue-clad trooper rode along just inside the Strip line, but the soldiers were too few to guard so vast a stretch. Suddenly a little girl sitting by her mother in a covered wagon began to bounce up and down, and call shrilly to one of the red-sashed riders, "Oh, Papa, look at that man! Over in the draw!" Everybody's glance followed her pointing finger. There in the distance was a man on horseback slinking out of the hollow where he had spent the night. The crowd took up a mighty cry of "Sooner! Sooner!" The man exploded into action. Apparently he expected a bullet from a soldier. He bent low over the horse's neck and dashed over the hill out of sight, while the crowd rocked with laughter. After that scare they thought he would hardly dare to contest his right to the claim.

The sun climbed overhead. Dr. Lindsey's watch showed ten minutes, then five minutes to twelve. The friendly conversation ceased. Faces were set in fierce resolution; each looked at his neighbor as at a rival who might outstrip him in the race. No soldier was in sight to give the signal, but all watched for a sign of movement elsewhere. Suddenly on a hill far to the west, they saw the line surge forward; and with a wild yell all were in motion. "I reckon we was all sooners," says old Will Sadler, looking back fifty years; "I think it lacked two minutes to twelve when we started."

Families and friends in the wagons stood up and yelled encouragement or they started racing across the prairie trying to keep sight of their men on horseback. The ground shook with thunderous galloping; the riders were enveloped in a cloud of dust and blackened cinders. But the tumult soon rolled over the horizon. The spectators lingered to exchange good wishes with the people still camped on the line — "Hope your husband gits a good claim," "If you all locate near Prairie City be sure to look us up," "Call on us if you need any help; we know what it's like." Then they turned slowly home, stopping at the store on the way to discuss the biggest event since the Run of '89.

Most of the homeseekers raced straight north to avoid tangling with the riders on their flanks. Will Sadler on a fine thoroughbred was in the lead, but one of the Alexander boys on a fleet cow pony was close behind. Both young men had their eyes on a level tract about half a mile from the boundary. Sadler reached it first, sprang to the ground and stuck his stake, while his horse, pulled up too sharply, whirled at the end of the rein. Alexander called, "You've got 'er; stay with it!" and raced on.

In a few minutes Sadler was joined by Jim Cobb with the wagon. The two men quickly located the corner stones, and noted the numerical description of the land. Cobb then took a spade from the wagon and began digging a well as evidence of possession. Sadler mounted again, and set off for the land-office on the Rock Island Railroad, thirty miles to the northwest, where the Government had platted the county seat town of Enid.

The young homesteader never forgot that wild ride to Enid. All over the prairie people were spreading out, driving stakes, hunting corner stones, arguing with other claimants, mounting and racing on. He saw several fine horses lying dead from the hard riding and the heat, their bodies already bloated until their legs stuck up in the air. He reached Enid about four o'clock. The "city" consisted of the frame shack that housed the Government land-office, but people were swarming all over the townsite, staking lots and setting up tents, and some lumber was already on the ground. He joined a rapidly lengthening line before the land-office, where he received a number giving him a date to return and file on his claim. He camped overnight at the spring on the Enid townsite, and returned the next day to the place he had staked. He found his brother-in-law still in possession; another claimant had come shortly after he started for the land-office, but Cobb had got rid of him without a fight. The two men camped on the claim a few days until the filing was completed; then Cobb returned to his farm and Sadler drove to Missouri for his wife and baby girl.

Other homeseekers were having similar experiences. The Alexanders rode about four miles before they separated, one turning to the east and the other to the west, and stuck their stakes. Their women and children followed in the wagon with a fifteen-year-old boy from Old Oklahoma who had come along to drive. The little girl who had spotted the sooner now became interested in the coyotes slinking across the prairie, their tails tucked under, frantic with fear. "They won't have the land all to themselves any more," explained her mother; "*people* will be living here now." The women soon lost sight of the riders, but they inquired of another homeseeker, who remembered the white shirts and red sashes and directed them on their way.

The fire had not reached the place where the Alexanders staked, and the grass though short was dry as paper. When the women came up, the men unhitched the horses, took a sod plow from the wagon, and plowed several furrows around the camp for a fire guard. Then they started to hunt the corner stones, not an easy task in the thick grass.

The women remained with the wagon. Soon they saw smoke rolling from the west, and then a fire racing across the prairie toward them. Their plowed furrows looked like too frail a barrier. One of the women took the children into the wagon, covered them with bedclothes, and quickly dropped the canvas sides that had been raised for ventilation. The other woman and the boy set a backfire, working with frantic haste, and the roaring menace swept by.

Meanwhile the men, not realizing their families were in danger, continued to hunt the corner stones. They saw the fire coming, with the deer and antelope running ahead of it, and they protected themselves by burning off a place to stand. Then, with the grass burned off, they found the corner stones, but to their dismay they discovered that both had staked the same quarter. They decided to camp there together trusting eventually to find a claim abandoned by some discouraged homesteader.

That night they made a shelter by lifting the overjets [1] with the

---

[1] The overjets were extensions, made of boards, six or eight inches wide and six inches to a foot high, fastened to the top of the wagon box; the bows that held up the canvas cover were fastened to these overjets. The purpose was to furnish a

cover from the wagon and setting them on the ground. Here sleeping quarters were arranged for the women and children, while the men prepared to lie on the ground under the wagon. They found a water hole in a nearby creek, and watered and fed their horses. They cooked and ate their supper and went to bed. The coyotes howled around them, but the wild prairie on which they lay had a feeling of home.

The next day they drew straws to decide which of the two men should file on the claim, and the winner rode away to the land-office, while the rest began to construct a dug-out. They camped there about a week, and then returned to Old Oklahoma to spend the winter. Before spring the landless brother filed on a deserted claim in the neighborhood, and the two families separated to settle on their own land.

Many of the "Strippers" returned to the line the evening of the Run. They joined their families camping around the parked wagons, or they gathered at the store to compare adventures. Lindsey and Le Rossignol came back with their faces so black from prairie cinders as to be unrecognizable. They were in high spirits, rejoicing over the good claims they had staked, picturing the "development of the country" that would take place, describing the town they would build, the populous city that would soon follow. Tired riders came by, stopping at the store, buying food, asking for water.

Some had raced half way across the Strip finding a man on every quarter until they met the swarm coming south from Kansas. One who had picked his land carefully before the President's proclamation against illegal entry, had been unable to locate it; "Bill thought about that place so much he expected to find a white house and a red barn on it," said his friends. Brother Hopkins came back in Clark's wagon; his horse had broken its leg, and he had lost the race. Some of the unsuccessful rode away from the store and never returned; others planned to stay in the neighborhood and try to buy out some claimant.

---

wider sleeping space during the journey. Most homeseekers packed their wagons solidly to the top of the top-box with goods; then their straw-tick (pioneer equivalent for mattress) was placed on top of the load, extending into the overjets. When night came, they slept in this snug bed, with the canvas cover forming the roof. The author has a vivid recollection of sleeping in this way on the road to Oklahoma. It was only at the end of the journey that the overjets and cover were removed and set down on the prairie.

Epic tales were told at the crossroads trading post that night. Lew Hoskins told the best one, a bit of sharp practice within the letter of the law that appealed to the lusty individualism of his hearers. Everybody knew Lew as a dashing young fellow who had been living with Perry Eaton waiting for the opening. Perry, already the owner of a homestead, was not debarred from entering the Strip He accordingly selected a fine piece of land, and undertook to train Lew's pony to find it. Every day he started at the line, raced to the location, and gave the pony a good feed of oats. The animal soon developed a strong partiality for the spot where oats grew so abundantly. When the signal was finally given for homeseekers to enter the forbidden land, young Hoskins' pony raced straight as an arrow to one of the best claims in the Strip.

Some of the riders reported grimmer experiences. One found the body of a man lying in a hollow; his throat had been slit and his skull crushed in. Another had met a man who appeared demented, wandering around in a circle and asking helplessly, "Where can I stake a claim? I want to get a home." Two others had found a man groaning with a broken leg; his wrecked wagon lay in a ditch, and his team had kicked itself loose and run away. They were able to carry him to a camp of strangers who cared for him. Another party laughed at a trick they had played on the Negro, frightening him from his claim by pretending they were going to hang him. "That's right; we don't want any niggers in this country," chorused the listeners.

Several had had adventures with sooners. A bunch of former cowpunchers of the Strip rode up shortly after midnight. They had kept together and staked fine claims in a locality they knew on the Black Bear. But just as Ed Smith stuck his stake, a sooner had ridden out of the brush and challenged his priority. Ed looked at the stranger's sleek, perfectly dry horse, and at his own lathered, heaving pony. "My horse is tired and yours is fresh," he cried. "But by God, I'll race you back to the line; and the one that gets there first gets the claim." The sooner refused, became ugly, and finally pulled his gun. Ed looked at him straight without moving ("I knowed he wouldn't shoot; he acted like a kid with a toy pistol"), and he put his gun back and began to dicker. He offered to trade the claim for Ed's saddle. The saddle was the pride of Ed's heart; he had paid $105 for it at Cheyenne, Wyoming just before he had ridden down the trail to prepare for the opening. "By God, you don't get my saddle or the claim either," he said. "I've got witnesses to prove when I rode in, and you've got nothing but a dry horse." By this time the other boys had ridden up and joined him, and the sooner slunk away.

The audience at the store was sympathetic. They all agreed that a sooner was a special kind of pole cat. While they were still talking, the sooner himself came in. He made a half-hearted attempt to sell out for fifty dollars, but he finally admitted his dishonesty. "I thought I might git a claim that way, or at least make something off of a man that wanted it. But the next time any of this land is opened, I'm goin' to git ready and make the Run right." Even Ed Smith joined in the good wishes when he rode away.

Thus with laughter, with chicanery and violence, with neighborly helpfulness and the age-old love of hearth and home, the Cherokee Strip passed from a prairie wilderness to a land of farms and striving towns. Prairie City had doubled its trade territory in one day. Out of this fact and the gambling spirit unleashed by the chances of the Run, the town entered into a period of feverish promotion.

VII

PRAIRIE CITY FEELS A BOOM

A NEW town was springing up on the Strip boundary that hope-filled spring of '94. Piles of lumber lay on the grass, a double row of skeleton frames was rising above the flat prairie, the air was filled with the staccato sound of the hammer. All this was the creation of the Prairie City Town Company organized by Le Rossignol, Dr. Lindsey, and S. W. Brown.

The new townsite lay on Dad Colby's land. Strangely enough Arthur Goodwin, having founded the town, had been unwilling to sacrifice his farm to its growth. But Colby agreed to sell twenty acres of his pasture for two hundred dollars. Under the special terms granted Old Soldiers he was already entitled to a patent. Shortly after the Strip Opening he made a trip to Kingfisher, forty miles southwest, where the land-office for that section was located, taking three of his neighbors as witnesses, and made formal proof of continuous residence. After he had thus "proved up," the land was his in fee simple title.

The townsite lay on the Strip border, a few rods off the north-south road. Le Rossignol made the survey, using skills he had picked up somewhere in his wanderings. ("Why do you make the streets so wide, Ross?" "For street car. W'en he build Chicago, he not tink a zat. Here we start eet right.") It was five years before anyone discovered that he had forgotten to lay out any road to reach it; people simply drove across Colby's land without question.

The town company had a well drilled in the center of their Main Street, and installed a pump and horse trough. They drove to the county seat and filed their plat with the register of deeds. The sale of lots began February 1; on that day ten of the Strippers and Arthur Goodwin bought business lots on Main Street — thirty dollars for a corner lot, fifteen dollars for others. Nobody bought a residence site; in this strange town every prospective business man professed to be a farmer, having stated explicitly under oath that he was taking his claim to live on and cultivate and for no other purpose. But the ambitions of the promoters did not run to turning sod and sweating over live stock. With the ideals of the gambler, the grafter, and the builder curiously mixed in their thinking, they expected to rear skyscrapers, deal in large affairs, and enrich themselves by what they would take from the undeveloped resources of a new frontier.

All this activity was good for the farmers, who made a few dollars selling stone for foundations, hauling lumber from the railroad, working on the buildings. Joe Spragg raised Goodwin's store on rollers, hitched on his traction engine, and hauled it to the new site. Dave Hodge's blacksmith shop and Dr. Lindsey's little drug store followed. Le Rossignol's lumber-yard sprawled over the prairie. Aunt Becky Newton came from one of the railroad towns and began serving meals in a tent till her bare, barn-like hotel was completed. Her daughter waited on table. "You're the prettiest girl in Prairie City, Miss Maud," Dr. Lindsey told her. For more than three years she was the only girl there.

Bachelors like Dr. Lindsey were able to live at the hotel, spending only an occasional night on their claims to comply with the homestead law. Married men were required to maintain an actual residence on the land. They built houses, established their families there, and drove back and forth every day to their business in town. Some of them rode bicycles exactly like present day models except that they cost seventy-five dollars and had no brakes. "Dude contraptions," said the farmers; nothing aroused their ire so much as the bicycle craze that had been sweeping the country the past eight or ten years.

The homestead law allowed a settler six months to establish a residence; hence the Strip had been almost empty of inhabitants while the promoters were laying out their townsite. Some of those who had staked claims had returned to families they had left in distant states. Those who had been living in Old Oklahoma had remained there in their temporary dwellings, gathering corn and kaffir they had planted, taking trips to their claims to make improvements. But all were settled by late winter or early spring of '94. The bare country across the line was soon dotted with dug-outs and kaffir patches, and the new society was breaking out into a fever of politics, visiting, and dancing. All these settlers bought

their supplies at Prairie City. Everywhere they went, they were
received with friendly interest as "new neighbors."

By the first of May the new town was humming with business.
S. W. Brown was selling sod plows to the "Strippers," binders to
the older homesteaders, nails and barbed wire, harness and horse
collars; he expected to sell a good many buggies and surreys after
harvest. All the older settlers knew him and had dealt with him
in Hennessey. C. T. Kingman and Son, both "Strippers," put in a
general merchandise store. C. T. was already a big man in the new
county across the line; an active Democrat, he had been appointed
by the territorial governor as county commissioner. Dave Hodge
sharpened more plow shares than ever; Dr. Lindsey sold chill tonic
and dispensed medical advice to homesteaders on both sides of
the line.

Another busy spot was "Matt's Place," established by a Stripper named Matt Kennedy. The opening of a saloon had revealed
a sharp division in the community. Most of the new city builders
had been in favor of it as an inducement to bring people to town.
Goodwin regretted it as a demoralizing influence. The farmers
were divided. The church people were sharply opposed; Matt had
been boarding with the Colbys while his shack was going up, but
when Mother Colby learned the nature of the business he planned
to establish, she told him reluctantly he would have to leave her
house.

Before this, there had been an occasional supply of liquor
brought to a dance, and some of the farmers always came home
reeling drunk from their trips to the railroad towns; but in general
the community was sober. Now everything was changed. The men
seemed to have no power of resistance. As soon as they tied their
teams to the hitch racks, they made for the saloon. Women waited
patiently in the stores, or sometimes in desperation they even in-
vaded the saloon to bring home drunken husbands. Girls made
detours to avoid knots of men gathered in the streets; for in such
groups there were sure to be some whose speech had been loosened by alcohol. And as election time approached, the candidates
not only found it necessary to drink with the men, but some of
them adopted the habit of buying a keg of beer and leaving it on
tap for all comers. After such a debauch dozens of men could be
seen lying along the roadsides, having failed to reach their homes.
But probably the saloon did bring more people to the town; it

had supplanted the blacksmith shop and the postoffice as the place of meeting.

Goodwin kept the postoffice for a year after Cleveland's inauguration in order to accommodate his customers, but when the new town started he yielded it to a Democrat. Young Ralph Evans, a Strip homesteader, had put up a little frame shack, purchased an old army press and a few cases of type, and was preparing to launch a newspaper. He consented to take over the postoffice, reasoning that it would bring people and therefore news to his office.

The first issue of the *Prairie Fire* appeared April 6. It was a four-page weekly, with its inside pages of ready print supplied by a Kansas syndicate. It carried no local advertising beyond an occasional brief notice: conservatives like Goodwin and Brown were satisfied to let business come their way by natural gravitation; and the boosting element operated on a margin too precarious to stand the extra expense. But it flaunted the legend, "The Only Newspaper in the World Interested in Prairie City, Oklahoma"; it extolled the accomplishments of the town in lyric tones; and as for the future — that was bounded only by the sky that overarched the plain.

It was packed with news, in print so small as to be all but illegible, written in the friendly, informal tone of neighborhood conversation —

Perry Eaton has bought a new buggy from our enterprising hardwareman, S. W. Brown. Who's the lucky girl, Perry?

A. T. Strickland has struck a fine vein of water on his claim in the Strip.

Dr. Lindsey reports a new merchant at the home of Arthur Goodwin. The father's condition is said to be serious.

And its "Territorial Topics," set under the recently adopted great seal of the commonwealth, gave the subscribers the first regular news they had ever had of happenings in Oklahoma.

Evans also supplied his readers with political comment, entering violently into the bitter personalities of an Oklahoma election year. He denounced the last legislature; "about one-third of its members should be in the penitentiary, and another third drummed out of the territory for being ornery and trifling." As to the county seat politician who served as Council member from the local district, "we know that he spent half of his time during the session chasing saddle-colored coons of the female sex up and down the alleys of the Capital City." And he quarreled as fiercely with the editors of surrounding villages over the merits of their rival settlements; one was "a thoroughbred ass with an enormous belly," and his town was "so dead it stinks."

But he published no local scandal. Although the hot blood and high spirits of the community often overflowed in violence and licentiousness, such lapses were never recorded in the home town paper. The subscribers were adept at reading the truth behind the news. "Two of our well known young people were married at the county seat last Monday" might as well have been worded, "It was a shot-gun wedding, and the groom skipped out immediately after the ceremony." When the most worthless family of all — shiftless, thieving, quarrelsome — sold out and moved back to Missouri, there was an edge to the friendly words, "Our loss is Missouri's gain."

The subscription price was a dollar a year, payable in cash, stovewood for the office, breaking the editor's claim, or butter and eggs, which the editor traded for board at Aunt Becky's. Nearly everybody subscribed for "our paper." But two hundred subscribers from an agricultural community would not have supported the enterprise. The life of the paper was dependent on the publication of "final proof" notices.

Homesteaders in Old Oklahoma were allowed to prove up at any time between five and seven years; hence those who came in the Run of April 22, 1889 and filed at the land-office during the next few days were eligible about the first of May, 1894. But not more than half the settlers had staked their claims in the Run. Many had come late, finding an overlooked or abandoned quarter. Others had bought out the original claimant; some claims had changed hands four or five times since the Run. And of the settlers who had come in the Run, many planned to wait the whole seven years in order to postpone the payment of taxes.

Four of the 136 homesteaders in the township had proved up early. One had "commuted" under a provision of the Organic Act permitting a settler after twelve months' residence to buy his claim at a dollar and a quarter an acre; he had taken this rash step because he had a chance to mortgage his land for $750 on the very day he made his payment. The other three had accepted the Old Soldiers' privilege; and all three of them had mortgages on their

farms within a year. About one-third of the other settlers proved
up from May to the end of the year 1894; and most of the remainder were distributed rather evenly through the next two
years, leaving only a few late comers who delayed even down to
1900.

Before proving up, a settler was required to publish his intention in a newspaper of general circulation — which in practice
meant politically acceptable to the register and receiver of the
land-office, at that time Cleveland appointees. Evans in spite of
Populist leanings managed to qualify as "friendly" to the Kingfisher office. He missed the first notices because of a required
twelve months' "continuous publication," but he got all of the later
business. On some weeks he had to use an extra sheet because the
notices almost filled his paper. The standard price was four dollars
— in real money. The homesteader would call at his office and get
the publisher's affidavit before going to Kingfisher with his three
witnesses to make his proof. Several neighbors usually made the
trip together and witnessed for each other. Often they took their
wives along and mortgaged their farms on the day they received
them, and the same neighbors witnessed these instruments also.

With the prospect of a broader tax base the people of the Union
school district decided to build a new schoolhouse. By this time the
sod building leaked where mice had burrowed, and an occasional
centiped dropped from the ceiling. The rafters sagged on each
side of the ridge log, so that the schoolhouse and its surrounding
district was known far and wide as "Wrinkle-Roof." In the summer
of 1894 the people held a special election and voted bonds to the
amount of $340 — the legal limit of 5 per cent on the district valua-
tion of $6,800 — to erect a frame building. They employed a car-
penter to supervise the work, but the men also donated their services, quarrying stone for the foundation, hauling lumber, and
working on the house. It was 36 by 24 feet in size, with walls ten
feet high — a plain box-like structure with a row of windows on
each side, a vestibule in front, and a steep roof. Glistening with
white paint it loomed up on the prairie as conspicuous as a lone
tree.

It was the pride of the district. The *Prairie Fire* characterized
it as "a magnificent structure, one of the finest in the territory," and
suggested that "it might be appropriate to change the name of this
township to University Township." The people voted a tax of

ten mills — the legal limit — to maintain a three months' term of school, looking forward confidently to the next year when they could levy taxes on the land. Other districts in the township followed their example, replacing their sod or log schoolhouses by these large, bare buildings as alike as packing crates.

The people now had a place of meeting unbelievably spacious and splendid in comparison with their cramped dwellings. As soon as it was finished they celebrated by an oyster supper and dance on the new floor. Then they decided on a "box supper" to raise money for lamps. These affairs followed a regular ritual: first came a literary program; then Perry Eaton held up gaily decorated boxes of lunch prepared by the girls, and with many jokes auctioned them off to the young men; and each purchaser opened his box, found the name of the girl, and the two ate their meal together with much giggling and blushing. Thus they raised six dollars for two "elegant" kerosene lamps that swung on chains from the ceiling. The literary and the Industrial Legion took on new life in these pleasant surroundings.

But it was apparent that the center of social activity was shifting to the new townsite, a mile and a quarter away. The Baptists decided to follow the trend and build a church there. By this time their congregation had been doubled by accessions from the Strip, but these new settlers were entirely without money. They managed, however, by the fall of '94 to collect twenty dollars, with which they purchased three lots a block off Main Street. By a mighty effort they raised sixty-five dollars more as the nucleus of a building fund. Their mission board came to the rescue with the remainder, and members donated foundation stones and labor. Brother Hayman was always ready with a team for hauling, and he worked all over the building with trowel and mortar or hammer and saw. By the spring of '95 the building was completed — a large, plain box like the schoolhouse. Will Sadler applied the white paint; and the congregation showed its appreciation by "a rising vote of thanks," carefully recording the action for all time in the minutes of the business meeting.

The men made fairly comfortable pews of twelve-inch boards for seat and back nailed to shaped uprights. They made a rather attractive desk for the pulpit, staining and varnishing the yellow pine. And the women by superhuman efforts managed to purchase a reed organ, which was hauled from the railroad and installed in time for the first service.

The whole community attended the Baptist church that Sunday. Brother Hayman's voice choked a little in his prayer of thanksgiving. Nothing seemed impossible in this new building erected for the glory of God and the salvation of Prairie City. Sister Hayman played the organ. And how the people enjoyed it! No more picking out tunes by "do, re, mi" and Fred Peters' tuning fork and his nasal tenor. After the benediction they would not leave; they clustered around the instrument, and sang "When the Roll is Called up Yonder," "Launch out into the Deep," and "Happy Day" loud enough to raise the rafters. No service had been scheduled for the evening, but they came back again and sang. A cloud collected in the southwest, but they stayed until they had to drive home in a choking dust storm. From this time on, the Baptist church vied with the saloon as the social center of Prairie City.

The erection of this building broke into the neighborhood solidarity of the union Sunday school. The Baptists and their Methodist friends withdrew to form a Baptist Sunday school there, Mrs. Lockwood still teaching the children, and Jerome Alexander, from the Strip, serving as superintendent.

The Sunday school at the schoolhouse became more and more a Campbellite organization. Brother Hopkins' time was increased to two Sundays a month. He spent the other two at "Highview," a sod schoolhouse erected by the new settlers a mile and a half across the line in the Strip; but he enrolled all who joined at this place with the Prairie City congregation. The two neighborhoods thus formed one church, with one set of officers. Most of the members loaded their families and their neighbors into their wagons, and alternated their attendance between the two preaching points, while their business meetings were held at the home of Dad Colby or some other centrally located residence.

In the spring of '95 the congregation purchased some lots on the side of town opposite the Baptist church, and the men helped Brother Hopkins to set up his house there. This was the first residence in the town. Sister Hopkins began to "do dressmaking" for the wives of the town builders, and soon she opened a millinery shop in one corner of Kingman's store.

Sister Hopkins in her home and Aunt Becky in her hotel found a serious problem in the town's water supply. All Oklahoma water was bad, but the Prairie City water was worse than bad. It curdled in great sticky flakes when it came in contact with soap, and it ate holes in cooking utensils. Apparently it was equally destructive to the human insides, but it tasted so bad nobody drank more than a few swallows. There was nothing to do but carry water a quarter of a mile from Dad Colby's well, and to try to catch rainwater for washing. But the farmers drank from the town well — spitting and making wry faces — when they came in to do their trading.

Thus the town was started. A bare little cluster of shacks, with the Baptist church shining in new paint, it was the pride and the hope of the builders. But these builders were to suffer much disappointment during the first years.

VIII
THE ECONOMIC BASIS

THE YEAR 1893 had been a bad time to start a town. The promoters had not realized the import of the calamitous depression that had struck the East. To a people busy with elemental tasks the closing of mines and factories had no meaning; and as for the freezing of credits, that condition was perpetual at Prairie City. One read about these things in the *Kansas City Weekly Star*, just as one read about cholera in India. When the price of wheat dropped that year to thirty-two cents, everyone talked of the inevitable "wheat boom" that would follow.

But the boom did not materialize: the price was 34 cents in '94; it had risen only to 38 or 41 cents in '96. The price of corn was 15 to 20 cents a bushel; most of it was fed to hogs, which brought from $2.50 to $3.50 a hundred. Only a few farmers around Prairie City had reached the place where they had cattle for sale, but the price ranged from $1.50 to $2 a hundred for cows and heifers, up to an occasional peak of $4 for prime steers. There was of course no market in Prairie City; these prices were paid at the railroad towns fifteen or twenty miles away.

The country was still too new and its people too restless for the production of much poultry and butter; but a few of the more energetic farm wives had begun to supplement the family income from this source. Hens hauled to the railroad towns brought $2 to $2.25 a dozen, or sometimes they were weighed and sold for 3 to 4 cents a pound; spring chickens were sold at $1.50 to $1.75 a dozen. Butter brought 10 to 12½ cents a pound in winter, 6½ cents in summer; eggs had a seasonal range of 6 to 11 cents a dozen.

It was of course impracticable to carry butter and eggs to these distant markets except when it was necessary to make the trip for some other purpose. Goodwin and the Kingmans bought this produce at Prairie City, keeping it without ice until they could haul it to the railroad. The local price of eggs in summer was as low as

2½ to 3 cents a dozen, but even then the merchants handled them mainly to accommodate their customers. Goodwin sometimes carried them to the back of his store and dumped them in the alley.

Worse even than the low prices were the crop failures of the middle '90's. The terrible heat and drought of the Strip Opening was the beginning of a dry cycle such as this new country had never before known. There was enough rain during the winter to produce good wheat in '94, but all other crops were seriously damaged. The next year was the worst of all.

Day after day without relief hot winds scorched the earth while the naked sun blazed its way across a metallic sky; the land lay lurid dark under a pall of red dust or blurred mirages shimmered over the burned fields. A few scattered heads of wheat stood up too thin for binding. The farmers removed the canvas from their binders, stood on the platform, and pulled the grain in with a hand rake; thus they managed to garner a little for seed. The oats were not worth reaping. The corn failed, but the farmers cut the stalks for fodder. This and some kaffir furnished the only feed.

The drought continued, with only an occasional break, through '96. That year there was a light wheat crop, which was threshed and hauled to market. But as soon as it was cut, chinch bugs swarmed from the stubble to the growing corn and kaffir. The farmers tried to spread an infection by loosing diseased bugs among them; they plowed a furrow along the field to trap the crawling mass of insects, trying then to destroy them with hot water or kerosene or to crush them with a dragging log; but all these methods failed. The corn and kaffir crumpled under the attacks of the pests as they moved across the fields. Only a few patches, not joining wheat fields, were spared.

The Strip settlers suffered terribly under these repeated blows. For more than three years they lived on their land without raising anything but some nubbins of corn, a fair supply of kaffir, and one light crop of forty-cent wheat. They found a few days' work on the claims of Prairie City business men or the farms of Old Oklahoma; but wages even in harvest had gone down to fifty or seventy-five cents a day, and the price of breaking prairie was seventy-five cents an acre. Probably the whole country would have been abandoned except for the financial reserves and the confidence built up during the good years by the older settlement.

A small amount of relief was offered them during these hard

beginnings. In the fall of '94 the Rock Island officials agreed to advance twenty-five thousand bushels of wheat for their first sowing. But most of the "Strippers" near Prairie City got their seed from Old Oklahoma; many had planted a crop there, which they returned to harvest in '94, and others bought from the farmers.

The next year this older settlement also was asking aid from the railroad. The county commissioners took the initiative. In July after the disastrous wheat failure, they advised the farmers to meet in their schoolhouses to determine the amount of seed needed to sow their fields. The meetings were held on the afternoon of July 15; each compiled a careful list of farmers requiring assistance, with the amount of seed needed by each. The average ran from five hundred to eight hundred bushels for each two-mile by three-mile school district with its twenty-four farms.

But the railroad officials declined to help. The failure, they said, had been general throughout the Kansas and Oklahoma territory served by their lines, and they were unable to assist the whole area. The farmers then held a mass meeting at the county seat — a hilarious, riotous meeting in spite of the grim need that inspired it — and drew up a resolution expressing "an abiding faith in our country" and a belief "that this extended drought is an exception and not the rule," and declaring their purpose "to redouble our diligence and try again." But the railway officials remained unmoved. One of the county commissioners then made a trip to Kansas; he found a man at Hutchinson willing to furnish ten thousand bushels of wheat to farmers in return for one-fourth the yield from their fields. And when oat planting came the following spring, the railroad refunded the freight on seed oats shipped to its trade territory in Oklahoma.

During that same July a number of ministers wrote on their own initiative to their church papers asking aid for the drought victims; the wheat and oats, they said, had failed, the garden seed lay in the ground unsprouted, the pastures were so dry that cows were dying of starvation, and the people were hungry. One minister from the county seat traveled through Kansas speaking in the churches and taking collections for the "Oklahoma sufferers." Editor Evans and other boosters writhed under the national publicity thus given to Oklahoma's somewhat-less-than-bountiful crops. Even the governor felt it necessary to defend the territory in his published annual report. There had been some lack of rain, he admitted, but the country was fairly prosperous; as for those who had taken it upon themselves to ask for aid, if conditions were as bad as they asserted their churches should withdraw from such a barren field.

Viewed from the outside, the plight of the Oklahoma settlers was enough to wring one's heart. But no outsider ever reckoned upon the hopeful spirit of the people that enabled them to find expedients and hold on. In only a few instances were they driven to desperation.

It was in July of '95 that a "Stripper" came into the Kingman store and bought a bill of groceries amounting to $4.35; he put the goods into his wagon and started to drive off. When the merchant demanded payment, he called back defiantly, "Git it if you can." The angry Kingman called the constable, who overtook the man four miles from town. At the examination before the justice of the peace, it was shown that his wife was ill and that his family was starving. The people took up a collection and paid for the groceries, and he went home heartened.

These hard years swept away the financial supports upon which the promoters had expected to build their Prairie City. Almost the only real money spent in the town came from Old Soldiers' pensions and from mortgages.

The Democrats had not been brave enough to withdraw the gratuities that the Harrison administration had distributed so lavishly. There were twenty-seven pensioners living on the farms — on both sides of the line — near Prairie City. The usual stipend was twelve dollars a month, given in four lump payments a year. That was more money than the average farmer ever saw during the depression years. Nearly all of it was spent in the town for groceries, clothes, and farm machinery.

Arthur Goodwin usually served as banker, cashing the checks when they came through the mail. He kept rolls of bills and sacks of loose change hidden behind bolts of goods or stuffed in kegs of nails. Every six weeks or two months he dug his money out of these caches and carried it to deposit in the bank at Hennessey; but he usually overlooked a few sacks, and his clerks often ran across them in unexpected places as they went about their work. One of them has never forgotten the time he sold a stove to a Strip homesteader, not knowing it contained one of these hidden rolls. He has a vivid memory of the merchant's excitement and the wild drive across the prairie to overtake the purchaser before he should start a fire.

It was probably just as well that the town had no bank. The whole Oklahoma country had been almost without credit ever since the Opening, for Eastern financial circles had been afraid to hazard their money there. The few banks in the railroad towns operated on short capital. Nobody could obtain a loan without mortgaging his live stock, and the interest ranged from 2 to 5 per cent a month. The legislature passed a law limiting the rate to 12 per cent a year, but the bankers easily evaded it by withholding a portion of the principal. Under these hard conditions farmers borrowed money only rarely.

But as soon as·the settlers received title to their land, they had a new basis for credit. All but six of the 136 homesteaders in Prairie Township proved up before the end of '96; of this number 73 mortgaged their farms almost immediately. The loans were usually from two hundred to three hundred dollars on a quarter.

The Deming Investment Company of Oswego, Kansas was the pioneer farm loan company doing business in the territory. In the spring of '93 it opened a branch office in Oklahoma City, and began to invest the money of its clients in Oklahoma mortgages. About half the loans in the Prairie City community were made by this firm. The average note ran for five years; on its face it bore 7 per cent interest, but the borrower gave a "commission note" to the president of the company amounting to 30 per cent of the loan and secured by a second mortgage. The interest and commission thus totaled 13 per cent, in addition to various fees.

S. W. Brown held almost half of the other farm mortgages in the community. He sold machinery on credit, and secured himself by mortgages on the farms; the notes ran from one hundred to two hundred dollars, and bore 10 per cent interest. Other farm loans were made by individual investors in the North Central States. On the face they carried 8 to 12 per cent interest.

The incumbrances on the farms of the township totaled about $18,000 by the end of 1896. Some of the money thus obtained went to pay debts and taxes — the tax on a patented quarter averaged about twenty-five dollars a year. The rest went into the purchase of live stock and machinery and the building of houses and other improvements on the farms. The new businesses in Prairie City could hardly have survived the depression years except for the money from this source.

Some of the settlers said they would starve before they would encumber their land. In general this was the more thrifty class: men who tilled their land well, cared for their live stock, husbanded their resources, whose wives were successful with poultry and knew how to save food and clothing. But a few of the more successful farmers mortgaged their land simply because they were shrewd; seeing in this new country boundless possibilities for the investment of capital, they stretched their credit and bought additional land. Eighteen farmers in the township who had come to Oklahoma with what they could haul in a covered wagon thus owned half sections of land (under mortgage) by the end of 1896.

An equal number of quarter-sections were sold to newcomers from neighboring states, young men who had made a start on rented farms in these older regions and who saw in Oklahoma's cheap land a chance to own a home. The price of a good quarter of patented land ranged from $750 to $1800, the purchaser assuming the mortgage and paying the remainder in cash. There was usually a mortgage; the homesteaders who kept their land clear were seldom the ones who sold. These land transactions of 1894–96 fell into a fairly constant pattern: proved up, mortgaged, sold — all within the space of two years.

The sellers, having acquired a small capital by grace of the homestead law, moved away to various places. Some returned to the old home. In general it was a disillusioned group that went "back" east against the tide of American settlement; Prairie City never heard of them again. More were attracted to the West: those who had come under Mormon influence settled in Utah; others went to California, forming the van of a famous migration. Most of those who went "out" west prospered and became leaders of their new communities; some returned after a few years, full of enthusiasm, to take up fresh opportunities at Prairie City.

During the same period a number of discouraged "Strippers" relinquished their claims, and — to use the expressive frontier phrase — "went back to live with their wife's folks." The first winter good quarters were abandoned, sold for ten dollars, traded for a mule. By the spring of '94, when the country became settled, the price had gone up to one hundred dollars or more; by the following fall the price was three hundred to five hundred dollars, where it remained in spite of the bad years. Most of this land was taken by homeseekers who had waited in the Prairie City neighborhood after failing to obtain a claim in the Run. Three or four quarters were purchased by young women, who thus escaped the hazards of the race. There was no legal way by which the occupant could transfer title, but he would relinquish it for a consideration, leaving the purchaser to file on it the instant it became vacant.

Some purchases were compromise settlements between rival claimants. In the confusion of the Run two or more homeseekers had staked the same claim in good faith; or perhaps it was a sooner who held out against an honest homesteader, trusting to his nuisance value to extort a cash payment. Sometimes these rival claimants lived on the same quarter for two or three years, each planting crops and making improvements. There was of course the legal remedy of a formal contest at the land-office, but the Prairie City homesteaders usually settled their disputes by holding on until one weakened and consented to sell out to his rival.

Four sections in each township of the Strip had been reserved from homestead entry: sections 16 and 36 as in Old Oklahoma for common schools, section 13 for higher education, section 33 for public buildings. The governor leased this land during 1894 and 1895. Much of it was taken by farmers in Old Oklahoma, who needed additional acreage.

Thus the Strip and the older frontier tended to merge into one community. Although the new section still lagged a little in material advancement — the orchards were younger, the fields were smaller, the houses were more primitive — one no longer marked a sharp difference as soon as he crossed the line. The Strip settlers belonged to a different county, and they struggled with more elemental problems of township government and district school organization. A further separation remained in the thought and speech of the people — a freemasonry of common experience that even yet has not faded from the minds of the old-timers. But the settlers on both sides of the line joined in the business and social life that centered in Prairie City.

IX
THE PEOPLE COME TO TOWN

ARD times never slowed the currents of ebullient life that swirled through the one street of Prairie City. Organized groups of every kind were formed around this center, and the whole population gathered there for Saturday afternoons and special celebrations. Some of this activity was fostered by the town builders to stimulate trade; more of it was spontaneous, springing out of the social vitality of the community.

The very first spring the young business leaders and half a dozen young men from the farms organized a band, meeting for practice in the Baptist church. At the end of the street where the two lines of shacks halted at the edge of the prairie, they built a stand; and there they played on Saturday afternoons. And the people filled the town to enjoy it, their talk and laughter quickened by the rhythm of the music.

Ball games also enlivened the Saturday afternoons. Young town builders and tall young men from the country made up the team. They played purely for fun, but it was good fun and they played surprisingly good ball. Their opponents were sometimes teams from rival towns, more often tough farm boys from some rural neighborhood. A playing field was marked out on the prairie near the Baptist church. The women sat in wagons and buggies lined up back of the diamond, while the men stood on the ground, yelling, crowding the players until they had to run in curves to reach the bases.

If other diversions were required, it was always easy to start a horse race. Perry Eaton's pony was about the fastest thing that ever skimmed over the prairie, but there were other young men rash enough to boast about their own mounts. Such arguments invariably ended in a challenge and a bet, a track was hastily laid off in Dad Colby's pasture, and the men streamed out from the town to watch and wager whatever money they had on the outcome. And sometimes footraces were held through Main Street and on to the section line. Sixteen-year-old Earl Peters could outdistance everyone in the neighborhood; but there was the never-forgotten occasion when the backers of a better runner from the county seat won all the bets and cleaned out the town.

Sometimes in the fall the men met in town to elect captains and draw up rules for organized "coyote drives." Each drive embraced a township, the men forming a line on the outside, closing their ranks as they came in and attempting to shoot the surrounded animals in the center. In the summer of 1895 they joined in a deadlier hunt.

Since the people had accumulated some property, the territory had become infested with outlaws, who robbed express trains, murdered country storekeepers and rifled their tills, and carried on an organized system of stealing horses, relaying them along an underground route from Texas to Kansas. Though Prairie City had escaped the worst of these depredations, the crimes had become so general that no community could hope for exemption. People began to suspect that there was a hide-out in the neighborhood; a shiftless family had recently settled on a school quarter and built a number of dug-outs — too many for any legitimate purpose — in the creek bank far from the public road.

The citizens decided to unite for mutual protection. In the spring of 1895 the more substantial farmers met in a room over the Kingman store and organized a lodge of the Anti-Horse Thief Association. The members were pledged to co-operate with the civil authorities in bringing criminals to justice, holding themselves subject to instant call.

In July they were warned that a notorious outlaw known as Dick Yeager and one Isaac Black were headed toward Prairie City. They placed the town under guard and watched the roads. While they were on the alert, a deputy sheriff rode into town and reported that he had seen a horseman — heavily armed and with muffled stirrups — and a covered spring wagon rounding a bend on a lonely country road leading to the school quarter. Quickly he deputized several trustworthy men to assist him. All mounted hastily and set out, some in the rear of the strangers, others riding around on another road to head them off. Their timing was perfect; they surrounded their quarry at a cross-roads where a cornfield and a creek furnished cover. The strangers ignored the command to surrender and began shooting. A considerable battle was fought there at the cross-roads; two of the farmers were wounded, one of the strangers was killed, and the others, seriously wounded, gave themselves up.

The neighborhood hummed with excitement. Everybody was sure that the notorious Yeager had been killed or captured. But the men turned out to be young Oklahoma homesteaders and a Kansas companion with no criminal record. Aside from their refusal to surrender and a veritable arsenal that they carried in the wagon they might have been peaceful citizens traveling through the country. The captives were kept in jail for a time at the county seat and then released. But the farmers who had taken part in the fight were completely exonerated. Prairie City to a man was on their side.

Meanwhile the real Yeager and his companion had slipped through the cordon of A.H.T.A. lodges and reached the western part of the territory. The embattled farmers of that region surrounded them, and after a hide-and-seek pursuit through gypsum hills and inaccessible canyons, Black was killed and Yeager wounded. The wounded outlaw then made his way back towards Prairie City, requisitioning fresh horses and food, always keeping a jump ahead of the farmers, who sprang to arms as he passed through. He stole his last two horses from Strip homesteaders a few miles from town. The men gave the alarm, the A.H.T.A. picked up his trail, and men from three counties converged upon a cornfield where he lay in utter exhaustion only three miles from the suspected hide-out. Officers from Enid took command; and two men entered the cornfield and shot the outlaw, wounding him fatally. The men loaded him into a spring wagon, while a good woman of the neighborhood brought him a drink of coffee and another furnished a straw tick from her own bed. He was taken to the train at Hennessey and carried to jail at Enid, where he died a month later.

The Prairie City lodge assisted in two or three other man hunts during the following years, but never again with such dramatic results. Then as the outlaws were cleared out, it gradually relaxed its vigilance and became in time a semi-social organization holding family picnics in Spragg's Grove. And the same spring the A.H.T.A. was organized, two fraternal societies were formed in the rooms on the upper floor of the Kingman building: the Odd

Fellows, through the efforts of a Strip settler, with twelve charter members, all farmers; and the Masons, with the town's business men and four or five of the more prosperous farmers of Old Oklahoma.

The next organization was a Methodist church — formed in the early spring of '96. For three weeks the Lockwoods with their wagon full of neighbors had been driving seven miles to revival services held by a Methodist evangelist in a country church. At the close of the meetings they arranged for him to come to Prairie City. The Baptists freely gave the use of their building, and the whole community, as always, turned out to attend the services.

The evangelist preached a more emotional gospel than the downright, practical-minded homesteaders had yet heard. He made mysterious references to a "witness of the Spirit"; warned against "joining the church without being converted," or "a change of purpose without a change of heart"; and held out hopes of a super-experience known as "sanctification." Some of his more conscientious listeners were deeply puzzled by a sense of their own inadequacy. The Campbellites were scandalized at his departure from logic — "The Methodist altar has sent more people to hell than the saloons," ranted Dad Colby.

But the meetings swept into an emotional climax, with more converts than Prairie City had ever seen before. The evangelist freely advised them to join the church of their choice: several united with the Baptists; more were persuaded to join the Campbellites; and about twenty were left to form the nucleus of a Methodist congregation formed at the close of the meeting and fully organized when a presiding elder came and held a quarterly conference. Mrs. Lockwood and the boy, Paul, left the Baptists and came with Tom Lockwood into their own church. But even the friendly Baptists were shocked at the ritual; "reading prayers out of a book" was abhorrent to frontier feelings.

The presiding elder arranged for the new congregation to be placed on a circuit that already embraced several neighboring churches. Under this system Prairie City Methodists were entitled to one Sunday a month from the pastor and one "quarterly meeting" a year from the presiding elder. They formed a Sunday school of their own, which according to their denominational practice became an integral part of their church organization. They held their meetings in the afternoon, the Baptists cordially granting them the use of their church. The two congregations attended each other's services, and Mrs. Lockwood served in both Sunday schools as teacher of the children's class. Thus Prairie City adjusted its community life to historical religious divisions.

It was also in the spring of '96 that the Old Soldiers organized. Their leader was Jonathan Cole, who had left a college classroom in Illinois to become a Strip homesteader. The men formed a post of the Grand Army of the Republic with twenty-seven charter members, while their wives organized a Woman's Relief Corps. On May 30 of that year they held their first Decoration Day observance.

The celebration was held in the Baptist church. There was an all-day meeting with a basket dinner at noon, music by the band, an address by Cole, recitations and songs by the children, a roll call of the veterans, and enthusiastic congregational singing of "Marching through Georgia" and "Tenting Tonight." There was no trip to the cemetery, for no Old Soldier was yet buried there, but Fred Peters had made a "Monument to the Unknown Dead" of wood painted to simulate marble and set it up outside the church. The children formed in procession at the band stand and marched to this place with handfuls of spring flowers, which they placed on the monument. To most of the people this act had no particular meaning, but Cole and others of the veterans were moved to tears. To their generation the great war was still very real and very tragic, and the decoration was an act of personal tribute to brothers and comrades who had marched away and were seen no more. They were greatly chagrined when their congregation gathered at the playing field to watch a baseball game at the close of the afternoon service.

In the fall the G.A.R. invited the posts and the women's societies of all the surrounding towns to a three days' encampment at Spragg's Grove. About five hundred came for at least part of the reunion; many brought camp equipment and stayed for the whole session. There were programs and speeches during the day, and personal narratives around the evening camp fires. After taps were sounded at night these graying men broke out in spontaneous antics; animal cries and the esoteric call, "O, Joe, here's your mule!" rang through the grove until it was time to start the breakfast coffee.

Several Confederate veterans attended the encampment, add-

ing their reminiscences to those of their former enemies, and
adopting a resolution of "loyalty to the old flag." Many years were
to pass before the Prairie City post relaxed its Decoration Day observance to include them — "I shall never be convinced that those
who fought to save the Union and those who fought to destroy the
Union should be on the same footing," said Jonathan Cole — but
two or three always attended the services, sitting as close as possible to the section reserved for the G.A.R.

Another patriotic gathering was the Fourth of July celebration
planned by the business leaders of the town. At sunrise the men
took the two anvils from Dave Hodge's blacksmith shop into the
street, placed one on top of the other with a charge of powder between, and set off the explosive with a fuse. There was music and
firecrackers and lemonade; some twisting of the British lion's tail
by the orators; and the reading of the Declaration of Independence
by Ralph Evans. In the evening were fireworks provided by the
business men.

But the third harvest picnic celebrated the month before the
Strip Opening proved to be the last. The people were so restless
in temperament that three years was about the lifetime of any
"annual" event; and the low price of wheat and the unfavorable
seasons put the people in a mood for protest rather than thanksgiving. In the election year of '94 the harvest festival was super-
seded by a Populist picnic. It was a political camp meeting lasting
three days — August 16–18. Farmers came from considerable distances to hear their candidates blast the Republicans and the trusts;
and denounce President Cleveland for his opposition to free silver.

"I hear you had a first rate howling time," said Jonathan Cole.

"Sure they did," said Pat O'Hagan. "I found a bunch of coyotes
in my pasture lined up listenin'; and niver a yip have they made
since they heard those Pops howl."

At the election in the Union schoolhouse that fall Prairie Township voted overwhelmingly Populist, but the Strip settlers holding
their first election in the new township across the line gave a slight
plurality to the Republicans. By plurality elections in most districts
of the territory the Republicans obtained control of the legislature
and re-elected Dennis Flynn to Congress.

The election of 1896 was the culmination of Prairie City's political striving. All through the preceding winter the Industrial
Legion had held township meetings the first and third Wednesday

of every month at the Union schoolhouse, and by February the
Populists had their party organization perfected and were confident of victory. In July when young William Jennings Bryan
voiced the agrarian revolt in flaming oratory and Populist ideals
captured the National Democratic Convention, the atmosphere
of Prairie City fairly crackled with political argument. Men of such
diverse beliefs as the O'Hagans and George Hadley united on the
common ground of blaming the Republicans for the low price of
wheat — and inferentially for the chinch bugs and the drought —
and Charles Lester expressed the hope of the new order in glowing
phrase.

The Democrats and Populists of the territory merged their
forces. Charles Lester was running for the Legislature on this fusion ticket. James Y. Callahan, a serious-minded young homesteader living near Kingfisher, was nominated for delegate to Congress; he was a real dirt farmer, and incidentally a Methodist
minister, preaching in country schoolhouses near his claim. He did
not speak at Prairie City during the campaign, but most of its people supported him. He was one of themselves.

Of all Populist dogmas the silver issue was the one that stirred
the settlers most. "The free and unlimited coinage of silver at the
ratio of 16 to 1" — they filled their mouths with the orotund syl-
lables. In their desperate need of money, it seemed so easy and
obvious simply to coin more. And the more astute understood that
if there were twice as many dollars the mortgages on their farms
and their debts at the store would be cut in half. When their world
was on fire, who would stop to reflect that a territory had no part
in deciding this burning question?

Even the Republicans had been converted by hard times to
this gospel of inflation. In their territorial convention they came
out for free silver as strongly as any Populists; they had to save
themselves as best they could when the national convention of
their party adopted the gold standard. When Callahan challenged
them to declare their faith, they tried to evade the issue and concentrated on "Free Homes."

The settlers in Old Oklahoma had taken their claims under the
general provisions of the homestead law, which gave them free
title to the land after the required residence; but in all subsequent
openings Congress had stipulated that before receiving a patent
the homesteaders should reimburse the Government for the

amount paid the Indians when the land was purchased. In the portion of the Cherokee Strip joining Prairie City this charge was $1.50 an acre with 4 per cent interest from the date of entry. The settlers had of course taken their claims on these terms, but they held meetings, formed associations, and agitated constantly for the cancellation of the debt. They used such noble expressions — "Lift the mortgage on our farms" and "Free Homes for Free Men" — that they convinced themselves it was a moral issue, "a great fight for human freedom." The settlers in Old Oklahoma had been very sympathetic, the legislature had made an appropriation to finance their campaign, all political parties favored them, and Dennis Flynn had been tireless in trying to get the measure through Congress. It was a safe subject for campaign oratory.

Flynn was running for re-election. Born in Pennsylvania, reared in New York, he had come to Western Kansas, where he had made a precarious living as frontier lawyer, townsite promoter, and newspaper editor; and he had settled at Guthrie the day of the Run and become its first postmaster. A slender, sprightly young Irishman with a pleasant voice and an eager, friendly manner, he was the most effective campaigner who ever ran for public office in Oklahoma. For four years he had gone out among the people, speaking in brush arbors, sod schoolhouses, country churches, on the street — always to packed crowds. Once he had greeted a man with his quick, close handclasp, he was his friend forever. He treated the women with a deferential courtesy that made them forget shabby clothes and work-roughened hands. And it was no figure of speech to say he kissed the grubby, tired babies; he not only kissed them but he learned their names and ages. Years after, he would greet a father with, "How's that little Bill of yours? Let's see — he's four years old now, isn't he? And you say you've got another baby? A girl this time? What do you call her?" And he remembered.

All the Republican leaders of Prairie City knew Flynn, having met him somewhere in one of these brief but permanent introductions. Now they invited him to come and speak, and made elaborate preparations for a rally. Ralph Evans through the *Prairie Fire* made preparations of another sort, striking with all the venom of his vocabulary at the delegate's political career and his personal morals.

When the day came, Prairie City was packed with people. A

solid line of teams stood at the hitchracks, and wagons were parked on the prairie all about the town. Men filled the saloon and gathered in groups on the street. Women collected in the shade of the tall Kingman building, where seats brought from the Baptist church had been placed before the bandstand. Children raced about, screeching with excitement, flaunting Callahan buttons and Flynn buttons —

"What are you wearing that old button for? It's no good."

"I wouldn't be an old Popocrat."

"I wouldn't be an old Republican."

Thus they argued, enjoying it all, snatching at each others' badges. And the young "Popocrats" formed in groups to chant:

"J. Y. Callahan is just the stuff,
    That's no lie and that's no bluff."

Then the candidate drove up. He was accompanied by one of the county seat politicians, and Dad Colby, Jonathan Cole, and other Republican leaders hurried over to greet him. Bertha Goodwin was put forward blushing to be his partner, a parade was hastily formed, and escorted by the band they marched through the street and up to the stand. He looked dusty and tired, but his step was light and the old magic was in his smile. He carried something in his hand that looked like a copy of the *Prairie Fire*.

Everyone took his place on the platform. The people crowded up. The band started to play. This was too much for the "Popocrats" in the audience. They all began to shout, "Hey, Ralph, come on down. You don't belong up there." The young editor sprang down laughing, his trombone in his hand. The band played a few numbers, the people sang "America" and "Marching through Georgia," and Jonathan Cole introduced the speaker.

When Flynn came forward, a great shout of "Hurrah for Callahan!" went up from his opponents. The Republicans tried to drown them out with "Hurrah for Flynn!" He stood there poised and smiling. Then he began to speak. He paid a tribute to the Old Soldiers; the night would never be too dark, he said, or the mud too deep for him to wade to the pension office and urge a case. From the paper in his hand he read some of Evans' intemperate editorials. "I think the writer labored under a misconception," he said reasonably, and he went on answering or adroitly dodging the arguments, winning the audience by his charm. Then with passionate earnestness he launched into his defense of Free Homes.

The people felt that here was a champion who knew what it meant to suffer on the bleak prairie, who understood the menace of this overhanging debt. Almost everybody was cheering when he ended.

But the stars in their courses fought that year for the fusion candidates. Even so, Callahan's majority was comparatively small. It was clear that the settlers in the area agitating for Free Homes were inclined to trust Flynn's leadership. Prairie Township polled only four Republican votes; but although the township across the line returned a strong fusion majority for all other offices, it divided its vote almost equally between Flynn and Callahan. Both counties elected fusion officers and sent fusion members to the legislature. Charles Lester at last sat in the lower house, with direct and unorthodox plans for making the territorial government an agency of the people who toiled on the claims. It was hard for the settlers to sit back without a vote and see McKinley and a Republican Congress and the gold standard win the national election; even to this day they invoke the name of Bryan with a rapture of adoration not bestowed on any saint.

Political rallies, band trips, G.A.R. encampments, lodge conventions — all were typical of a population ever in restless movement. There were business trips to the larger towns, journeys here and there in search of work, visits to relatives in distant communities. And "Strippers" came long distances to buy nursery stock of Tom Lockwood, eating their meals with his family, spending the night as a matter of course in his home. Other "Strippers" with upland claims drove through on their way to "the jacks" for wood to supplement the fuel known in the ironic frontier phrase as "cow chips" or "prairie coal."

Thus the whole of the Oklahoma country became one neighborhood through which the people moved freely with mutual friendliness. If night overtook them on the road, they camped by a farmhouse, where they spent the evening as guests. In the towns they put up at the camp houses — great, spreading frame buildings with stalls for horses, a rude kitchen with pine tables and a cook stove or two, and tiers of bunks filled with hay. Settlers who had come thirty miles from opposite directions met in the camp houses of Enid or Guthrie and exchanged news about crops and happenings in their communities, invariably finding common friends and common experiences.

There were a few exceptions to this homogeneity of the population. Hermann Koch, the lone German the people had noticed in the Strip Run, had succeeded in staking a claim and was putting it under cultivation. The whole family worked in the field — the indignant neighbors saw his wife walking beside the breaking plow with her hands on the beam pushing it into the ground as it cut through the tough sod — but even in the leanest years his horses were fat and strong. Although they had lived ten years in Iowa, neither Koch nor his wife ever understood the frontier spirit. Surly and self sufficient they refused to accommodate their neighbors just as they rejected all friendly overtures.

The settlers laughed at the sparerib episode. Koch had come to the home of James Alexander in search of a stray calf. The Alexanders had just butchered a kaffir-fed hog, and according to frontier custom they gave him the sparerib. An hour later — with one eye blacked and his face covered with scratches — he was returning the meat,

"Meine vife she versteht nicht. She tink I haf de meat stolen. Mit de broom she hit me. She say I must de meat back bringen."

But there was tragedy in this aloofness when their baby died from lying in the hot sun while its mother planted corn. They dug a grave on their claim and buried it, in bitter loneliness of spirit without a single hand extended to them in sympathy. The neighbors were distressed over their own negligence, but they had not even known the child was ill until they saw the little fresh mound on the prairie.

The people knew even less about Anton Jezek. He lived on a claim at the west edge of the settlement with a fresh-looking young wife and an increasing family, attended the Catholic church at Hennessey, and found all his social activities in a Bohemian settlement several miles west. When he came to town he always wore a coat even in the warmest weather, with a red handkerchief knotted around his throat. Nobody knew why; long afterwards his grandchildren told how for more than two years he had been without a shirt.

Antoine Le Rossignol did not hold himself apart; it was the people who never accepted him. He was variously believed to be an English nobleman, a Swiss baron, or simply a "dago." Even the wildest boosters ridiculed his dreams for Prairie City; for while they balanced their promotion schemes with a certain humor, he believed every word he said. And the farmers told stories — true or apocryphal — about his ignorance of agricultural techniques.

"I was up to Ross's place the other day, and he was tryin' to milk his cow from the wrong side. She finally got her foot in the bucket, and he cussed a blue streak. I laughed till I couldn't stand up."

"That wasn't as bad as the way he greased his wagon. He propped it up with boxes and things and then he took off all four wheels. It settled down a little, and he wanted me to help him git the wheels back on."

"I know a better one than that. When Dad Colby put up his windmill, Ross said in that Dutch brogue of his, 'I see how ze wheel go 'roun' an' pump ze water out, but when ze win' change, why don' eet put eet back down again?'"

But all this was marking time. The real development of Prairie City had to wait till the rains came.

X

THE PASSING OF THE PIONEER ERA

THE RAINS began in the fall of '96; and the wheat and oats harvest of '97 was the precursor of bountiful crops. How the settlers reveled in the sight of their level acres that summer! On both sides of the line the land lay tamed and productive, the clean weedless fields of a young country. Here and there across the shock-dotted reaches, a feather of smoke and a mist of chaff marked the location of a thresher, and whistled blasts from the engines cut into the clear, bright air. The corn and sorghums stood rich and green against the yellow stubble, and the little orchard trees were weighted to the ground with fruit. A "Stripper" still points to a careful entry in his diary —

"August 19. Eat the first peach that grew on our place, the Southeast Quarter of Section 28, Township 20, Range 4 West."

The first wheat hauled from the threshers hit the Hennessey market at 65½ cents; early in August it reached 75 to 80, with some good days at the unheard-of peak of 88 cents. By the following May the market manipulations of a Chicago speculator had shot the price up to $1.10. Old-timers still date events by "the year Leiter cornered the wheat."

Of course only a small portion of the crop sold for the fabulous price of $1.10, but all the farmers got a good price and a few made a killing. Pat O'Hagan, owner of a half section by sweat and by mortgage, sold three thousand bushels at $1.03. He used his profits to buy two more farms. From that time he was a rich man. He had brought nothing but a team, a cow, and a few pieces of machinery to the claim he staked in '89.

The money was even more important to the "Strippers." And they knew how to enjoy it. The diary quoted above has the laconic entries:

"Sept. 23 Finished thrashing wheat from stacks.

"Sept. 24 hauled 140 bu. wheat to Hennessey

"Sept 25 Went to Ringling Bros. circus in Enid."

Wheat prices declined somewhat after this good year, but not to the former disastrous levels. Other farm prices rose steadily. Wheat was the principal crop, with supplementary acreages planted to feed, and with cattle and hogs an important source of revenue. The farmers were acquiring good horses and mules, having raised them from colts or bought them from carload lots shipped in from neighboring states.

Large scale wheat farming had been attempted as early as '94 when five Old Oklahoma farmers planted from three hundred to seven hundred acres each, using hired labor, and leasing school quarters and breaking the land of Strip homesteaders. The next year Joe Spragg attached his traction engine to a John Deere gang plow with five "bottoms" and began to plow up the Strip prairies. But wheat failures drove such adventurers back to subsistence farming on their own land. In 1900 on both sides of the line 85 per cent of the farmers owned and operated quarter sections. By this time about 10 per cent of the land was in the possession of absentee owners. S. W. Brown owned half a dozen quarters he had obtained through the mortgage route; but the transactions were voluntary sales, and not foreclosures, for the mortgagor could have borrowed elsewhere to pay his note to the hardware dealer. Such land was usually leased to farmers in need of additional acreage.

The more prosperous farmers employed "hired hands" the year around for thirteen to sixteen dollars a month except for a dollar-a-day rate during harvest and threshing. Most of these hands were farm boys, who lived in the home of their employer with everything furnished except oats for their ponies. A few were landless married men who had drifted in from other states; they were furnished living quarters on the extra quarter sections of the land owner with the use of a cow and the privilege of raising chickens and garden. There was no difficulty in finding employment on these terms; from '97 on, there was always a shortage of labor.

The farmers worked moderately most of the year, husking corn, cutting fodder, caring for live stock; but the wheat and oats harvest was a time of nerve-racking toil. Every social activity stopped while the reaping was in progress. Probably half the farmers cut on Sunday, although there was a general feeling that such a misappropriation of His day was an ungrateful return to the Giver of the Harvest.

Some of the grain was stacked to be threshed in the fall, but an increasing amount was threshed directly from the shocks. Each threshing outfit had its own crew of bundle-haulers and pitchers, who slept on comforts spread everywhere about the place, and ate their meals at a trailer-like "cook shack." The number of locally-owned threshers increased rapidly after '97. They were bought on credit; the purchase price was underwritten by farmers, who signed the purchaser's notes and deducted the obligation from their threshing bills.

The mountainous stacks of straw left by the threshers became a familiar feature of the landscape. They fitted into the pattern of brilliant sky, clean fields, straight roads, young orchards about bare buildings. After '97 the country blossomed out rapidly in new houses and barns and granaries. The houses were usually plain, story-and-a-half structures, L-shaped or T-shaped, but a few were fanciful with cupolas and dimension shingles and spindled balusters. The barns were red-painted but small, in keeping with the mild, open winters. Only a very few straw stables and sod houses were to be seen — and then only in the Strip — after 1900.

A reed organ, or in rare cases a piano, went into every one of the new houses. A bachelor girl holding down a Strip claim and a daughter of Jonathan Cole drove about the country giving music lessons to farmers' daughters. Each had about thirty pupils taking weekly lessons. The parents were touchingly grateful that at last they were able to give "advantages" to their children.

By the end of the century the school terms in Old Oklahoma had lengthened to five or six months; and in the Strip, with its unpatented land, the people were taxing themselves twenty mills — now the legal limit — and voting bonds and erecting frame buildings. But in spite of the high spirits of the people it was an adults' world. No provision was ever made for the children's recreational needs; they found their fun in their own way — in obscenity on the playground, insubordination in the classroom. Baiting the teacher until he was compelled to resign — "running out the teacher" — became a recognized sport. Most of the teachers were middle-aged incompetents or bright boys and girls from rural schools who had managed to pass the teachers' examination, but were too inexperienced to control young rowdies as old as themselves.

But the schoolhouses were still in constant use as community centers. Old Bareheaded Jenkins, now retired from teaching, conducted singing classes, charging a small fee and instructing adults in do-re-mi's and part singing. Sometimes a traveling "professor" came through the country showing magic lantern pictures. And Fred Peters traded for a second hand phonograph, which he played for the literary at Union. The people held their breath in wonder when barely recognizable words came out of the scratching and whining of the machine, but they laughed when it sang "Jesus, Lover of my Soul." "I knew the blamed thing could talk, but I didn't s'pose it had a soul," said Perry Eaton. But the literary was beginning to decline with the growth of other interests, and the Alliance and the Industrial Legion died with the advent of prosperity.

An "elocutionist" came to the community in '97 when young Rufus King from Kansas bought out a Strip homesteader. Mrs. King was a graduate of a good school in Wichita; and she read with restraint and good taste and real dramatic feeling. The people thronged to the recitals she gave at the schoolhouses or the Baptist church; and she gave lessons to young farm girls, who responded instinctively, finding joy and power through this means of self expression.

The people were as avid for pleasure as ever, but they were more dependent on paid — or at least on formal — entertainment. There was less visiting and sharing of food. And while there was some dancing — with considerable drinking and license — among the more irresponsible, the old joyous neighborhood dances had disappeared. Even the young people met formally in the "sitting rooms" of the new houses and listened to programs of songs, readings, and instrumental music. Young and old gathered around the organs to sing, but the wagon loads of people singing all the way home from church or literary had given place to single families in surreys or courting couples riding alone in buggies.

The "old settlers" — the expression was used generally, and without ironic intent — noticed the change and spoke regretfully of the happy pioneer days "when everybody was on a level." Their words implied that social distinctions based on money were responsible. It is true that in ten years from the date of the first Run the thrifty settlers had become well-to-do, enjoying comforts, wearing good clothes, carrying themselves with assurance, while the shiftless had retired to a position of confessed inferiority. But there may have been other causes. Everybody was older, and therefore more critical, more inclined to pick and choose friends and social activities. And the forming of organized groups — churches, lodges, ball teams, a band — with specific membership and peculiar interests, may have contributed to the division. Whatever the cause, not only economically but socially the pioneer days passed with the wheat crop of '97.

The people drove their new buggies recklessly, the young men especially often racing with each other. And with better horses there was an appalling number of runaways. A week seldom passed without a serious accident — a farmer thrown in front of a mower's slashing sickle, a family spilled along the highway. Broken bones were frequent, and there was an occasional fatality. There was no official deploring and keeping of statistics, but it seems probable that the accident toll of these horse-and-buggy days was greater than it has ever been since the coming of the automobile and power machinery.

New harness, shiny buggies, lumber for the new houses, furniture, good clothes — all were purchased at Prairie City. The merchants who had held on through the lean years found their profits mounting. Arthur Goodwin's low, dark cluttered store was so packed with goods that he and his clerks could hardly pick their way through it; he put up another store across the street and opened a big stock of hardware, buggies, and farm machinery. The Kingmans had sold out at a loss during the hard times and left the country; but young J. Q. Walker who had started a store in a tent in one of the Strip towns the day of the Run, bought the tall ramshackle building and moved his family and his business to Prairie City. A young woman homesteader of the Strip built a little frame shack and opened a millinery store, living in the back part and returning at infrequent intervals to sleep on her claim. Several Old Oklahoma settlers, tired of farming, leased or sold their land and moved to town. One with the help of his wife and daughters started a restaurant. Another bought a stock of furniture and coffins, and took orders for musical instruments. A carpenter and a painter left off farming to practice their trades; they were able to find work most of the time at the standard wages of two dollars a day for skilled labor.

Thus the town began to gain actual residents — probably fifty people by 1900. Half a dozen little boxes and four or five good, substantial houses ringed the business street. The settlement was so compact that every minor incident — a dog fight, the quirks of a balky horse, a family quarrel — was shared with the whole populace. A few little trees and shrubs and even some exotic weeds were beginning to break the clean sweep of the prairie. There was a bare little Methodist parsonage among the new houses, and three churches now rose conspicuously on the edge of the settlement.

The Methodist buildings were among the first fruits of the good harvest and soaring wheat prices of '97. The people gave thankfully of their first real money, and borrowed the remainder from a denominational fund used for church extension on the frontier. In their building they followed a historic tradition rather than a mystical need by the upward lines of pointed, colored-glass windows and a steeple rising into the vivid arch of the sky. They left the interior unfinished, and their pews were home-made, but they managed a reed organ and some new song books. The building was ready for use in the spring of '98. The parsonage stood on the same lots, with a stable in the back for the preacher's team and cow.

The Campbellites started their venture without the blessing of a denominational board in the very depths of the depression. The women took the initiative; they organized a Ladies' Aid and formed the nucleus of a building fund by every possible means from serving ice cream on Saturday to raffling off quilts and other mild forms of gambling. They next drove through the country spotting the cottonwood trees along the creeks and begging them of the farmers; and they got Joe Spragg's promise to saw them into lumber. Then they announced to their husbands that they had the material, meeting every objection, answering every argument, until the men catching their enthusiasm agreed to cut the trees, haul the lumber, quarry the foundation stones, and work together on the building.

They held meetings at each other's houses and planned and worked all through the year of '97. There was the election of a "stone boss" and an "assistant stone boss," the listing of teams for hauling, the piling of lumber, the decisions about the size and type of building, the election of a "head carpenter." In January of '98 all the material was on their lots, and the building was started. It had been their intention to box it up with the cottonwood lumber, leaving the siding and inside finishing for better times. In that form it was ready for use before the end of April. It stood thus for nearly a year, big and naked, with the green lumber shrinking and warping.

But even as they were working in this limited fashion, the good crop came, with the possibility of cash donations. They postponed their own buying to swell the building fund.

"The first thing I'm going to get with this wheat money is some chairs," Mrs. Clark told Mrs. Hodge; "I've just got the two we brought in the covered wagon when we came."

"You'd better put up with what you've got a little longer," said the other woman. "Children don't mind standing up to eat, and when company comes you can always use boxes and beds. I don't think any of us ought to buy furniture till that church-house is finished."

And the money went into the building fund. Thus by individual subscriptions of five dollars, eight dollars, ten dollars, and with the Ladies' Aid holding an ice cream supper or a box supper in the building every few weeks, the congregation raised $274 with which they purchased siding and paint. The exterior was finished before the close of '98; and the building stood white and shining, the work of their own hands, as plain and practical as the gospel they preached. Their last purchase was a small, not very deep-toned bell, which they placed in the fall of '99. Its challenge rang out exultantly over a tamed and settled country which a scant ten years before had heard no sound more civilized than a coyote's howl.

The congregation had carried out all these plans without the leadership of a regular pastor. Brother Hopkins, always restless with the urge to see beyond the horizon, had found a newer field in the Strip. Other preachers arguing from the same texts had come to the community to hold "protracted meetin's" but none had settled down there. Now with an adequate building the members "accepted a proposition" — so reads their minutes — from one of these wandering preachers to employ him half time at a salary of $180 a year. And so like the Baptists and Methodists they adopted a conventional religious program centered in the town.

Thus Prairie City had three churches, several resident families, and an exceedingly profitable trade with a prosperous farming country. But the voice of the town was stilled even with the coming of the good times it had so confidently predicted. When the Old Oklahoma settlers had proved up and the Strip settlers were not yet ready to apply for patents — to say nothing of Republican control of the land-offices — the *Prairie Fire* languished for want of homesteaders' notices. It suspended publication in the spring of '98. Ralph Evans commuted his claim, sold it the same day, and with the capital thus acquired through his brief experience as a "farmer" he went into business at the county seat. The postoffice, again in Republican hands, went back to Goodwin's store.

It was easy to sell a farm. Investors throughout the United States now had their eyes on Oklahoma. Early in that fecund June of '97 when the tall wheat was just ready for the sickle the president of the Deming Investment Company drove through the Prairie City community with two shrewd Pennsylvania German farmers sent by their neighbors to investigate the safety of his mortgages. Everything was growing with the fierce intensity that characterized a good year in Oklahoma. The Easterners' eyes bugged out, and their comments dwindled to a hushed, "Did you ever see such wheat?" and an awed, "No, I never did." And from that time on the thrifty citizens of that snug state loaned their money on Oklahoma farms. In 1899 Bradstreet reported "a great commercial awakening" in the territory, and opened an office there at the beginning of the next year to handle the inquiries that were pouring in from the East and North. By that time the railroads were running two excursions a month, bringing in thousands of people from the North to view the country.

In '98 Dr. Lindsey entered into a partnership with Hermann Koch and opened a real estate office. In all the splendor of new clothes purchased with dollar wheat, Koch visited his former home in Iowa and told his countrymen of this new land of cheap farms and mild winters. They began to buy before the year was over, and the partners branched out, Koch visiting German settlements in Iowa, Illinois, Minnesota, and Wisconsin, bringing in prospects, Lindsey keeping up the office and making out the papers. Other clients were native Americans who came to Orlando or Hennessey on the homeseekers' excursions and were driven across the country; they owned high priced land in the North — Iowa, Illinois, eastern Nebraska — and saw in Oklahoma an opportunity to increase their acreage. These newcomers came with plenty of money;

they brought adequate furniture, live stock, and farm machinery, shipping their goods in emigrant cars rather than traveling by covered wagon.

The price of land rose rapidly under the bidding of these well-to-do purchasers: twelve hundred to two thousand dollars for a good quarter in '99; three thousand to five thousand in 1902. Few of the settlers could resist such prices. Many had taken their claims purely for speculation, and this seemed a favorable time to cash in. Others had sincerely intended to establish a home, but their prosperity was so sudden and unsettling that the serious business of homesteading seemed like a lucky gamble; it might be well to try another venture. By 1902 more than two-thirds of those who had proved up claims on the Old Oklahoma side of the line had sold out and left the country.

The people who sold out still found the West — California, Oregon, Idaho, Colorado — their favorite field of investment. But a good many went to western Oklahoma, where the land, largely unclaimed by homesteaders during the dry years, had begun to settle up rapidly after 1897. It was only in such ventures that they could find agricultural opportunities for their sons.

An unwanted generation had already grown up at Prairie City. There were enough bachelor homesteaders to absorb the girl crop until about the end of the century, but there was no place for the boys. They had been too young to take claims in the Strip race, and the price of land was rising faster than anybody could earn money to pay for it. The community was full of young men marking time at blind alley jobs in the stores or on the farms; and there was a constant drift to the growing Oklahoma cities.

Some of this surplus population was drawn off in 1901 when a fertile tract in southwestern Oklahoma was opened by lottery. For weeks this "New Country" was the all-absorbing topic of conversation. All the young men and a few young women went to register, and about twenty-five drew lucky numbers with the right to file on land. For two or three years they made trips back and forth in covered wagons, finding work at Prairie City, driving back to their claims to make improvements and attend to their crops, their parents helping them with food and implements. Some established themselves and entered permanently into the building of that new frontier; others sold out at a good profit and came back with the money burning holes in their pockets.

There was enough speculative excitement at Prairie City to arouse the sanguine hopes of its more unstable citizens. Early in '98 Le Rossignol got title to his land through commutation and began to organize a company to drill for oil. It was practically a sure thing; there was a place on his creek where the topography was exactly like that of a producing field in Pennsylvania. To make twice sure, he did some amateur "witching" with a forked willow stick. But the project languished. Le Rossignol sold his farm to a thrifty neighbor and his lumber business to a company operating a chain of yards, and took his unquiet quests to other places. Two years later Mike McGraw found a place on *his* creek that looked exactly like the coal country of the Choctaw Nation. This time a company was actually formed and several farmers invested in hundred-dollar shares. A hole was bored to a depth of several hundred feet; then the money gave out, and the enterprise died.

There was a scheme current in 1900 to make a new county of the surrounding area on both sides of the Strip line with Prairie City as the county seat. There were great expectations of obtaining a railroad that was building into the territory from Kansas; the community offered a bonus of ten thousand dollars to induce the officials to route it through the town. And fifteen men at one time were working on patent devices of various kinds, five of which were machines to generate perpetual motion. But the people lacked the ruthless concentration and the practical knowledge to carry their plans to completion. The people on the Strip side of the line struck one bonanza; in 1900 Congress passed the Free Homes Bill.

During the hard times, when the required payment had loomed as an insuperable obstacle, Congress had extended to ten years the maximum time for proving up; but Callahan like Flynn before him had failed to obtain remission of the debt. Then came Republican victory in the election of 1898.

The Spanish War was a contributing factor in the Republican success. It was a very satisfactory war, with excited talk on the streets, exultation over spectacular victories, the rise of a flamboyant patriotism. On the Saturday after Manila Bay the whole countryside gathered on the prairie south of the Baptist church to plant a "liberty pole" and raise a flag.

The people knew that Theodore Roosevelt was raising a cowboy cavalry regiment from the Western territories. On April 29, ten days after the declaration of war, four young men from Hen-

nessey came riding through on their way to the recruiting office at
Guthrie. One of them was a black-eyed, guileless-looking youth of
seventeen, with a gay, rash spirit showing through his rustic shy-
ness. He gave the name of Roy V. Cashion, and he carried in his
pocket his parents' written consent to his enlistment. The boys
stopped and talked a few minutes with Dick Martin, who was
cultivating his corn by the road. Dick was sick with longing for a
tough horse and a fast ride and the remembered taste of danger;
but he saw his new house standing high and shining above his
well-kept fields, he thought of his growing family, and he knew
his adventuring was over. Other tamed and maturing cow-punch-
ers felt the same stirrings and the same inhibitions. And the unfet-
tered boys of the new generation found the call too remote from
their experience. There was no enlistment from Prairie City.

News filtered back to the neighborhood of the doings of the
Rough Riders. Roy Cashion wrote home from Tampa, "I never
enjoyed anything so much as I have this trip. Everything I see is
new and has a lesson in it." And there was his letter written on the
voyage, "The ocean looks like the great prairies of Oklahoma, and
the most interesting thing of all is the great fleet sailing in two
columns." The people felt a tingling excitement along with their
sympathy for the sister town, when he fell at San Juan, the first
Oklahoman to make his rendezvous with death and glory on foreign soil. And some of their money went into the memorial statue
that still stands overlooking the Oklahoma prairies he saw in memory when he looked across the sea.

Even today Prairie City idealizes the career of "Teddy" Roosevelt, who became in imagination a son and champion of the West.
And the fierce joy of winning a war by proxy spilled over into a
Republican majority at the fall election. "This is a patriotic year
and an American year, and the people voted accordingly," exulted
Dad Colby. The Populists, moreover, were alienated by the in-
gratitude of the Democrats in grasping all the spoils of fusion; at
a joint convention that year Callahan and the Populist ideas had
been completely ignored. Most of all, the rains and the rising farm
prices had changed many a howling Populist into a smug Republican.

Dennis Flynn was out in front winning everything — "A vote
for Dennis is a vote for Free Homes and Statehood," urged his ad-

mirers. But the indefatigable Irishman worked until June 17, 1900 before the Free Homes Bill became a law. By that time the slogans should have lost some of their emotional appeal; in that prosperous year no Strip homesteader near Prairie City could honestly say that the obligation to pay three hundred dollars for his farm was an oppressive burden. Still it was a sizable handout. Of the 128 quarters exclusive of school land in the adjoining township 43 had already been proved up and sold; but Free Homes for the remaining two-thirds of the settlers meant that more than twenty-five thousand dollars that would have been sent to Washington remained in the immediate trade territory of the town.

The news was flashed on the wires to the larger towns of the territory. It was flashed almost as rapidly across the Strip prairies by the waving of sheets and tablecloths from house to house. When it reached Prairie City, the clanging of the anvil roused the whole countryside. Jonathan Cole remembered that the date was the anniversary of Bunker Hill, and nobody saw any blasphemy in classing together "these two momentous events in the age-old struggle for human rights." When Flynn spoke at Enid in October the whole township joined the milling, shouting crowd that welcomed him; the delegation carried a banner with an oil painting of an Oklahoma farm scene and the words, "NO MORTGAGE ON THIS FARM: DENNIS FLYNN PAID IT." The year 1900 was not a Republican year at Prairie City or in the territory, but both voted enthusiastically for Flynn, and he was returned to Congress by a comfortable margin.

Relieved of their financial obligation, the remaining two-thirds of the Strip settlers nearly all proved up on their land during 1901. Most of them had it mortgaged within a month; some mortgaged on the same day they made their proof. Lindsey and Koch now acted as the agent of a loan company; the debts were still small — three hundred to eight hundred dollars a quarter — and the interest had gone down to 7 or 8 per cent.

A few homesteaders willing to postpone the payment of taxes, waited the maximum ten years and proved up in 1903. A small amount of land that had changed hands several times during the homesteading period remained under homestead tenure still longer — even as late as 1907. Such land sold almost as readily as patented land; it was even listed for sale with the real estate dealers as freely as though the title had not been vested theoretically in the United States Government.

Thus in land tenure as in farming practices and social life the pioneer days were over. But the growth of the town waited on a railroad. That development came with the commercial expansion of the early twentieth century.

XI

THE COMING OF THE RAILROAD

Iɴ the spring of 1902 the community was thrown into a fever by rumors of railroad promotion. The talk spread in waves along the hitchracks and swirled into the saloons and stores —

"They say it'll be a main line from Denver to New Orleens."

"I don't believe it'll stop at Denver; I heard it was goin' clear out to some place on Puget Sound."

"They's goin' to be two railroads; the surveyors is at work right now."

"You bet they are; they drove their stakes right through my bottom land."

This last brought the inevitable reaction —

"That's the way the railroads do. They cut right across a man's farm and he can't help it. The law always favors them big corporations."

The prosperity of the whole community was curtailed by inadequate transportation. Freighters with mule teams made twice-a-week trips over the execrable roads to Orlando, hauling for the merchants at fifteen to twenty cents a hundred pounds, which was added to the price of the goods. Farmers dreaded the heavy haul with wheat, the suffering and shrinkage of their fat hogs. The women counted up their poultry losses from smothering and thirst on the long trip; they hung their butter and even their eggs in the well, trying to save the produce for the next trip to market. And every time the farmers sold anything in the railroad towns they made purchases there, to the loss of the Prairie City dealers.

The town, however, had continued to grow. By this time it had a hundred and fifty residents, all packed together like one big, riotous family. Along Main Street were two saloons, two real estate offices, eight or ten stores, two restaurants, and a harness shop. At the edge of town close to the lumber yard was a livery barn with spreading wings, where one might stable his horses

or rent a team. The town swarmed with agents who put up at the
hotel while they canvassed the community selling life insurance,
threshing machines, or enlarged photographs. Everybody was
making money, but all expected to make more with the coming of
a railroad.

Two lines of stakes crossed the wheatfields and converged upon
the town, and rumors were flying thick and fast of several other
proposed roads. The most likely project was being pushed by a
group of territorial promoters — mostly Enid men — backed by St.
Louis capital, who combined railroad construction with the sale
of townsites along the right-of-way. In April an official of this
company came to Prairie City and worked out a scheme with the
business leaders. The latter organized as a town company, with
Arthur Goodwin as president, S. W. Brown as vice president, and
Dr. Lindsey as secretary; they agreed to undertake the sale of the
townsite, and entered into a contract to pay the construction company twenty-five thousand dollars if the road should be built to
the town within six months. This extortionate sum was really a
tribute levied on the ambitious spirit of the little settlement; for
the larger cities of the territory were obtaining their railroads for
less. Possibly the Prairie City leaders might have got better terms
if their eagerness had not been so apparent. But the alternative
was too frightening; this decade was to see the Oklahoma country
haunted by the ghosts of many once-lively towns that had died because the railroad passed them by.

The plan provided that the station should be located and the
townsite laid out one-half mile south of the old site, thus compelling everybody to remove and buy new lots. The town company
accordingly purchased a half section of land — two farms at five
thousand dollars each — and prepared to plat it on an ambitious
scale. When the transaction became known, a few conservatives
were bitterly resentful, but most of the people accepted the expense and inconvenience as the price of the railroad. So large a
bonus could hardly have been raised by voluntary subscription.

Late in April surveyors arrived from Enid and began setting
up tripods and peeking through instruments in the heading wheat
that covered the new townsite. This time it was sober, steady
Arthur Goodwin who insisted on wide streets. "People laughed at
Ross, but he was right," he said. "All those Eastern cities made
their streets too narrow. We don't need to make that mistake in

Oklahoma. When the time comes for street cars we may not be here, but somebody will be glad we laid the town out right." A beautiful level tract two blocks from the Main Street was laid out for the school ground; another on the opposite side was reserved for a park. A strip joining the "old town" was purposely left un-platted to forestall any merging of the two townsites; thus every business would be forced to remove.

The community watched the survey with mounting excitement. New business and professional men were coming in almost daily — from the surrounding farms, from the railroad towns, even from distant states — finding accommodations as best they could until they should be able to build on the new townsite. Two newspapers were started in May; one, the *Prairie City News*, swallowed up its rival before the month was over and emerged with 270 subscribers and brisk local advertising. A photographer opened a "gallery"; a physician located in the town, the first it had ever had whose major interest was in his profession; a dentist from a neighboring town opened an office one day a week; a new man bought the drug store and put in a soda fountain.

A. T. Strickland sold his Strip claim and started a bank, with his brother and sister coming from Kansas and serving as vice president and cashier. As the Pioneer State Bank it opened with a capital stock of $5,000 and a surplus of $1,000. All the business of the community immediately centered there. It soon had $25,-189.56 in individual checking accounts, and $31,231.29 extended in loans. Farm couples — the woman frightened, the man bursting with business — were often seen signing papers at a table behind the railing, for Strickland also served as local agent for an Oklahoma City farm mortgage company.

With the coming of these new people, living conveniences mul-tiplied. A man with a mule team started hauling water in from the country, filling the housewives' barrels at the rate of a penny a pailful; and a restaurant owner began to keep ice — hauled from Orlando — on hand for the local trade. A barber opened a shop, shaving the opulent and eliminating the "cat stairs" that had marred the wife-sheared heads of pioneer Prairie City; he also collected the town's dirty clothes, sending them every Saturday to a steam laundry at the county seat. A line of telephone poles marched across the country, connecting Dr. Lindsey's real estate office with the outside world.

The town buzzed with social activity. The churches were always full; each now had preaching every Sunday morning and evening, an active young people's society, mid-week prayer meeting,
and a dizzy round of picnics, ice cream suppers, parties, and special programs. The lodge directory in the *News* showed Masons,
Odd Fellows, a newly-organized Modern Woodmen of America,
the G.A.R., and the W.R.C., each with weekly or fortnightly meetings. The band boys went out one morning among the business
men and collected $110 with which they purchased seventeen sky
blue uniforms with gold braid; thus arrayed they played on the
street every Saturday. The baseball boys bore the name of the
town proudly emblazoned on new uniforms.

The saloons drew more people than ever; the proportion of
drunken men on the streets increased with the accelerated speed
of town life. The new saloon had a pool hall, and the rumblings
from the ten-pin alley could be heard from early in the morning to
early the next morning. The place was whirling with Klondike
cages and roulette wheels, and busy with tables of seven-up and
poker. Most of the players here were farm hands and other young
men from the country. But the same saloon had a special room in
the back, a secret hide-out, where most of the business leaders,
infected with gambling fever by the chances of the Strip race and
the excitement of townsite promotion, played late at night for high
stakes. Dramatic transfers of property took place in this close,
smoke-filled room — a store would change hands overnight, or a
high-stepping team would pass to a new owner. But nobody really
won. The more successful, heady with victory, went to the surrounding cities to flaunt their winnings, and were mowed down by
better men.

Meanwhile preparations were being completed on the new
townsite. A contractor was employed to grade the streets — and
the Saturday afternoon crowd repaired there to watch a horse race
on this new track. A town well was sunk — with water only slightly
less bad than that in the "old town." The lots went on sale Saturday, May 24. The *News* that week carried a full-page advertisement setting forth the future of "This New Railroad Center in the
Finest Wheat Belt of Oklahoma." But through Arthur Goodwin's
insistence the sale was conducted quietly, a private sale at fixed
prices, without auctioneering fervor or by-bidding. Even so, the
prices were good for an undeveloped wheat field.

On Main Street the best corner lots sold at seven hundred dollars, others at two hundred to three hundred. Residence lots sold at fifty to seventy-five dollars according to location. All lots were so narrow — twenty-five feet — that two were required for a building site. Property owners in the "old town" received one of their lots free, and the churches were given free sites to induce them to remove.

Within a week 158 lots had been sold for $18,000. The plat in Dr. Lindsey's office was always surrounded by an interested group, and inquiries were coming in by telephone from neighboring towns. The actual building waited until the harvest rush was over. Even the town company thriftily cut and threshed the wheat on the new townsite. But by July men were swarming like ants all over the place. Farmers on their way to the "old town" stopped to marvel at the size of the new foundations, and the *News* went into ecstasies over the "magnificent," "elegant," "immense," "mammoth," and "splendid" buildings in process of erection. Best of all, three grain elevators along the line of railroad stakes were raising skeleton timbers against the sky. The hotel was packed with workmen, and barn lofts were at a premium.

During the same month contractors began to raise the old buildings, set them on trucks, and pull them to the new site with traction engines. Goodwin's store went first. The people watched, stirred as always by the prospect of change. "Well, the old town'll soon be a thing of the past," they exulted. An "old settler" attempted reminiscence — "When I came to this country in the Strip Opening, that store was on the corner of Goodwin's farm." There was a polite "Is that so?" or two, but in their minds the "old" town with its eight years of brimming life was already relegated to antiquity. It was typical of the impatient, changeful spirit of the settlement that Prairie City had had three sites in thirteen years.

By October although the road between the two townsites was still blocked with trussed-up buildings and laboring engines, most of the business was being transacted in the new location. A double line of much better frame buildings faced the broad Main Street — new ones built on the spot, old ones enlarged and improved. The "First" Baptist Church stood on its new site; the "First" Methodist Church, and the "First" Christian Church were on the way. Comfortable dwellings spaced at decent intervals were rising around the outskirts; the business men who had homesteaded Strip claims now moved to town, but Arthur Goodwin, loving his land, continued to live in the sturdy house just off the edge of the town-site.

Meanwhile the construction of the railroad had paralleled the building of the town. A right of way agent arrived in May, a breezy Kansan full of talk and optimism. He bought most of the land without difficulty; nobody wanted the track to cut across his farm, but all were too eager for the road to interpose serious objections. All, that is, except George Hadley, who stood out alone against the corporate enemy. "They ain't no damned railroad goin' to cross my land," he shouted. "I've got a patent from the United States Gove'ment, and I'd like to see anybody take it away." It was necessary to serve papers and institute condemnation proceedings.

In June the president of the company announced that the grading contract had been let. Within a week camps of sub-contractors were strung out all along the right of way, families living in tents and shacks on wheels, men holding scrapers and driving sweating mules over cuts and fills. The settlers made friendly advances to these temporary neighbors, soft-voiced people with native courtesy and charm, but often illiterate, and with their women addicted to the strange habit of dipping snuff. Some of the farmers took their own teams and found employment at the construction camps.

In September a machine grader began working on the yards at the station site. The men watched it fascinated; it was pulled by fourteen mules and removed a thousand cubic yards of earth a day. The excitement boiled over when the president telephoned Dr. Lindsey that a gang had started laying steel out of Enid. Two weeks later Jerome Alexander came to town with a report,

"Yes sir, I can stand right on the roof of my barn and see the smoke of that ingine. I don't think it's more'n fifteen miles away."

At the next report the pointing finger of steel had reached a new townsite eight miles north, and trains were running between that place and Enid. The last two weeks people drove up every day to the advancing terminal to watch the track laying; on the last Sunday the whole town and country was there. On Monday morning, October 27, the train was whistling on the townsite.

People saw it approaching, three or four flat cars in front, an obsolete little engine behind pushing. It moved erratically, starting and stopping, throwing out rails and ties. Men were carrying material ahead laying a temporary track, and a crew followed behind, placing more ties and spiking the rails. Women left their houses, men left their stores, farmers left their fields — all gathered along the right of way. When the first shrill blast came from the engine, the crowd went wild — men's hats sailed high in the air, and a shout went up that almost drowned the sound of the whistle. All day the town was full of people talking over the greatest event since the Run into the Strip.

But in a more significant way, without noise or drama, the community was realizing the value of the railroad. Even a week before the first whistle cut the air with its new note, one of the elevators started buying wheat. Loaded wagons began to converge on Main Street and pass on down to the gaunt structures that stood beside the right of way — the first of a mighty procession that still rolls through the town. In deep thankfulness business man and farmer accepted this gift of time and space. In their minds the "City" had become a reality.

XII
CITY WAYS

PRAIRIE CITY had the best location on the new railroad; although townsites were being laid out eight miles apart along the line, it was the central station of the sixty mile stretch between Enid and the county seat. It had a population of possibly three hundred. It had swallowed up several rivals — three or four country stores and postoffices and one considerable village missed by the railroad — and captured their trade territory. Now its more ambitious promoters met early in 1903 at the real estate office of Lindsey and Koch and formed a Commercial Club.

First a committee of this organization engineered the incorporation of the town. But the election of officials by ballot proved too rigid. The voters met in caucus, and with conversation and discussion, with persuasion of the reluctant — "You might as well let us put your name down, Doc; somebody's got to do it" — they made up a "citizens' ticket." The legal election that followed was a mere formality.

With incorporation launched, the Commercial Club next planned a Fourth of July "to eclipse every celebration ever held in Oklahoma." Probably this holiday marked the high tide of the exuberant, riotous life that flowed through the town. Early in the morning wagons and buggies began rolling in and parking all around the outskirts; by ten-thirty an estimated five thousand people were jamming the streets. There was a grand parade with the band leading: floats showing the Thirteen Colonies, the Ship of State with Columbia at the helm, the Goddess of Liberty and her lovely sisterhood of states; other floats representing the churches, the lodges, the business firms; decorated buggies with pretty young women driving; young men on horseback representing Indians, cowboys, clowns; and trailing all, the inevitable small boys. In a large shade pavilion of rough lumber was a program and an oration by an Enid speaker, glorifying the achievements of Oklahoma. The boys kept up an unearthly din of exploding fire-crackers and popping pistols, the little girls with arms linked about each other fought their way abreast through the crowds, the babies cried, the men and women stood on the streets and talked, every-body ate too much, a good many drank too much. Nobody sus-pected at the time that Prairie City was never to see its like again.

The Commercial Club was not so successful in bringing indus-tries to the town. In the spring of 1903 the *News* proclaimed the opening of "one of the largest stone manufacturing plants in the territory"; enough concrete blocks were finally completed for one residence and a small produce house before the enterprise died a natural death. Then a farmer of the neighborhood invented a pat-ent shocker, which was going to revolutionize the harvesting of wheat — but never quite did. There were nebulous plans to erect a ten thousand dollar hotel, but the "model two-story stone struc-ture" never took visible form.

In the summer of 1904 a suave gentleman came to shower gold on the community by tapping its hidden rivers of oil. He was backed up, he said, by enormous capital; and his company was ready to begin drilling at once without local assistance. By this time oil excitement was entering into the common fabric of terri-torial life; and he talked so glibly of "structure," "pools," "over at Tulsa," and "proven territory" that his listeners were completely mesmerized. Said the *News*, "Fortunes may lay at our feet and we may die in poverty unless we put forth our hand and take it."

Dr. Lindsey took his team and conducted the fine-spoken stranger around over the country, helping him obtain leases to a solid block of land ten miles square lying on both sides of the Strip line. The leases ran for twenty years, carried no consideration, pro-vided no guarantee as to drilling, and fixed the royalty to the land owner at 5 per cent of production. Lindsey was as innocent as the farmers of the usual terms of an oil lease.

The promoter next organized the Prairie City Oil, Gas, and Development Company. He undertook to transfer to this company his leases on two thousand acres of land; and farmers and business men subscribed $3,250 in stock, with plans to increase it to $7,000. The steadiest men in the community were elected as directors. It was confidently asserted that drilling would begin within thirty days.

But before thirty days had passed, Prairie City had done some figuring —

"He gives us back a little block of our own land, and keeps all the rest. Then if we get oil he cashes in."

"He said he had big money backing him up. Now he sits back and we pay all the expense of drilling."

"How much money do you get if we do strike oil?"

"Five per cent."

"That's what my lease says, too. That's one-twentieth. I've found out they pay a tenth or an eighth over in the Indian Territory."

"Sposin' they don't drill at all?"

"Well, we've just got our land tied up for twenty years. They ain't no way we can make him do a thing."

"Where does he come in anyhow? It's our land, and we're expected to dig up all the money? Why can't we have the profit?"

"We could, if we could git rid of them damned leases. We could raise enough money right here in this town to drill to China."

"Le's git together on this. I don't think he can hold 'em, when he didn't pay nothin' for 'em."

It was an angry but chastened group of farmers who got together for a meeting of their own. They elected a president and a secretary and assessed themselves to hire a lawyer. They instituted a suit in the territorial courts, but the speculator surrendered before the case came to trial. The final act took place in the Methodist church, where all the lessors met to canvass the releases on their land, checking the numbers and wording to be sure nothing had been overlooked. Then out of the simple goodness that always underlay their striving they prepared a statement for the newspaper —

"We, the undersigned lessors, believe we should forgive and forget. No doubt we were hasty in some of our remarks. We understand the man who got the leases lost money on the deal. Let's not crow over him. We hope all will remember the golden rule."

Prairie was equally unsuccessful in its bid for a second railroad. The line of stakes that had been so fervently exploited at the time of the lot sale had already been abandoned when three enthusiastic strangers submitted another proposition to build a line from Kansas to the ranch country of West Texas, and on to Old Mexico — if Prairie City would pay for its share of the survey. The Commercial Club quickly raised one thousand dollars to purchase this third line of stakes. The survey was completed in the spring of 1903. Everybody expected construction to follow immediately. But nothing happened, although the project was revived periodically during the next ten years.

The railroad the town already had came somewhat short of expectations. The trains ran off the track every few days, but they inched along so slowly that nobody was hurt. Construction reached the county seat in the spring of 1903; two years later a second spurt of building extended it north of Enid, and on to the Kansas line. In 1907 the Santa Fe system took it over as a convenient connecting link between its north-south line across Oklahoma and its east-west line to California. From that time on, it was operated efficiently.

But even in its worst days its facilities were in constant use. Its passenger service to Enid or the county seat displaced the frequent horse-and-buggy trips to neighboring towns. And the whole town went down to the station, especially on Sunday evenings, to watch the train come in.

The marketing of the new wheat in 1903 was the consummation. From early in the morning till ten or even twelve at night the loaded wagons crawled through the dust-deep streets and down to the elevators. Sometimes a dozen or more were lined up waiting their turns to unload. The average daily sale through July and August was six thousand bushels, and the checks paid the farmers — the price was low that year — totaled three to four thousand dollars. During that first twelve months after the road reached the county seat Prairie City shipped 344 carloads of wheat, 30 carloads of cattle, and 8 carloads of hogs that would formerly have been hauled to distant points.

For the first time the women's products became an important adjunct to the farm income. The prices were good and steadily rising: eggs ranged from eleven cents a dozen in summer to twenty-five in winter; chickens from eight to eleven cents a pound; turkeys ten to twelve cents; butter ten to twenty cents. In the spring of 1904 several farmers purchased incubators from the local dealers and two or three bought cream separators; all the women went to see these labor-saving innovations, exclaiming over the downy chicks, and dilating on the convenience of separated cream.

Wagons loaded with hogs, corn, wheat; herds of fat cattle; buggies piled high with cases and pails of eggs — all were pointed towards Prairie City. The town was full of people, always buying — everything from a threshing machine to a dish of ice cream. The spirits of the merchants rose and dipped, sensitive as a barometer, with every change of weather. Part of the wheat lay in the ground unsprouted during the dry winter of 1903–4; when the rains began in April, sober Arthur Goodwin dug up a stock of left-over fire-crackers and grown men exploded them in the street.

During the winter of 1905–6 the business leaders sought to increase the purchasing power of their trade territory by persuading the farmers to plant cotton. Through an active campaign in the *News* they obtained a total planting of twelve hundred acres, and induced a gin to locate in the town. The following September Joe Scott drove up Main Street with the first load ever marketed there. Quite a crowd gathered at the gin to watch the whirring teeth remove the fiber and to see the plunger compress the snowy mass into a bale. The Commercial Club offered a bonus of ten cents a hundred for the largest load. Pat O'Hagan won the premium with 5,400 pounds, which at the market price of $3.20 plus the bonus brought him a check for $178.20. The next year a Prairie City business man constructed a second gin. The community seemed to be successfully launched on a new enterprise.

At the same time the town was the center of new conveniences going out into every rural home. A telephone exchange was established in 1903. When one of the new society leaders in town gave a reception to the Baptist choir, a general ring called the farm families to their telephones to enjoy the program. Rural mail delivery also was instituted in 1903, largely through the efforts of Arthur Goodwin, who was still serving as postmaster. Four routes radiated out from the town, serving 518 families with 2,074 members. The people dubbed the white delivery wagons "white angels," and they filled their mail boxes with cake, orchard fruit, slices of melon with salt, and fried chicken for the carriers. With railway mail service and rural delivery, people in both town and country began to subscribe to daily newspapers — still mainly from St. Louis, Kansas City, or Wichita, but also in increasing numbers from Oklahoma.

In one respect the railroad had a diffusive influence; the mail order firms — Sears and Roebuck, and Montgomery Ward — began to cut into the trade of the Prairie City merchants. The *News* paid the debt to its advertisers by many editorials denouncing the practice. But even the merchants could not resist buying in the best market; they ordered family supplies from their wholesale houses, and their wives — and the editor's wife — took many train trips to the cities for a day's shopping. The *News* also sought to bring pressure on the territorial delegate to force him to fight the parcels post measure then pending in Congress. Here a battle raged between the small town interests and the express companies on one side, and the farmers, the Kansas City farm weeklies, and the mail order houses on the other; and the opponents of the measure managed to stave it off until 1913.

In one sense Prairie City had an active mail order business of its own, through the advertising circulars sent out by its real estate men to attract Northern immigration. The movement reached its climax in 1905. Many of the farms changed hands two or three, or even four, times during the first six years of the century. The price of a good quarter stood at five or six thousand dollars in 1906; by that time only 20 per cent of the land in the Old Oklahoma township, 30 per cent in the Strip was still owned by the men who had proved up. Most of these changes increased the size of the holdings, whether a successful "old settler" acquired an extra quarter by buying out his neighbor, or whether a well-to-do Northerner bought out three farmers at once; by 1906 only about half were of the traditional one hundred and sixty acres. Even the farmers who owned only one quarter usually managed to rent additional acreage, school land or the farms of absentee owners. There was little farm tenancy except in this limited sense. The large farming unit had become so general that the rural population in the two townships declined from 1279 in 1900 to 959 in 1907, a decrease of 25 per cent. Some of the rural schools by the latter date had dwindled to an enrollment of ten or twelve pupils.

Families quitting the farm disposed of their goods at public auction. These sales came at the rate of two or three a week during the slack seasons in the summer after harvest and in the fall after wheat planting. Perry Eaton, now promoted to "colonel" by virtue of his profession, did a rushing business as an auctioneer. Everybody attended — to take leave of old friends, to see all the neighbors, to listen to the jokes and the strange gurgling and warbling of "the Colonel," and to bid on a table or a buggy or a span of mules.

About half the farmers who sold out moved to town to manage an elevator, start a store, open a produce house, sell real estate —

engage in any of the expanding occupations of Prairie City. The others went to newer frontiers to repeat their pioneering: some acquired great tracts of level land in the Oklahoma and Texas Panhandles; others obtained irrigated land in Arizona, settling in a neighborhood close together; several joined an American colony in Old Mexico, with Harry Hayman as pastor of the Baptist church.

Thus the farming population was largely displaced by a new element. But the Northern newcomers did not like Oklahoma. They were dismayed by its unpredictable climate — the hot winds that alternated with violent rains, the sudden blizzards that swept down into the mild winters. And there was the fine, thin soil that packed like mortar, swirled into dust clouds, or washed down the creek leaving great gullies in the eroded fields. Five years was about the limit of their stay. But very few ever returned to the North. They sold their land at a good profit, and invested in California.

A slower infiltration of people came from Kentucky — friends and relatives of Dave Hodge. A tall, sturdy people, friendly in manner, soft in speech, ardent in temperament, inclined to religion or violence, they found a congenial atmosphere in Prairie City. They farmed on a comfortable, but not an ambitious scale, and they held on to their land.

The Germans also stayed. They bought good land, tilled it well, and lived in comfort. When they prospered — as they almost invariably did — they bought more land and settled their sons around them. They associated only with each other. Even their children attended the public schools only irregularly, partly because they were busy, but mainly because their parents opposed any influence tending to break down their separate culture. The furniture dealer at Prairie City learned to keep pictures of the German Kaiser in stock; the hard, narrow face with its absurd mustaches looked down strangely upon this new American scene.

The winter after the town moved, Germans of various beliefs from Lutheran to Methodist united to form an Evangelical church. For a time they used the Methodist building; then early in 1904 they dug deep into their comfortable bank balances, and the men all went to work with hammer and nails and good German concentration and erected a building. The other churches joined in the all-day service of dedication, rejoicing in another community achievement. They employed a pastor who had come from Germany by way of Indiana — a man with a pointed beard, and stiff, measured walk, and pale, intellectual face, who looked as strange on the streets as some character from a picture book. Their children were grounded in the faith with a thoroughness unknown before in Prairie City, and ponderous preparations worked up to their Easter and Christmas celebrations.

The Catholics also built a church when the town moved. But they held their first services in the Union schoolhouse, where Father Ledoux, a missionary priest, came occasionally during 1903 to celebrate mass. Here in this plain, schoolboy-scarred room a group of children — the girls lovely and innocent in white, the boys solemn and self-conscious in new suits — affirmed their faith and knelt before an improvised altar to receive their first communion. Along with the Irish children were a young daughter of Anton Jezek and the son of another Bohemian family recently arrived from Nebraska.

The next year a little frame church with a graceful spire was built and opened for services. The Catholics raised the money to complete the payment at the biggest picnic Spragg's Grove had seen since the early years. There was a program with Arthur Goodwin presiding — an address of welcome by Father Ledoux, music by the band, songs and recitations by young people of all religious faiths. And everybody danced, and ate ice cream, and drank lemonade to swell the building fund. Then followed another exultant day of dedication, with Protestant well-wishers sitting friendly and interested, but afraid to stand or kneel lest they seem to countenance some idolatrous rite.

The surrounding country was still dotted with Sunday schools, meeting at the schoolhouses, with an attendance of forty or fifty crowded into the diminutive seats. They met now in the afternoon, for most of the leaders attended morning services in town; and young-men-about-town liked to drive out to court the rural girls and contribute special musical numbers.

It was one of these rural schools that sponsored a community Sunday school picnic in Spragg's Grove the summer of 1904. Seven or eight Sunday schools from the town and country contributed special numbers to the program, and there were addresses by the four Prairie City ministers. The new Evangelical school entertained the audience greatly by a song in German. Only the Catholics did not participate, but the women of the Altar Society sent a five-gallon freezer of ice cream. This meeting, held the year the two new churches were built, marked the climax of religious co-operation in Prairie City.

Nobody suspected at the time that this year also marked the high tide of religious interest. Even the following winter saw a decline of the rural Sunday schools, and before many years they all passed out of existence. The town churches continued to function; but so imperceptibly that no one saw it happen, the life of the community ceased to focus there.

As soon as the new town was established the people turned their exuberant energies to the pursuit of culture. During the first winter a group of young people organized a Reading Club; soon after, the first woman's club was organized with weekly meetings and an appalling program of study. A four-room school building was erected — the first brick in Prairie City. An "opera house" was in constant use for plays, musical recitals, readings, and lectures; any entertainment — home talent or professional — could pack this building and collect twenty to seventy-five dollars in paid admissions. There was a lyceum course, sponsored by the woman's club and underwritten by the business men.

Society took on a self-conscious elegance. There were elaborate weddings and banquets and "balls." Flinch made its appearance the second winter of the new town, and soon the social leaders were forming flinch clubs, with progressive tables, late lunches, and music filling the gaps. Already the reed organs that had once seemed so fine were rapidly being traded in for pianos.

Prairie City's young and active bodies found exercise in sports that seemed more city-like than the earlier recreations. The business men and their wives organized a tennis club. The women formed a basket ball team, wearing blue uniforms with vast, pleated bloomers, and taking time off from housekeeping duties for daily practice. The baseball enthusiasts contributed lumber and built a fence around a vacant space used for a ball park; during the last stage of the work there were so many volunteer carpenters there was hardly room to swing a hammer.

Some of this abounding vitality splashed over in public and dramatic flouting of the seventh commandment by the town's social and business leaders. The community was shocked whenever a scandal broke, but such affairs were soon forgotten by a people too friendly to hold a grudge, too lively to remember. There was

the same light hearted tolerance of crime. There were store robberies and chicken thefts, attempted — but never successful — rape,
promiscuous shooting at windows and trains, fights and shooting
scrapes. These offenses were usually committed by country boys.
Most of them were warned and forgiven. But the A.H.T.A. did
engage in two organized man hunts when outlaws passed through
the community, and the embattled town rose to arms in an unsuccessful attempt to prevent the robbery of the bank.

The center of all this activity was at first a stark little place,
with the new buildings standing bare in the brilliant sunshine.
But the second fall the town council purchased black locusts of
Tom Lockwood's nursery, and planted the park and checker-
boarded the whole townsite with rows of straight little saplings.
The trees grew rapidly for the first ten years, shooting up tall and
graceful, shading the houses and filling the air with the spring
fragrance of many blossoms; and the people joyfully repaired to
the park for every summer outing.

Water was still a sore subject to the civic minded leaders. A
windmill was installed at the city well, and the water was pumped
into an elevated tank and piped to a couple of hydrants on Main
Street and to a watering trough for teams. People constructed cisterns at their residences for household use; nobody realized at
the time that the lack of iodine in this rainwater was disposing the
population to goitre. In times of drought when the cisterns, and
sometimes even the public well were dry there was a certainty
that any blaze obtaining a good headway would sweep the town.
But every incipient fire was arrested in its early stages by the volunteer firemen and the little chemical engine they drew by hand.

The growth of Prairie City did not keep pace with its ambitions or its civic development. Its leaders were gamesters rather
than builders. Its business population was unstable; men came to
town and moved away, bought in and sold out, traded a store for
a livery stable, closed a produce house and started a dray line.
Only J. Q. Walker and Arthur Goodwin seemed settled into permanence.

And yet curiously enough there was a certain rhythm in all
this movement, a continuity in all the shifting life, a community
spirit growing even out of a common restlessness. The *News* carried a dizzying succession of names at the mast head, but every editor no matter how briefly he spoke, voiced the aspirations of a self-

conscious social unit. One of these editors — recently arrived, as it happened, from Kentucky — attempted to analyze the intangible essence that gave form to this chaos.

"The Oklahoman is a distinct type," ran this editorial. "His main characteristic is to be previous. This trait may have originated in the days of soonerism, but it is getting stronger every year.

"We have a passion for priority, supremacy, dominance. Our motto is 'Get there first.' We have made a harmonious solution of the North, South, East, and West."

In the main he was right. It may have been a compound with the elements in unstable solution, but it was none the less a homogeneous society. This community of spirit was shown in the neighborhood reaction to tragedy.

XIII
THE SHOCK OF TRAGEDY

It was February of 1905. The land lay ice-locked in the coldest weather it had known since the Opening, and its irrepressible people had turned eagerly to their first winter sports. The school had given a play in the opera house that Friday night; and the young and gay had come to town, shouting and laughing, skimming over the snow in wagon beds set on makeshift runners.

Fifteen-year-old Virgil Lockwood had driven the family equipage up with a flourish — his parents and his sisters snugly settled in the robes, and a set of sleigh bells used before only in Christmas celebrations jingling from the harness. And Helen Lockwood had been the star of the play that night, so lovely with the delicate bloom of her eighteen years that the whole audience had felt a thrill of pride and affection. But the crowd had dispersed, the shouts and the laughter had died away; the night lay dark and still with the threat of a storm coming.

About one o'clock the young man at the telephone switchboard saw a lurid red cutting into the lowering sky. It seemed to come from where Tom Lockwood's big house stood back from the road in the bend of the creek surrounded by its orchards. The operator began hastily calling one number after another to rouse the town. Men threw on their clothes and sprang on horses or hitched up teams, while women piled robes and extra coats in the buggies. "What a terrible night for a house to burn down," was the thought in every mind. Then over the wire came the incredible message from Joe Spragg.

"Listen, central, I want you to get this straight. My phone is down, and I'm calling from Pat O'Hagan's. Tom Lockwood tried to kill his family and set his house afire. Tiny got away. She is at my place. Send a doctor to her as quick as you can. And get help to the Lockwoods; some of them may be alive in the house. And

tell everybody for God's sake to be careful. Tiny says her father's
got a gun."

In a few minutes the whole town and countryside was aroused.
Dozens of men were converging on the place where the burning
house stood outlined against the trees. Joe Spragg was carrying
Tiny. It had been impossible to keep the desperate child away. As
the men approached the house, she screamed wildly,

"Don't go, oh don't go! He's hiding in the timber. I know he's
hiding in the timber."

"She may be r-right," said Pat O'Hagan. "If he's waitin' out
there with a gun, we'd make a good tar-rget 'gainst that light.
I don't suppose anny wan's alive annyhow."

And they waited in the shadows until the walls fell.

Then they saw the pitiful, blackened bodies. Tom Lockwood
lay near the twisted stove; his head was gone, and a burned shot-
gun with two empty shells lay by his side. They found Mrs. Lockwood, Helen, and the boy with their skulls crushed. By this time
the snow had begun to fall, and before they finished removing the
bodies a wild blizzard was raging, with the wind howling through
the orchard and piling drifts over the cooling embers.

They carried the bodies to Pat O'Hagan's and arranged them
as decently as possible. Two of the men kept vigil beside them until
morning. Tiny was taken to the Spraggs' and put to bed. The doctor gave her a sedative, and Mrs. Spragg sat beside her with a hand
on her head to quiet her starts and sobbing. It was Pat O'Hagan
who stood at the telephone to notify the county officers, and to
inform the older Lockwoods — Paul, married and living in the
New Country, Martha working at the county seat — of the misfor-
tune that had overwhelmed their family.

During the forenoon hundreds of people fought their way
through the swirling snow — walking, picking their way on horseback, or driving far out in the fields around blocked roads — and
came to the Lockwood place. The men milked the cows, cared for
the horses, fed and watered the hogs and chickens, even coaxed up
a slinking dog and some frightened cats, but for the most part they
stood around the ruins. For once the community was shocked out
of its ready speech.

Martha Lockwood came up on the morning train, stunned with
horror and grief. Joe Spragg drove to town after her and brought

her out to his place to sit with her arms clasped about her heart-
broken little sister. The sheriff and the coroner arrived on the same
train. The inquest was held that afternoon. Tiny fought to control
her rising hysteria, and in response to kindly questions she told a
coherent story —

"I'm twelve years old. Yes, I know what an oath means. My
mother taught me. . . . Yes, we all went to the play that night.
Was it yesterday? . . . We had a good time. We went in a sled,
and my father put some sleigh bells on the harness. My brother
drove. My father said, 'You're a better horseman than I am.' My
sister was in the play. . . .

"My brother put up the horses. Yes, we talked a while before
we went to bed. About the play mostly. My father went to bed last.
Well, no, I didn't see him go to bed at all. He was still there when
the rest of us went. By the fire in the sitting room. I kissed him
good-night. I always did. . . .

"I woke up when I heard my mother scream. . . . I sat up in
bed and just then my father came in. He had a lamp in his hand,
and he was carrying an ax. He said, 'Lay still and I won't hurt
you.' I laid back down. Yes, I was awful scared, but I didn't know
what else to do. He took hold of the bedclothes and pulled them
away from me. It was the hand that had the ax in it. He had the
lamp in the other. Then he raised the ax and I thought he was
going to hit me. But I dodged and slipped out on the other side
of the bed. Then he threw the lamp right down on the bed. And he
went out and started down stairs. But before he went out he said,
'Don't follow me.' I tried to put out the fire in my bed but I couldn't.

"Then I ran to my mother. She was in bed. I shook her and said,
'The house is afire.' She groaned, but I couldn't wake her up. . . .
I thought she was dead. I ran to the other rooms and found my
sister and my brother. They felt limber and I couldn't wake them
up. I was sure they were dead.

"I ran downstairs, and there was my father in the sitting room.
He had the shotgun by him. The stove door was open, and he was
shoveling out hot coals with the fire shovel and scattering them
on the carpet. He didn't see me. I ran out the back way and came
to Mr. Spragg's house. And Mrs. Spragg took care of me. . . .

"Yes, my father was always good to us. He was quiet sometimes. My mother told me, 'When he is quiet like that you mustn't

go near him or vex him. He isn't very well.' No, I didn't think it was queer. I didn't think much about it."

Joe Spragg told how the sobbing, gasping child had come bursting in to throw herself upon them as they slept. She was barefooted and clad only in her night dress, her teeth chattering until she could not speak. They tried to warm and quiet her, and they finally got her story. Spragg threw on his clothes and started for help, but she grasped his arm and screamed, "Oh, don't leave us. He followed me. I know he followed me. He's got a gun. He'll come and kill us." Spragg hesitated, but his wife said, "You'd better go. They've got to have help. I'll lock the door, and I think we'll be all right." But it was a dreadful strain, waiting there with the frantic child in the silent house and an unknown terror outside.

The Spraggs testified that they had known of their neighbor's mental lapses. He had acted queer that fall when the two men butchered together, and Mrs. Lockwood had told them, binding them to secrecy.

"It's been coming on for almost a year," she had said. "And he knows it, too. But when he is among people he tries so hard to act the same as usual that I haven't the heart to let anybody know. And I don't think he's at all dangerous; I can manage him. Next spring Paul is coming to take over the farm, and the children and I will move to town while he goes away for treatment."

Martha also testified that she had known of her father's condition. "Helen knew it, too, but I don't think the younger children ever suspected. I wanted to stay at home to be with my mother, but she thought I'd better keep my job. She said we might need the money after they broke up farming."

The verdict of the coroner's jury was "murder and suicide because of insanity." The physiological causes that had undermined Thomas Lockwood's mental health were never known. It was certain that there were no outward circumstances that could have driven him to that condition. He had never had a mortgage on his farm, and he owned another quarter, which he had paid out clear; he was singularly fortunate in his family life; and until the last year — when his neighbors looked back and remembered that he had "seemed to be studying about something" — he had been a man of serene and open nature.

Paul arrived on Sunday. By that time the trains were blocked by drifts, but he managed to make the last miles by team. His young wife came with him; it was plain that she would have walked if necessary to share his tragic homecoming. Neighbors with their spades worked in relays at the hard labor of digging the graves in the frozen cemetery, and it was neighborly hands that wound the poor, charred bodies in sheets and placed them in the coffins. Other hands measured and cut and sewed for desolate little Tiny.

The funeral was held at the Methodist church on Sunday afternoon. The building was crowded in spite of the cold and the drifted roads. All were thinking of the Sunday only one week before. Thomas Lockwood had sat there in his accustomed place, and men had deferred to his judgment. The tall boy and his lovely sister had raised their young voices in the choir, standing untroubled and confident, secure in home and love and protection. Mrs. Lockwood had taught the little children in the Sunday school, just as she had taught them since that first gathering of new settlers in an open grove. Now her friends remembered that her eyes were haunted, that her sensitive color had faded during the past year; they had supposed that she was tired, or that middle age was wearing down her vitality. Prairie City always shed sympathetic tears at a funeral, but this time men, women, and young people felt their hearts torn by personal grief.

The people were accustomed to tragedy — the result of recklessness and uncurbed spirits and the natural gravitation of the abnormal and the emotionally unstable to the frontier. Suicide and insanity were appallingly frequent. Children played with fire and burned to death; many farmhouses from one cause or another went up in smoke. There was violent death from runaways and the accidental discharge of firearms. Rabies went all the time unchecked, and there was one horrible case of hydrophobia. But never before had a calamity struck so deeply at the heart of the community.

The young people — in school, in Epworth League, in the new sport of skating — thought constantly of their missing companions, incredulous that death could be.

"Do you remember how pretty Helen looked that night? Once she looked down at me and smiled. I never thought — "

"Virgil was going to help clean the snow off of the pond. He always liked — "

The men soberly filled the vacant place on the church board,

the school board, the township board; and the women tried to
gather up the neighborly tasks that fell from Mrs. Lockwood's
loosened hands.

"Nobody can ever take their place in this community," they
said.

The week after the funeral Paul and Martha took their forlorn
little sister and left the country. None of them ever returned, even
for a brief visit, to the place where they had spent their childhood.
They disposed of their land as quickly as possible to farmers who
needed additional quarter-sections. The house was never rebuilt,
the outbuildings were removed, the trees died. Not a trace now
remains of the gracious farmstead nestling in the timber where
Thomas Lockwood broke the sod to found his home in love and
neighborly kindness. Only the old-timers still point out the scene
of "the Lockwood Tragedy."

The shock slowly passed from the consciousness of Prairie City.
The talk ceased to go around and around on the same subject. The
snow melted and spring work came, and the people turned with
their old zest to other interests. The first of these was a promotion
scheme.

XIV

PRAIRIE CITY GAMBLES WITH ITS FUTURE

THE RAILWAY promoters through their initial arrangement with the town company had a lien on the unsold lots in Prairie City. They had many townsites along this and other railroads, and their Enid offices had extensive facilities for advertising. The town company made a few tentative plans for a lot sale to be conducted by Lindsey and Koch, but the power that worked in the background had other designs. The sale was placed in the hands of a high pressure promoter in Kansas City. Booklets entitled *Prairie City: Queen of the Wheat Belt* were printed and distributed throughout the North Central States. Contracts entitling the purchaser to a lot, a free excursion, and a chance at the new artificial-stone building on Main Street were offered at thirty-five dollars each, payable in installments.

The home people should have known the false assumptions that lurked behind the fervid words of the advertising booklets. The town showed no signs of becoming a great metropolis where a rectangle of vacant land taken at random would rise to fabulous values. Some of the lots were within the town — three or four were in the heart of the business section — but most of them lay in the vacant land stretching half a mile beyond the farthest limits of building. And even a desirably located lot standing alone was virtually worthless. But the advertising made good reading:

"Oklahoma, land of marvelous opportunity — "

"This thriving town, a wheat field less than three years ago — "

"Two railroads, one already in operation — "

"These examples of rising property values in Oklahoma towns — "

Prairie City was innocent; its own citizens joined the investors.

By the fall of 1905 about one thousand purchasers had bought and paid out contracts for from one to ten lots each. The date for the distribution was set for November 23. It was apparent that the two hotels and three restaurants the town boasted would be inadequate to accommodate the crowd; so the Rebekahs fitted up the Odd Fellows' hall with cots, and the women's societies of the churches prepared to serve meals.

Many of the contract holders remained at home and sent proxies, but about three hundred came in on a special train — well-fed Northerners fairly shining with good clothes and prosperity. The weather might have been ordered by the promoter. A gentle rain during the night had freshened the fields and washed the sky. In the morning great, soft clouds rolled back before such a day of blue and gold and tingling warmth as comes only in an Oklahoma autumn. The new town with its rows of little trees stood up clean in the sparkling atmosphere, and all around it to the low horizon stretched the living green of young wheat.

The visitors were enchanted. They strolled about enjoying the mellow sunshine, or they gathered in animated groups to repeat the language of the advertising pamphlets. Prairie City caught snatches of their conversation:

"This town's bound to grow; it's got everything."

"I wouldn't mind living here myself."

"Oh, there's no use talking; Oklahoma's the coming country."

"I knew a man that bought lots in Oklahoma City, and in three years — "

Just the words Prairie City wanted fervently to believe. Three or four pioneers stopped to greet each other and to watch the visitors — tanned, graying men, lank with the struggles of the past sixteen years.

"Wonder what they'd 'a' said if they'd 'a' got here in a dust storm," sneered George Hadley.

"Too bad they didn't," said Fred Peters. "The whole business is a swindle, and now the weather joins in to fool 'em still more. They'll swallow anything now."

"Mebbe it's not such a swindle after all," reasoned John Clark. "All the big cities had to start sometime. I wouldn't mind buyin' a few lots myself."

"This is the best thing that ever happened to this country," declared Dad Colby. "Those fellows have all got money. Most of them will move here and start a business. Then the town will really boom."

Before the day was over all Prairie City had joined the optimists.

In the evening the promoter shepherded his contract holders into the Methodist church —

"Now, ladies and gentlemen," he announced, "this is your meeting. You have bought all my lots, and I am turning them over to you. It is your privilege to choose your own method of distribution."

The contract holders quickly formed an organization, electing a breezy citizen of Missouri as chairman. They voted to apportion their property by lottery; and chose an allotting committee with one of the few lady investors — a trim woman from Nebraska — serving as secretary. Slips of paper, each with the numerical description of a lot, were then placed in a box and thoroughly stirred; and each contract holder for himself or by proxy drew out as many as he had purchased. The secretary recorded the results, placing the name of each purchaser opposite the number of his lot.

It was a good-natured and orderly crowd that filled the dimly lighted little church. The work lasted far into the night. Finally the last slip had been drawn and the last name recorded. Then it developed that these strangers from many states were unwilling to trust each other with the records. They finally agreed to give the books into the custody of the secretary, reasoning in some obscure way that a woman would not be dishonest.

The next morning it became known that someone during the night had tampered with the records. For a few minutes things looked dangerous. But when the secretary was confronted with the facts she tearfully admitted that she had juggled the numbers in order to claim eight choice lots for herself and three of her friends. She made some rapid erasures, signed an affidavit that her corrections were accurate, and departed in haste on a freight train. Everybody was happy again.

The purchasers spent most of the morning exploring the lots they had drawn. The fortunate were full of plans and enthusiasm; some even showed their faith to the extent of buying out the holders of adjoining lots at a considerable advance over the contract price. The unfortunate accepted the result with cheerful good humor. One man was seen starting out with a box of cartridges and a shotgun. "I'm going out to kill varmints on my lot," he explained.

He had drawn a gulch down by the railroad bridge on the far edge of the townsite. The drawing for the building was held in the open at the close of these exploratory tours. The winner was jubilant; before he left he made a good rental contract with a Prairie City farmer who planned to move to town and start a produce house.

At the station the editor of the *News* distributed fresh copies of his paper. Almost everybody subscribed. He spent some time fraternizing with two or three newspaper men he found among the visitors; it was evident that they would do their duty in spreading the fame of Prairie City. When the special train pulled out, it bore away a happy group of true believers, singing praises of the Oklahoma climate, the agricultural wealth of the community, and the future of the town.

Prairie City settled down to enjoy its prospects. Nobody showed any curiosity over the books of the town company. If the railway promoters had made money by the sale, it was in a good cause, for had they not given the community the precious boon of transportation? As for the speculative enthusiasm of the investors, the people felt happily that their own faith in their town had been vindicated by the judgment of these well-to-do visitors from the North.

During the next few months lively letters came back to the *News*, expressing satisfaction with the sale and a continuing interest in civic affairs. But realization slowly dawned on the purchasers that a twenty-five foot frontage was too narrow for a building site, and that the lottery had distributed the ownership until it was virtually impossible to bring adjoining lots into the same hands. The paper carried many offers from owners of two lots — five lots — ten lots — scattered singly over the townsite: "I am willing to sell one or all, or buy the lot joining each if I can find out the name and address of the man who owns it." As soon as the promoter of the sale finished making out the deeds to validate the drawing, the editor published a list of lots and owners and mailed it to his Northern subscribers; but long-distance purchases and sales among the investors turned out to be difficult.

At first the absentee owners had an inflated idea of the value of their property; then they lost interest entirely, and it became almost impossible to trace them. After three or four years they began to neglect the payment of taxes. People in the community bought up the tax titles and grew crops of fodder or potatoes or even wheat on the vacant lots. These islands of farm land gave the town a ragged appearance; at the same time it was impossible to enforce ordinances for the care of trees or the cutting of weeds when so much of the land lay virtually unclaimed.

The uncertainty over titles hindered legitimate development. When a citizen of Prairie City prepared to build a residence he wanted a spacious site with room for trees and garden; but the purchase of several lots together was a tedious process. Worst of all was the effect on community morale; it was a bitter dose to swallow — that strangers who had bet their money on the town had crossed the transaction off their books.

Thus in selling patches of raw land to deluded buyers the promoters had unwittingly set limits — physical and spiritual limits — to the future of Prairie City. The whole movement was part of the unreal development that made life in Oklahoma such a feverish striving in the years preceding statehood.

XV
THE MAGIC OF STATEHOOD

Prairie City had been talking about statehood ever since that starveling summer of 1890 when its people first met to form their political institutions. As land rush followed land rush, adding new frontiers to the growing area of settlement, they felt with increasing intensity that their own calloused young hands should forge its destiny. But the question was complicated by the uncertain status of the Indian Territory.

The border of this undeveloped area lay about sixty miles east of Prairie City. It was a land of romance and irresistible appeal. Farmers and business men made hunting and exploring trips to the region, returning with glowing accounts of its virgin fertility. Some of the homesteaders who sold their farms settled there, finding some method of residing in the Indian country. All expected it to fall by inevitable gravitation into the hands of the white man.

In 1893 the Federal Government had begun to liquidate the Indian régime, and subsequent agreements with the tribes had set 1906 as the final date of dissolution. This was too far in the future for impatient Prairie City to wait for statehood. All agreed on that. But the relationship between Oklahoma Territory and the Indian Territory in the statehood plan was good for an argument on any Saturday afternoon.

"Why do we want to wait for them Indians anyhow? We've got enough here in Oklahoma Territory to make the greatest state that ever come into the Union. Let's have separate statehood, and have it now. We'll have to wait ten years if we come in together."

"Not necessarily. Just join the Indian Territory on to Oklahoma now, and make one state out of the whole business. It won't take long to get things organized over there if they just give the white people a chance at it. And we'll have a bigger state and a richer state."

In the spring of 1902 Flynn managed to get a bill through the national House of Representatives providing separate statehood for the Territory of Oklahoma. When it reached the Senate it was amended to permit the eventual annexation of the Indian Territory after the termination of tribal control. Thus matters stood when the session ended.

Flynn was ready to retire from Congress. The Republicans nominated Bird McGuire of Pawnee, and adopted a platform strongly endorsing the pending statehood bill. The Democrats nominated Bill Cross of Oklahoma City, who advocated single statehood for the two territories. Both men spoke at Prairie City. The people took time off from moving the town and watching the railroad to hear them. Neither aroused much personal devotion, but most of the voters accepted the interpretation of the *News:* "A vote for Cross means waiting four or five years for the Indian Territory; a vote for McGuire means statehood this winter." McGuire carried Prairie City. He carried again in 1904 by the same argument. But he never had the slightest chance to win statehood for Oklahoma alone.

There were practical political considerations against multiplying the number of Western and radical states. And in a deeper sense there was an essential unity underlying the superficial separation of the "twin territories." The whole area had been set apart three-quarters of a century before for Indian occupation. Beginning with the Run of '89 the western half had been opened, tract by tract, for white settlement; the eastern half was longer in transition, but by a somewhat different method it was passing through the same change from Indian to white tenure. Thus even the great Runs and the crowded years of life in Oklahoma Territory were only incidents in the larger movement.

The Enabling Act admitting the two territories to single statehood under the name "Oklahoma" was finally passed by Congress and signed by the President on June 16, 1906. Prairie City would have preferred the other method, but everybody was too happy to complain. The territorial officials divided the country into election districts, and the governor set November 6 for the election of delegates to a constitutional convention. Prairie Township as usual was joined with a tract of Negroes and sand along the Cimarron, but it prepared to assert its own judgment in the making of a constitution. The Republicans made their nomination by the usual convention method; but the Democrats introduced the new primary system, which agrarians of all parties believed so ardently would eliminate political chicanery and place the government directly in the hands of the people.

This was Charles Lester's day. While he followed his corn rows and plowed his wheat land he had thought deeply and independently on political and economic issues. He had seen the powerful financial centers of the country exact tribute from the hard-run Oklahoma frontier in inflated freight rates and excessive costs of farm machinery and usurious interest; and he had seen the sharp and predatory in Oklahoma exact a similar tribute from their humble brethren. It seemed so simple to stop it all. Just to make a constitution in the interest of the common man. It was like writing a great charter of human freedom on a clean sheet of paper.

Something of the same political ferment stirred Prairie City. Even the *News* — its editor an Iowa Republican — supported Lester. In the Democratic primary he polled 111 votes in the township, with none for an opponent from another part of the district. In the election he received 155 votes to 29 for the Republican candidate. His lead was strong enough to overcome the united Negro opposition, and send him to the constitutional convention. Thus Prairie City voted its deepest convictions.

Charles Lester at least was never disillusioned. During occasional visits home from the sessions at Guthrie he talked freely about his impressions. He found that most of the 112 delegates were men of kindred faith; they were young, ardent men of many vocations — lawyers, farmers, editors, ministers — agrarian in outlook, shrewd in practical politics, naive in political philosophy. They went to work enthusiastically to create everything a constitution ought to have; they would attend to every detail so there would be no growth of tyranny through elastic clauses and implied powers.

The completed document contained forty-five thousand words, one hundred and fifty pages of close print. It placed everything directly in the hands of the people; and those overshadowing giants, the corporations, were brought under strict control. There were the initiative and the referendum, a multitude of elective offices, two-cent passenger fare, provisions protecting labor, commissions for this and that and everything.

But this was not all. Prairie City in fact was engaged in two moral crusades at once. Here was the chance to destroy the liquor power. The saloon element and the churches had been fighting over this issue ever since the first drunkard reeled out of Matt's Place at the beginning of the town.

In the spring of '97 a national organizer of the W.C.T.U. from Indiana addressed a union meeting one Sunday evening at the Baptist church. She made a fine impression — a silvery-haired, cultured woman, who conducted herself with dignity and ease on the platform, and appealed to her audience in terms of wrecked homes and human wastage. The following afternoon a branch was organized with about fifty members, and an almost equal number of husbands standing in the offing ready to help. It carried on an educational program, organizing the children into a temperance society with marches and songs, enlisting the older girls in dramatic readings, and inducing young men to sign the pledge.

Others attempted to curb the liquor traffic by direct action. In the fall of '99 the territorial organizer of the Anti-Saloon League called a mass meeting at the Methodist church, and assisted in forming a local branch. Under territorial law saloon licenses were granted by the county commissioners upon petition of the voters; hence this society attempted to defeat these petitions. But they generally went through; the number of saloons increased from one in 1899 to four in 1903 and five in 1906.

As statehood approached, the controversy was intensified by outside influences; for Oklahoma became a battleground between the liquor and anti-liquor forces of the country, each seeking to control its admission to the Union. Both sides entered the contest in Prairie City; one of the great brewing companies spent money freely to maintain its hold on the community, and prohibition lecturers from the surrounding states aroused *their* adherents by intemperate oratory. The fight reached its culmination in 1905.

In January an elderly minister from Texas gave a week of lectures in the Methodist church attacking the saloons and their works in fiery language. At the close of the series he organized a "Law and Order League" with over sixty members, farmers and business men, all determined to take decisive action against the liquor traffic. But on his way to the hotel that night he was knocked down and beaten by a saloon partisan. He had barely left town — with the embarrassed apologies of all good citizens — when Carry Nation came to give a lecture at the opera house. Saint and sinner alike came out full of curiosity to hear her, for all knew how she had wielded a hefty hatchet against illegal saloons in prohibition Kansas. She had a packed house — admission, ten cents — and sold innumerable hatchet-stickpins and crudely written little pamphlets glorifying her career. She proved to be a woman of nimble wit and an appearance of candor that won the unsuspicious heart of Prairie City. Those who had come to scoff remained to join up — this time a "Prohibition Federation" of Republicans and Democrats who were expected to renounce their parties.

On the evening of Decoration Day a traveling troupe with a tent played "Ten Nights in a Barroom" to a packed and deeply moved audience. And the Law and Order League defeated one saloon petition after a fight that almost tore the town asunder. In revenge the opposition managed somehow to "spike" the fruit juice served at one of the genteel meetings of the W.C.T.U. The effect was rather appalling, but the women — young and lively, as they were — accepted it as a joke. By this time, although the liquor dealers found their business as brisk as ever, the "dry" forces were in control of public sentiment.

Just before Congress convened that fall, an outside organizer went through the country and obtained many signatures to a petition asking the law-makers to fix prohibition on the proposed state for twenty-one years. The petitioners had a good argument: the United States had always attempted to guard its Indian wards against firewater, and the tribal governments of the Indian Territory were requesting the continuance of that policy. When the Enabling Act finally passed Congress late in the session, it did contain a twenty-one year prohibitory provision for the Indian country comprising the eastern half of the embryo commonwealth.

"Statewide Prohibition for Oklahoma" then became the battle cry of the fighting "drys." They were not successful in pledging the delegates to place this clause in the constitution. Charles Lester told his neighbors, "I don't drink, do I? You know I'm not a saloon man. But let the people decide this for themselves." The convention accordingly wrote the provision with a stipulation that it be submitted separately to the voters.

The constitutional convention completed its work July 16, 1907. The governor set September 17 as the date of the statehood election. If the usual Oklahoma political campaign was a circus, the campaign of 1907 was a three-ringed circus. There was the election of state officers, the adoption of the constitution, and the question of statewide prohibition. Prairie City was passionately interested in all three.

There was unexpected leisure that summer. It was the most disastrous crop year since 1895. In the spring the "green bugs" attacked first the oats, and then the wheat. On the fields appeared disfiguring red-brown patches rapidly changing to bald spots, which quickly spread and merged and blotted out the green expanse. June passed strangely without the familiar gold on the landscape and the sweat and strain of harvest. Drought in the summer burned up most of the corn and even cut short the kaffir crop. In the fall the wheat acreage was seriously curtailed because it was too dry to plow and plant. It was a good year to talk politics.

The Democrats nominated their state officers by primary on June 8. The Prairie City vote was light — only 41 for the township. The voters were overwhelmed by the complexity of issues and the unfamiliar personalities in the enlarged area that would comprise the state. The Republicans took more interest in the convention, which met at Tulsa in August to make their nominations. Dr. Lindsey, Jonathan Cole, Arthur Goodwin, and "Colonel" Eaton made the trip over to the roaring Indian Territory oil town; they never forgot the uplift of spirit that came with their first glimpse of the diversified interests, the unknown reaches of land, and the varied historic backgrounds that were uniting to form their state.

Both parties held primaries for the nomination of county and township officers and members of the legislature. Candidates were as thick as the weeds in the empty fields; forty-two were registered for the various county offices. But this time Prairie City was on familiar ground; and there was a stronger vote — 71 Democrats and 84 Republicans. The Republican lead was due apparently to revulsion against the constitution, which had been held up to ridicule by the *News* and the opposition dailies. Prairie City above all things liked the feel of worldly wisdom; an embarrassing suspicion of its own innocence began to undermine its faith.

All through the summer the constitution was the all-absorbing topic of conversation on the streets, in the saloons, wherever a farmer stood with foot on wagon hub to talk with his neighbor. It was published serially in very fine type on the ready print pages of the *News*. Several of the voters plowed through every word — "A man's got no right voting on a thing unless he knows what's in it," they said. Most of those who read it pronounced it "the greatest constitution for a poor man ever written." Others preferred to be guided by the arguments of the press and the political leaders. The greatly admired President Roosevelt was known to disapprove of its radical provisions. Secretary of War Taft came to the territory, and in his calm and masterful way pointed out its defects. William Jennings Bryan, still the inspired prophet of the common man, came and lauded it in extravagant panegyrics; he said it was the greatest constitution ever written, greater than the constitution of the United States.

Meanwhile as the political campaign and the constitutional arguments increased in intensity the prohibition battle was working up to an even higher climax. There were marching, singing children, pins showing the forty-sixth star and statewide prohibition, orations and dramatic readings, personal appeals to voters. The saloon crowd watched helplessly, and several old soaks — pathetic wrecks of men — prepared to break their shackles by one desperate vote against the destroyer.

The election was held on September 17. Somebody remembered that it was the one-hundred-twentieth anniversary of the day when the great convention finished its work on the Federal constitution. Never before in the eighteen years' abounding life of Prairie City had the voters come to the polls so deeply moved by a sense of historic portent.

When the returns were in, it was found that the township had expressed its reaction from its constitutional orgy by voting for Republican officials — an average of 108 Republican votes to 88 Democratic. But it had not dared to postpone statehood by voting against the constitution itself. The heaviest vote of all was cast on that question: For, 126; Against, 93. And the prohibition section carried: For, 101; Against, 94. The Democratic Party, the constitution, and prohibition carried the area soon to comprise the state.

Soon after the election several members of the W.C.T.U. attended a convention at Lawton, a six-year-old city that had sprung into lusty being the day the New Country was opened. They returned full of thanksgiving and uplift; they reported a gathering swept by exultant emotion, exchanging experiences on "What we did in our town on election day" and breaking into waves of song — "Praise God from Whom all Blessings Flow," "Blest Be the Tie That Binds." On the way home the delegates had filled the train, singing their campaign songs, and by permission pinning their white ribbons on seventy-five men passengers between Lawton and Oklahoma City.

The date set for statehood was Saturday, November 16. On that day the President would issue a proclamation declaring Oklahoma to be a state of the Union, and the new state officers would be inaugurated at Guthrie. The train ran on convenient schedule, making the trip down in the morning and returning in the evening. But Prairie City's enjoyment of the ceremonies was curtailed by the money panic of 1907.

The blow struck without warning. Prices were good. The community was busy as usual, picking cotton, raising live stock and poultry, trying to salvage as much prosperity as possible from the bad crop year. Suddenly, the last week in October, the territorial governor proclaimed a week's banking holiday, and the Pioneer State Bank closed its doors. The bottom dropped out of the cotton market, and the price of produce fell so low that "I want to put an ad in your paper for an egg-sucking dog," a farmer told the editor.

On the evening of Friday, November 1, the business leaders met with A. T. Strickland and the other bank officials and worked out an agreement to carry the community through the crisis. The following Saturday afternoon Strickland explained the situation to a mass meeting in the opera house. The people knew him well — this tall, unsmiling pioneer — and they sensed the confidence in his quiet voice.

"Our community is solvent. All Oklahoma is solvent. Your money is perfectly safe. All we need is a little time to get our funds from Eastern depositories. But a run right now would ruin everything.

"The bank will open Monday. Depositors will be allowed to withdraw only five dollars cash in one day, a total of ten dollars in one week. You may have a certified check for the whole amount of your deposit. With these checks we can carry on our business until money is circulating again. All this is for your protection. The business of the community is built around the stability of this bank."

The people accepted his statement. They passed through the following weeks with no sign of tension. But these developments overshadowed the inauguration ceremonies and kept most of them at home on that momentous Saturday.

It was a warm, golden day with every little tree a plume of

color. A crowd went down to the station in the morning to see the train pass through, but only half a dozen purchased tickets. Laughing boys in uniform were spilling out on the platforms — the territorial militia coming from stations up the road to take part in the inaugural parade. Their olive-drab looked strange to a people brought up on song and oratory glorifying "the boys in blue."

Shortly after nine o'clock the news began to circulate through the stores and pass along the streets that the President had signed the statehood proclamation. There were quiet expressions of joy — "We're living in a state now" — but no demonstration. In the afternoon for the first time since the panic struck, the town was jammed with people. The merchants were giving prizes — postponed for two weeks — to cotton growers. Pat O'Hagan won again with the largest load — 10,165 pounds, in a long, especially constructed rack drawn by four mules. It would have brought $406.60 at four cents a pound if he had marketed it before the panic. Now with the price at $2.85 it brought $289.70. And he had paid $1.25 a hundred for picking. The man who won a prize offered for the longest haul had brought 2,500 pounds from a ginless town eighteen miles away in the Strip. The people watched the great loads roll through the street and down to the gin; and through all the interest in weighing and photographing ran the exultant thought, "We're living in a state now."

When the visitors to the capital came in on the passenger that evening, they had a story they would tell as long as they lived. Said Mrs. Sadler,

"The sidewalks were packed all along, and near the library where the ceremony was, the streets were solid with people. Every few minutes they broke out cheering at nothing at all. We jammed our way and worked around to where we could see and hear. I had the baby in my arms and so everybody helped me through.

"There was a Cherokee Indian band that played. And there was a wedding; an Indian girl representing Miss Indian Territory was married to a cowboy, Mr. Oklahoma. When the governor took his oath everybody got quiet. And he made an awful good speech. All about what a great state it was. The people surely cheered when he said, 'Glory, glory, long live the state of Oklahoma.'

"We talked about it all the way home. The train was crowded, and we got acquainted with a lot of people."

All that day in Prairie City the men visited the saloons in droves. As night came on they drank with a concentrated intensity as though they were obligated to exhaust the stock. The saloons were expected to close at midnight, but clocks were turned back and they remained open till dawn. The "drys" stepped softly fearing some sort of reprisals. They could afford to be patient.

"It is the last time," they said. "Now we will have a generation growing up that never saw a saloon, never saw a drunken man on the street, never tasted liquor. It is the greatest thing that ever happened in Oklahoma."

Thus with headlong idealism and headlong debauchery, with joy and exultation, and with supreme self confidence Prairie City came into statehood. The days of strain and stress were largely over. The years that followed were quiet years, filled with the deep, creative power of growth.

XVI
THE PEACEFUL YEARS

T HE PERIOD between statehood and the outbreak of the First
World War was Prairie City's golden age. The ambitions and the
strivings had largely passed; the community reached fulfilment.

There was an agreeable realization of the economic benefits of
statehood. Two-cent passenger fare was very pleasant — until it
was thrown out by the courts. The Corporation Commission, a new
agency of the constitution, made drastic cuts in freight and express charges, and these savings went into the pockets of Prairie
City producers and consumers.

Even more satisfying was the privilege of voting for President.
There was poetic justice in the fact that Bryan was again a candidate in 1908. But the community had changed since the lean Populists had longed so passionately to vote for the Great Commoner
twelve years before. And was not Taft running with the blessing
of the incomparable Teddy? The township went for Bryan — but
only 103 to 99. The keen edge of appreciation for the franchise had
worn down to the dullness of familiarity by 1912. The Democrats
supported Wilson, reasonably, logically, with no flaming fanaticism. They carried the township 93 to 67.

The community regularly returned a small Democratic majority in state and local elections. But the people soon discovered that
they had failed to realize utopia by the constitution method. The
ultra-democratic devices had clogged the democratic process; the
voters stamped the ballot at random and hoped for the best. And
predatory forces that formerly operated on the territory from outside were now entrenching themselves within the state government itself. Unable to specialize on the intricacies of the constitution, some of the voters sought a remedy in socialism.

The Socialist Party had been organized in the territory in the
fall of '99; and one lone Socialist vote — the first ever cast by Prairie

City — had been recorded in the statehood election of 1907. The number increased to 22 in 1908, to 32 in 1912. By the last date the doctrine was spreading with all the enthusiasm of old time Populism.

Everyone knew that Mike McGraw had cast the pioneer vote of 1907. Mike still spent most of his time in the coal mines, but when he came back to look after his farm he carried on missionary work among his neighbors. With his own money he prepared his field by gift subscriptions to *The Appeal to Reason*. This publication from the mining region of southeastern Kansas was buoyant, hopeful, even Christian in tone; it condemned the exploitation of the many by the few and proclaimed the coming liberation of the masses through collective ownership.

Mike's converts were unpromising enough — a farmer who had failed through shiftlessness, a business man who had retired by the poker route, a doctor who had lost his professional ambition. Listening to their arguments one gained the impression that they were capitalists all, that their convictions were personal, that they ached with hunger for the rich man's money.

"A poor man ain't got no chance in this country," raved George Hadley, looking over his untidy acres. "I've worked like a nigger all my life, and look what I've got. I should 'a' been rich by now, and by God I will be if we ever git any justice in this country."

But Mike gathered them all together and organized a "local." They were required to renounce their former political faith and subscribe to the Socialist platform, and they sent monthly dues of ten cents a member to the state secretary. They brought lecturers to town to harangue the crowds on the street or to address meetings at the opera house. These speakers all tried to present the agrarian argument.

"You have made a little during these 'prosperity' years, but the capitalists have made millions. You sweat to raise your hogs and cattle, and the packing trust and the railroads get most of the profit. Under socialism the people would own the packing houses and the railroads, and no bloodsucking capitalists would grow fat off your labor."

But if the people had failed to cure all economic ills through statehood, they were fairly well satisfied with one of their efforts at reform. Nobody even attempted to deny that the closing of the five saloons had brought an abatement of the drink evil. Some men

ordered liquor by express, since the state had no control over inter-
state commerce; but ordering was a deliberate process very different from the mass emotion that drew them to the saloons. Bootlegging developed slowly, under cover and not too obnoxiously.
By the fall of 1909 there were two illicit dispensers: a small grocer
who added "cider" to his stock, and a restaurant keeper who was
bold enough to obtain a Federal license. There were a few mild
attempts at prosecution, but it was almost impossible to obtain
evidence that would stand up in the courts. Only once was there
any suspicion that the town officials were corrupted; then the next
town election became a real contest with two tickets in the field,
and the discredited officials were defeated by an overwhelming
vote.

The saloon keepers easily adjusted themselves to the closing
of their establishments; most of them had tried their hands at half
a dozen things before they engaged in the liquor business. Even
those merchants who had favored the saloons as bringing trade to
the town were converted to the new order; they sold shoes and
sugar to men who had formerly spent their money on drink. The
people supported the prohibition policy. In 1908 they voted against
a referendum petition setting up state agencies to distribute alcohol for medicinal purposes. Two years later they defeated a petition for prohibition repeal 117 to 70.

Other influences than the closing of the saloons were slowing
down the turbulent life of Prairie City. There was of course the
dramatic quiet while the headache cleared away that Sunday
morning after statehood; but there was a gradual decrease of violence during the years that followed. Insanity, suicide, accidental
death, sporadic crimes were as frequent as ever in 1909; they had
diminished appreciably by 1914. Even adultery and the more spicy
divorce trials became uncommon.

By 1914 most of the ardent city-builders of the promotion era
had left the community or had become discredited by personal
financial failure. The Commercial Club died; the affairs of the
town passed into steadier — and slower — hands. The people accepted the fact that the "City" would never be realized; that part
of the name was gradually dropped from common speech. The
smaller the town, the less the competition, was the prevailing
philosophy. When in 1912 talk of the second railroad became current for the last time, there were penurious souls ready to argue,

"Another railroad would kill Prairie. There'd be new stations eight miles on each side to cut into our trade territory." Even the *News* changed its superlatives from a future "Prairie City will soon be the biggest — " to a present "Prairie is the best little town on earth," or "Prairie is the best town of its size in the state."

The population, however, was increasing: 364 in 1907 by a special Federal statehood census, 480 by the census of 1910 — a growth of 32 per cent in three years. In September of 1909, following a bountiful harvest of dollar wheat, the Pioneer State Bank reported over $210,000 in deposits. The same fall the postoffice was raised to third class status, with a fixed salary for a full time postmaster. Fifty thousand dollars was spent in the erection of permanent buildings in the town during the following year. Two frame corners on Main Street were replaced by solid two-story brick: Goodwin and Sons (one of the "Sons" being Earl Peters, married to Bertha Goodwin), and Walker's General Merchandise. Another building year came in 1914, following a more gradual increase of community capital. And all of this development came from the production of the surrounding farms; never before in its history had the town grown on such a stable foundation.

The five years following 1909 were dry. The season of 1910–11 was in fact the driest the country had seen since 1895; not a nubbin of corn was raised, the pastures failed, trees died in town and on the farms. Some of the people found it hard to think beyond the immediate experience of burning wind and brazen sky; they began to create a universal disaster, a sort of indigenous eschatology. Could this be the end of the world? They quoted Rev. 8:7 and Joel 1:15–20.

But this was only an aberration of the human spirit tortured by the terrible heat. There was a fair wheat crop every year, with the price from seventy to ninety cents a bushel. Hog prices were high — usually seven or eight dollars a hundred — but a good many pigs were sold off in 1911 with the failure of the corn crop, and hog raising was never so important again. Beef prices ranged from four to six dollars a hundred, and a good many carloads were shipped from Prairie in spite of the unfavorable seasons. Every farm raised colts; horse and mule buyers came to town regularly and shipped away the surplus animals. Eighty to ninety cases of eggs (2,400 to 2,700 dozen) was a not uncommon take for the produce houses on any brisk Saturday. These houses now bought cream also (butter-

fat, sixteen to twenty-eight cents a pound); almost every farm had
a separator, though the production was curtailed during the dry
years by the scarcity of feed.

But these years marked the beginning of a change from diversified farming to wheat farming. Men who toiled through the year
with corn and kaffir and live stock became one-crop farmers in
spite of themselves by the failure of their spring crops and the
scarcity of feed. It seemed simpler to plant in accordance with the
facts.

Cotton was the first to go. It had justified itself during the
"green bug" year, when it had been the only crop raised, but succeeding years were disappointing. There was the boll worm and
the web worm, drought or rains at the wrong time, and prices
which three years out of six were less than four cents a pound.
Worst of all was the labor problem.

The men hated to work in the cotton field — "farming with a
hoe, gittin' down on your knees and crawlin' around with a cotton
sack, workin' thirteen months out of the year." As for their wives,
it was out of the question, and they were unwilling to take their
children out of school. In 1907 James Alexander, who had out
eighty acres, visited a factory in Chicago and invested in a cotton
picker; but when he tried it out in his field it proved to be a failure.
The same year Hermann Koch employed Japanese workers from
the beet fields of Colorado, but they were unable to do the unfamiliar work. Negro labor was the only solution.

While a Prairie farmer by stiffness and groaning might pick one
hundred pounds a day, and his children might loaf through the
field on Saturday with a haul of twenty-five or fifty pounds, a
Negro man or woman, with the ease and grace of water flowing,
could pick two hundred to five hundred pounds, and every little
woolly-head stuck to his row with the tenacity of a boll worm. The
farmers went to the county seat and brought them out, quartering
them in tents or empty corn cribs or hay lofts. A few built shacks
for them and employed them the whole year. They accepted inconveniences in high good nature, working tirelessly, and spending their free time in epic battles with dice or razors.

Prairie was troubled by their presence. They were a challenge
to its most precious ideals of frontier democracy. Old Jonathan
Cole was true to his convictions. "Anybody who works for me can

eat at my table," he said, and his cotton pickers ate with the family to the scandal of his neighbors and the embarrassment of the Negroes. Most of the people tried self-consciously to model their conduct after that of the Southerners in the community. But they never acquired the Southerner's instinctive guardianship. When they attempted segregation, they succeeded only in being cruel. "I'm not a nigger doctor," said one of the physicians, refusing to minister to a dying cotton picker. And they were uneasily aware that their laborers lived under sub-human conditions and that the children were out of school. While the farmers wrestled with their problem, the town protected itself by an unwritten law — enforced by the marshal — forbidding any Negro to remain within the city limits after sundown. It was a relief to the community conscience when cotton farming was abandoned, and it could practice its democracy without reservations.

The acreage had declined so much that one of the gins did not operate in 1909. The other continued until 1915. They were eventually dismantled and the machinery was shipped to another part of the state. On the eastern edge of the township where the land was too rough for wheat a few farmers still planted small patches of cotton as late as 1920, but they hauled it to other towns.

Not so noticeable at the time, because it developed more slowly, was the decline of fruit raising. After their orchards were well started, the farmers began to plant fodder crops between the rows as they had done in less rigorous climates. But the trees could not endure the hard seasons without cultivation. Every dry spell took its toll; in the terrible drought of 1910–11 whole orchards died and were pulled out with traction engines. Most of the farmhouses were surrounded by ragged trees for a few more years, but nobody ever planted a second orchard. Commercial fruit raising was conducted on a large scale in "the jacks," and it seemed easier to buy from the wagons that always stood on Prairie's streets in season than to undertake the labor of growing and picking.

Possibly the impermanence of land tenure also discouraged the planting of orchards. Farms changed hands more frequently than ever. Although buyers — especially Germans — continued to come in from the North, an increasing proportion of the land transactions took place between Prairie people: farmers who sold one farm and bought another, business men who bought a farm as an investment. In the prosperous year of 1909 the price of a good level quarter shot up to eight thousand, nine thousand, or even ninety-six hundred dollars. Some farmers who sold out took the old trail to the Far West, and flourishing Prairie colonies were now settling along the Gulf coast in Texas.

In spite of land sales and emigration the farm population increased during the years immediately following statehood. The Federal census of 1910 listed 1,126 people living on the farms of the two townships, an increase of 17 per cent since the special census of 1907. This reversal of population trends was due in part to cotton growing; although few of the Negro workers had been enumerated as residents, this crop had brought a tendency to break the farms into smaller units leased to white tenants. A deeper cause was an increased demand for farm land, which made it more practicable for a large landowner to rent out his land rather than to operate it with hired labor. Thirty-eight per cent of the farms surrounding Prairie were operated by tenants in 1910. Most of them were community young people born too late to acquire homesteads; some were landless families from other parts of the state. They paid one-third of the grain, one-fourth of the cotton to the landowner, and were as far as possible removed from the popular connotation of "share-croppers."

Everybody was prospering. The farmers visited the stock shows at Enid and Oklahoma City — now the capital of the state — and invested some of their profits in blooded horses and cattle. But too much money still jingled in their pockets. Some of the surplus was spent in a land lottery in the Florida everglades, and half a dozen families even went there to live. The speculation ended in an unsuccessful suit to recover from the promoters, who had neglected to drain the area. Other Prairie citizens — business men and farmers — organized oil companies, which leased land in the eastern part of the state, and were perpetually on the verge of bringing in a gusher.

The people read in their newspapers of "The High Cost of Living" — fact, slogan, personified evil. They hurled a few orthodox anathemas at the current demon, but few marks of his cloven hoofs were visible. The prices of their farm products were rising, but the goods they bought — thanks to better transportation — cost little more than in the days of thirty-five cent wheat and three cent eggs.

The farmers complained, however, that there was too large a gap between the selling price of their products and the cost to the consumer. In 1907 branches of the Farmers' Union, which had absorbed the Alliance and other farm organizations, were formed in several rural schoolhouses. Before the year was over, in spite of the money panic they subscribed ten thousand dollars in capital stock and established a clearing house in town for the marketing of their poultry and dairy products and the sale of staple groceries. But they failed to provide adequate management, and after a few years the "Farmers' Store" was discontinued. Plans to purchase one of the cotton gins and lease one of the elevators evaporated in nothing but talk. But the conviction developed that Prairie was a poor market, that it paid less for farm products than the surrounding towns.

If their customers were becoming alienated, the business men ignored the danger. Townspeople and farmers alike were turning with their usual light-heartedness to a new diversion; none knew it was a revolution.

Ever since the turn of the century an occasional automobile had come chugging through the country, puffing out foul smoke, leaving runaways and wrath in its wake. It was not until July of 1909 that Dick Martin from the proceeds of that lush harvest purchased Prairie's first motor vehicle. The day he came to town he forgot how to stop it and bumped the hitching post; the men laughed uproariously at his loud, involuntary Whoa's. The doctor, always harassed for time, bought the next one; he was followed by a liveryman with an eye alert for business; a merchant and two farmers came next, happy as children with a new toy. Before the end of 1910 the town recognized the phenomenon by an ordinance imposing a six-mile speed limit on Main Street, ten miles on other streets. By the next year the automobile had a fixed place in the amusement pattern, as owners treated their friends to rides, ran a free taxi service to parties and picnics, and packed in their neighbors for ball games or Fourth of July celebrations in surrounding towns. At first the blacksmith shops made the repairs. Then early in 1913 two garages were opened: one by Dave Hodge as a natural evolution of his blacksmith shop; the other by Joe Spragg, who sold his farm and his threshing outfit to invest in the new business. By the next year about forty automobiles were owned in the community, distributed about half and half between town and country.

The rapid acceptance of the new mode of transportation was due to the low price of the Ford car. All but the first two or three automobiles were of that lowly make. The owners felt a strong personal loyalty to the little machine and its builder: they acquired Ford joke books and repeated Ford jokes; they created a Ford Legend that in a measure supplanted the Bryan Legend and the Teddy Legend. Owing a new and exciting sensation to Henry Ford's mechanical genius and financial insight they were ready to accept his judgment on matters political and international.

The little cars were miscreated agglomerations of error. When they were cranked, they were likely to kick and break the wrist of their driver; if they struck a clod in the road, they turned over; they developed trouble with their radius rods and wandered off into the fields. But everybody drove so slowly and carefully that few injuries resulted from highway accidents. And there was an exhilarating sense of power in holding the steering wheel, a godlike feeling of mastery over time and space. Even the children drove — boys and girls of nine or ten expertly twisting a wire here and there and poking their little feet in and out among the pedals as they chugged about on family errands.

In spite of this new gift of distance Prairie was still the community center. But the social activities changed with the inconstant spirit of the people. The band showed a fluctuating, but generally declining vitality. Baseball suffered a depression about 1907; revived on a semi-professional basis with a Sunday schedule, it furnished good entertainment, but it was no longer an instinctive expression of community life. The universal visiting had ceased; parties were less frequent. After 1907 the Fourth of July usually brought a deserted town, with its people eating ice cream and chicken somewhere in the country or packing the trains — and automobiles — to an out-of-town celebration. But when a moving picture theatre was opened in 1911, it was packed to the doors.

In October, 1910 an agricultural fair sponsored and financed by the business men was as adequate an expression of the maturing achievements of the community as that first harvest picnic was of its budding promise. For three days thousands of people lined the sidewalks along the roped-off Main Street watching a shifting progression of pageantry, exhibits, amusements. It began, fittingly enough, with a parade of the Eighty-Niners, followed by those who

Waiting for the signal on the south line of the Strip. Sep 16th 93

Forbidden to enter, they spent much time looking across the border trying to figure out the lay of the land. (42) Settlers gathering and waiting on the line for the signal to start the run into the Cherokee Strip, September 16, 1893. Western History Collection, University of Oklahoma.

Suddenly on a hill far to the west, they saw the line surge forward; and with a wild yell all were in motion. (44) The run into the Cherokee Strip from the Kansas Line, noon, September 16, 1893. Western History Collection, University of Oklahoma

It looks so bleak! Do you suppose trees will ever grow there? (4) A Cherokee Strip family and sod house north of Marshall, O.T., Spring, 1896. Courtesy of the George Beeby family

Even yet they hold it as a grievance that these hard-won slips of paper were never called for. (42) Registering for the run at Orlando, O.T., where 36,000 registered in September, 1893. Western History Collection, University of Oklahoma

Tom Lockwood looked distressed a few days later when he stood with the rest of the crowd at the 'babtizin' hole' to watch his wife and boy go down into the stagnant water. (36) A baptizing in the Cimarron River near Perkins, 1894. Robert E. Cunningham Collection

It was a shabbily dressed but sturdy group of young people with a strange blending of self-confidence and diffidence who walked bare-footed across the prairie to the sod schoolhouse carrying books from many different states. (19) Sunnyside school, Cherokee Strip, near Marshall, O.T., winter 1895-6. Courtesy of the Beeby family

Hard times never slowed the currents of ebullient life that swirled through Prairie City. (66) Typical Saturday crowd on first townsite, Marshall, O. T., July 19, 1902. Courtesy of Mrs. Bert Scott

MARSHALL HIGH SCHOOL

I never heard a man say just because he only had one child he wanted it to grow up ignorant. (145) Above: Rosenberg School, District No. 97, southwest of Marshall, O. T., winter 1901-02. Author's collection. Below: Marshall, Oklahoma "High School" in the 1920s. Western History Collection, University of Oklahoma

Early in the morning wagons and buggies began rolling in and parking all around the outskirts; by ten-thirty an estimated five thousand people were jamming the streets. (98) Floats on their way to Main Street parade. (Note Baptist church in permanent position on new townsite.) Marshall, O. T., 1903. Courtesy of Mrs. Grover Diedrich

Four boys went to Oklahoma City and enlisted the first week. (152) An Oklahoma soldier in his World War I "doughboy" uniform, about 1917. Author's collection

*They defiled into a pasture, where the watching thousands
saw a cross burst into flame, and sheeted figures moving
about in ghostly ritual. (165)* A Ku Klux Klan rally near
Lone Wolf, Oklahoma. Western History Collection,
University of Oklahoma

'Looks like we got more'n we expected when we settled this claim in '89, don't it?' (185) Country store and #1 Discovery Well on McCully farm southwest of Marshall, Oklahoma, June, 1927. Courtesy of Ida McCully Schwarz

Roustabout row, where oilfield workers lived on McCully lease southwest of Marshall, Oklahoma, 1927. Courtesy of Ida McCully Schwarz

But on the edge . . . stood one whose presence twisted his neighbors' hearts — old Joe Spragg, long a leader of the town, reduced in his old age to this extremity. (222) Man walking home with relief provision, June, 1937. Western History Collection, University of Oklahoma

'I've seen lots of country but I wouldn't trade Prairie for all of it. (240) A Marshall, Oklahoma, GI during World War II. Courtesy of Mrs. Wesley Van Hauen

had ridden that burning September day to take their homes in the Strip. People cheered the lean, vigorous men who were still among the leaders of the community, but they broke into wild applause when "Surprise," a grand old horse known to all old-timers, and "Gilbert," a noble sorrel aged twenty-six, came arching their lank necks as proudly as though they sensed the import of the history they had helped to shape.

Registered cattle, combed and curled to the last hair, blooded horses, beautiful colts, sleek mules were led in constant procession through the street; mighty porkers grunted from pens; grain and cotton and potatoes, fine poultry, cooked foods and canned foods, fancy work and art – all were on display. Nobody had realized that the community was so rich in the products of its farms and its homes. And there were foot races and riding contests through the same street, and the band played and everybody greeted old friends. Altogether it was the culmination of twenty-one years of intense, creative living. "Let's do it every year," was the universal reaction.

The next year's fair was surprisingly successful in spite of the drought; and it was a heartening experience to add up what the community had salvaged from the general failure. The third fair brought almost a thousand visitors on a special train from the county seat. Then the project was dropped. Three years was still about the limit of Prairie's fleeting enthusiasms.

Only Decoration Day survived as a permanent institution. Was it that even effervescent Prairie could not deny the finality of death? Or possibly it was due to the constancy of the Old Soldiers, who always had the observance in charge. There were plenty of flag-marked graves in the cemetery now, and the surviving veterans were gray-haired, aging men. Their ranks were reinforced now by their former enemies; it was in 1909 that they began to invite Confederate veterans to join in their ceremonies. They deplored an atmosphere of general hilarity with baseball games, gay crowds filling the streets, and the all-day din of "squawkers" and firecrackers; and they were inclined to decry an increasing tendency of civilians to visit the cemetery and place flowers on the graves of their own dead. But the voice of the Old Soldiers had become feeble; only thirteen in faded blue, three in quiet gray made the trip to the cemetery in 1914 – conveyed for the first time in automobiles furnished by kindly neighbors. It was remarked that seven had died during the preceding year.

All these activities showed a social life in transition, with a corresponding variation, a greater complexity of pattern. But Prairie was united on one community achievement — its overmastering faith, its rapturous pride in "our school."

XVII

PRAIRIE CITY GRADUATES

Prairie had come a long way since Arthur Goodwin had set up his little store in a grassy waste. Its school had come a long way since that first group of ragged men had built their earthen hovel to the cause of education.

For years it was simply a rural school — one of six in the township — with the accident of a village within its district. The first families living in the town sent their children to the one-room box a mile and a quarter down the road. Then railroad prospects brought more people, and the building overflowed. The board hired an additional teacher and herded the younger children into the Methodist church, where they sat without desks or blackboard, their legs dangling from the high, homemade pews.

When the railroad came and the town moved — closer, as it happened, to the schoolhouse — the board lengthened the building, stretching it to form two rooms. School opened that fall with 38 pupils in the upper room and 52 in the lower, arranged for the first time in the rigidity of a graded system. There was a seven months' term, with salaries of forty dollars a month for the "professor" in the upper room, thirty-five dollars for the young woman who taught in the lower. It was still a district school, but the town promoters of that febrile era liked to call it "the Prairie City School." One farmer and two business men served on the board.

For the first years the school had had no objectives. The children had returned term after term to mull over the same lessons until they were ready to "quit school" and join in adult activities. But the spring the railroad contract was signed, the community had its first common school "graduates."

About thirty young people from five or six districts gathered in the frame schoolhouse under an "examiner" appointed by the county superintendent and labored for two days on a written examination prepared in the office of the territorial superintendent;

and the papers were sent to the county seat to be graded. About twenty passed. Their diplomas came by mail from the territorial superintendent's office; before long most of them were framed and hanging in living rooms. They bore the picture of a brave new building standing starkly on a prairie; it was good for these children to know that it stood there, the territorial university, and that they were qualified to enter its preparatory department. None of them entered, however: the older ones took another examination and began teaching in rural schools, or their parents sent them to business college at the county seat to return no more to Prairie City; the younger ones settled down in their various districts to another year of McGuffey's Fifth Reader and the same old problems in Ray's Arithmetic.

The next year with the town settled on its new site, and with a Commercial Club and a corporate government and a people bursting with civic spirit, a strong effort was made to move the school to town and erect an adequate building on the plat reserved for it. It met stubborn opposition from the south end of the district.

"The town children can't walk half a mile to the schoolhouse; our children already walk two miles, and they think it's all right for them to walk half a mile further. Well, we own land and pay taxes, and our children is just as good as theirs. We're goin' to keep the schoolhouse right where it is."

The board decided that the school could not be moved from the center of the district without unanimous consent. Meanwhile as the town grew, a third teacher was employed, and again a church was requisitioned to hold the overflow. The term was lengthened to eight months. A year of high school was added; four young people who had passed the territorial examination wrestled, not very successfully, with Latin, algebra, English composition, and physical geography.

In 1904 removal carried, and bonds were voted 90 to 5 for the erection of a building. The four-room brick was the pride of the community. After all, it was only fourteen years removed from the sod for which the pioneers had been so grateful, only ten years from the frame box that had seemed so fine to the developing settlement. In salute to the Latin and algebra, proud lettering over the entrance blazoned the name, "Prairie City High School."

"It was a memorable day in our history," said the *News* when the children assembled on Main Street and marched down with flags and singing to the new building. One hundred and twenty-eight reported to the four teachers. Of this number thirty-seven were enrolled in the "professor's room" — ten in the ninth grade, the remainder in the eighth — of whom about half were tuition pupils riding in on ponies from surrounding districts to round off their education by a year in "town school."

But the school had outgrown the educational leadership of the pioneers; and the new city builders were occupied with promotion schemes. After two good years, fickle public interest shifted to other things. The school settled into a dreary routine of unenlightened direction and half-hearted teaching. Finally the "high school" was justified by only one student — a boy from an outside district who constituted the ninth grade. In this time of expanding prosperity and ease of living, the educational opportunities offered the young people lagged far behind every other phase of community life.

Conditions might have continued thus indefinitely except for the vigorous action of new people. Mrs. A. J. Webster, wife of a business man from the North, had been the founder and was now the president of the woman's club; she was a college graduate, and most of all a mother, who regretted the educational inertia of the community. Under her leadership the club women became actively and sincerely concerned. They found an ally in B. F. Abbott, another recent arrival, who had come from New York to establish the town's first up-to-date drug store. Abbott had children of his own, but above all he was a builder, a strong man who liked the feeling of clay in his hands.

"Prairie will always be a little town," he reasoned. "But we can make it a good town. We can make it an educational center. There is no reason why we can't build the best school in the county."

It was easy to elect Abbott and Mrs. Webster to the school board. There was always difficulty in finding persons willing to serve. In 1909, with a passive third member, they employed a new kind of "professor." The school had occasionally had good classroom teachers, who had come up the hard way by much reading of a few text books; but young Mead was a recent university graduate with an engaging combination of juvenile "college spirit" and fresh and inspiring scholarship. He found ten boys and girls with common school diplomas and collected them into a "freshman" class, a "Class of 1913" — magic words, expressive of vistas ahead.

He organized a girls' basket ball team and a boys' basket ball team, and matched games with neighboring towns; the colors they adopted and the songs and yells he helped them compose are even yet the official expressions of the school's spirit. In the spring he started a baseball team, and his young huskies actually won a victory over the big high school at the county seat.

The town was almost beside itself with pride over these athletic achievements. And the young people studied their lessons with an interest they had never known before. The next year it was a heartening experience to see a class finally pass out of the ninth grade, to see two classes in the high school. Once more tuition pupils came in from outlying districts, this time with a prospect of continuing their studies. Out of this practice came the annexation of the district just across the line in the Strip.

"Consolidation" just at that time was the sacred shibboleth of educators. "Consolidate the districts into larger units to form a graded school, and transport the pupils there. The days of the one-room country school are over." As a matter of fact, on the common school level the one-room school under a superior teacher with its system of individual instruction and its absence of distractions had some advantages over the crowded, graded school with its lock-step routine geared to the speed of the slower pupils. But few rural school boards employed superior teachers; and in a one-room school if the teacher failed, the school was a failure. Nobody could deny that failure was far too general. It seemed easier for educators to abolish the system than to correct it. In a deeper sense consolidation of schools was only one phase of a general tendency to displace the direct but often bungling processes of local democracy by a system of overhead control.

In 1908 with the encouragement of their county superintendent the Strip townships near Prairie began to vote on the question of merging the separate districts into central township schools. The measure always failed to carry by small margins — nine votes, one vote, three votes — but some of the more progressive farmers kept the issue alive.

Will Sadler was the most influential champion of consolidation in the Highview District. He had served on the school board ever since that first spring of '94 when a group of young pioneers had met in a dug-out, elected officers, and made a laconic entry in a new book:

"The question was taken up of deviseing some means, of Erecting a School house. And was decided to build a Sod House, and a building Committee was apoinded."

Will had increased in more ways than one since that inchoate day. He owned a half section of land without a mortgage. He lived in a big house on a hilltop with a fine bearing orchard around it. He won ribbons on mule colts and registered Herefords and corn and hogs and potatoes at the community fair. And he had ten sturdy children ranging from a tall girl he had brought as a baby to his claim down to a petted two-year-old.

One day B. F. Abbott called Sadler into his store.

"Let the rest of your township go, and bring your district in with ours," he urged. "We have a good school started, but we need more land to support it. And you need the school."

From that time on the two men worked together. Sadler argued with his neighbors, he called special elections, he warded off a court injunction; and he finally won, 23 to 21. At the same time Abbott called an election in the Prairie district; but here the issue was never in doubt, and it carried almost unanimously.

Even to the present day some of Sadler's neighbors are resentful over this election.

"You wanted to get into the Prairie school just because you've got so many children," they accused. "Now we'll all have to pay high taxes to educate your family."

"I pay taxes, don't I?" he countered. "I pay more than anybody else in the deestrict. Suppose I *have* got a big family. I never heard a man say just because he only had one child he wanted it to grow up ignorant."

The *News* tried to smooth the situation by treating it as an equal proposition. "This action adds $110,000 in taxable property to the Prairie District, or $300,000 to Highview, whichever way you want to look at it." But it was a "consolidation" of the two districts only in a technical sense; actually it meant that a larger constituency had been added to the Prairie school. One courtesy was carefully observed, however; it became an unwritten law to elect one of the three board members from the Highview neighborhood.

That year the school employed five teachers; the old Union building, which had stood vacant for seven years, was hauled in and set up on the school ground for the additional room. A specially constructed "kid wagon" with a closed body and two long seats running lengthwise was built in Enid at a cost of $125, and a young man was employed at a salary of $37.50 a month to collect the Highview children and bring them in. The first morning it brought twenty-seven pupils — two high school students who had formerly paid tuition, the others pleasantly excited over the strange ways of a graded school. Only high school students now sat in the "professor's" room; and the "Class of 1913," with two classes immediately following, was becoming a reality.

With these good prospects it was easy for Abbott to win converts in other districts to the idea of consolidation. Two held elections the next summer, but the measure was defeated.

"We'll run our own school," said the opposition. "We don't want any town people interfering in our affairs."

One of the schools had only eight pupils, and was paying a teacher fifty-five dollars a month, but even the "economy" argument failed to move the conservatives.

"We're educating our own children," they said. "If we join the Prairie Deestrict, they'll raise our taxes to educate the town children."

Schooling at Prairie *was* expensive; but the people received good value for their money. Abbott and Mrs. Webster, with all deference to the member from Highview, chose the best teachers they could find. They had none of the bucolic humility, the hidden fear of intellect, that had made the community unconsciously seek mediocrity in its schools.

The high school was put on a departmental basis with three teachers. Mead served as superintendent, coached the debate team, and carried a full teaching schedule, at the fabulous salary of $125 a month. The other two were the pick of the graduating class at the state university: a young man of nineteen, who served also as athletic coach; a young woman of twenty, who conducted high school classes, coached choruses and plays, and taught the eighth grade in her spare time. Younger than some of their pupils, but assured and competent, they walked among them in glamour, the embodiment of everything young Prairie had missed.

Four teachers were employed for the grades. The combined salaries of the seven were $559 a month — higher than the salaries paid at the county seat. But the little town and its outlying farms found it impossible, even by taxing to the constitutional limit, to stretch its term beyond eight months. There was an enrollment of

216, with 49 in high school and 167 in the grades. Nine – three
boys and six girls – were high school seniors.

The personal histories of this small first graduating class formed
a composite of community history. Only two had been born in
Oklahoma, one the son of an Eighty-Niner, the other the daughter
of a man who had made the Run into the Strip; two others were
the children of pioneers who had come in the early '90's; five had
come since the railroad. Four of the nine were tuition pupils from
outlying districts, who drove in or "did light housekeeping" in
town; four, including one from the former Highview, came from
the farms of the district; and one lived in town. They ranged in
age from two girls of twenty-three and twenty-one, who had
waited long for high school opportunities, to a bright sixteen-year-
old who had come straight up the road.

The high school year was one solid blaze of glory for Prairie.
The young teachers were tireless; everything they had ever done
in college they tried out on their students. There were programs
and plays at the opera house, football games and basketball games
in dizzying succession. The young coach himself played unde-
tected on the football team. Prairie had no illusions about sportsmanship; why play, except to win? And it usually did win. The
culmination of the year's activities was a two days' meet in April,
when a school many times as large came to compete in baseball,
track, debate, and literary and musical contests. The invaders
came in automobiles, sixty strong, contestants and supporters. All
Prairie was there; the field was surrounded with shouting mad-
men, and the opera house was packed until there was scarcely
standing room. And the school won almost everything – all but
the ball game, which it might have won "if it hadn't been for – "
At the close of the second evening's program the woman's club
gave a reception to the visitors and the home high school and
faculty. In that relaxed atmosphere both schools fairly outdid
themselves in sportsmanship and good feeling. The *News* that
week carried the headline, "SKINNED 'EM ALIVE," in black letters clear across the front page.

There was not much time for studying, but the young people
worked like threshing hands. Literally they burned the midnight
oil; one could almost count the high school students after the rest
of the town had gone to sleep, by the kerosene lamps shining dimly
from their windows. Their scholarship was not impressive – there

was too much to be overcome in crude beginnings, and even then the eight months' term was too short — but no students ever worked harder.

Prairie found its greatest pride in their achievements, its most interesting entertainment in their performances. And nothing was too good for the seniors. They were given a banquet, with the juniors as hosts and the woman's club as humble cooks and waitresses, with hothouse flowers and a formal program and fearful concentration on forks and etiquette; their graduation clothes were the finest that fathers could buy and mothers could make; and the whole town showered them with presents. Their "commencement" was worth a packed opera house, a college president, and the whole front page of the *News*. To a people less than twenty years removed from a three months' term of school in a sod building, high school graduation represented the ultimate in academic achievement.

The members of the class carried themselves soberly, mindful of their responsibilities. They felt as strongly as the first settlers had felt that they were making history. They made up a yell glorifying themselves as the "pioneer class," and their historian traced their progress through school in somewhat limping verse beginning,

"This is the song of the Seniors, the class of the year 1913,
      Who traveled an unknown road to the beautiful country of
         knowledge,
      Making through trackless wilds a trail for others to follow."

The week after their graduation the alumni — how they delighted in the new word, expertly juggling the Latin endings! — went to the creek one green and gold day for a final picnic. Pleasantly sad and sentimental after the manner of young graduates, they were nevertheless confident that the future belonged to them. Their young woman teacher had gone along as chaperon.

"You must begin to assert yourselves," she told them; "ten years from now, you will be the leaders of this community."

They believed every word. On the creek that day they organized an Alumni Association, electing officers, writing a constitution, and appointing a committee to plan the reception of the next year's class.

The next year most of the graduates taught in rural schools

near Prairie. Some of the girls eventually worked their way through a term or two of college before they married — well or badly, according to the whims of fortune. The boys settled into humble niches in unskilled employments. Prairie was still off the highroad of opportunity. Ironically enough, none ever became a leader in his home town. Only two remained there; the others scattered far, finding their living in cities. But they did blaze "a trail for others to follow" in their influence on succeeding classes; and the Alumni Association they formed is still one of the functioning organizations of the community.

The year following the graduation of the first class Prairie High entered into even more ambitious contests with larger schools. The little town soon became known throughout the state for the honors it won in football, in track, in debate, in music, in dramatic readings. As victory followed victory, the people were in ecstasies of celebration. Everything else was subordinated to this major activity.

Even the churches sank to second place. Their finances were healthy, their buildings were improved, their members were as numerous as ever, but their interest was declining. There was a whole chapter of unwritten ecclesiastical history in a brief paragraph of the *News* in December, 1913:

"None of the churches will have an elaborate Christmas celebration this year. The children have been so busy with school programs that it is a kindness to give them a little rest."

But just as the interest of the community became centered on its young people, unreckoned forces in the world outside were at work to claim them. All unknowing, eyes fixed as always on a roseate future, Prairie was suddenly touched by the agony of the First World War.

XVIII
OVER THERE

P<small>RAIRIE</small>'s whole philosophy was based on the continuity of human progress. It had seen crossroads store grow into pleasant town, sod subscription school become high school, raw land free for the asking rise to unheard-of values, young pioneers with little but their courage work their way to affluence. What more proof was needed that mankind was headed toward the stars, with Oklahoma riding at the head of the parade?

True, there were some complications on the other side of the Rio Grande. The trouble touched the community directly in the spring of 1914, when Brother Hayman and his fellow colonists were forcibly removed by the Mexican authorities. It was the general conviction that "somebody ought to go down and clean up that place."

But when the war broke in Europe the people were stunned with grief and horror. They were genuinely and sincerely neutral, not by grace of Presidential proclamation, but through complete unfamiliarity with the issues involved. Only the Germans were outspoken in support of the Kaiser's government; five young men, recent arrivals, even returned to take up arms in defense of the Fatherland. Since they alone had convictions on the subject, Prairie was willing for them to have their way.

It was pleasant to listen to the Socialists. Through personal influence, visiting lecturers, and *Appeal* editorials they were urging an isolationism incredibly naïve.

"If you favor war, dig a trench in your back yard, fill it half full of water, crawl into it and stay there for a day or two without anything to eat, get a lunatic to shoot at you with a machine gun, and you will have something just as good, and will save your country a lot of expense."

But the sinking of the *Lusitania* in May brought the war very close to Prairie. Some people clung more passionately than ever to their neutrality — "Served 'em right; they'd ought to stayed at home." Others, as in times of drought, took refuge in eschatology; this really looked like Armageddon. And before the end of the year a few were cautiously advocating "preparedness."

Before the election of 1916 the voters of Prairie Township were listed, under a new registration law, as 85 Democrats, 68 Republicans, 42 Socialists, and 5 Independents. But the slogan, "He kept us out of war," was a powerful inducement to Socialists and even Republicans to vote for Wilson. "If Wilson is re-elected, we'll have peace; if Hughes is elected, we'll have war," urged the Democrats with sincere conviction. Prairie voted for peace: Democrats, 103 and Socialists, 31; Republicans, 62.

Meanwhile the town continued the building that had been so notable before the war. In 1914 two more firms on Main Street replaced their wooden structures with brick. The same year the Campbellites abandoned their pioneer "church-house" for a comfortable modern building. By this time they had won their battle with the "denominations" and were known throughout the community as "Christians." The name brought ambiguous implications — "Are you a Christian or a Baptist?" — but Prairie understood. Many contributions from members of other churches went to help the building fund.

In 1915 the town voted $25,000 in bonds, and established water works, sinking deep wells, and a municipal light plant. The next year by a three to one majority the school district voted bonds of $17,000 — sold immediately at 103½ — and enlarged the school building with four additional classrooms, an auditorium, and a gymnasium. The following year the term was increased to the nine months required as standard by the state department of education.

The prospect of oil wealth was coming pleasantly close. Early in 1916 several shoestring promoters began leasing, sometimes paying an annual rental of a dollar an acre, more often obtaining the contract free because of the farmer's eagerness for oil development. Soon the community was ringed with wildcat tests, from eight to fifteen miles in every direction. The material for some of the rigs was unloaded from the cars at Prairie; the people saw it hauled out to the locations, and they watched the tall derricks rising above wheatfield and pasture. On Sunday afternoons automobile owners packed in their friends and drove out to the wells, standing around fascinated, watching the practiced rhythm of the

drilling crew. Tall farm boys starting in as lowly roustabouts, became regular company employees, working up to the specialized
labor of the industry, drawing fabulous wages, sent here and there
— to Drumright, to Shamrock, to Kansas.

But Prairie still had to depend on its farms. The agricultural
pattern was not yet affected by the war, but wheat had already
become the dominant factor in economic life. The price fluctuated
dangerously and then rose to unprecedented peaks. There was an
immense crop in 1914, largely sold at prewar prices. The next
year the yield was greatly curtailed by a wet harvest; the market
started at 85 cents, but the farmers held their crop for better prices.
Some even kept it until the spring of 1917, and sold it with the light
1916 crop for the unbelievable price of two dollars a bushel.

By that time of course the United States was in the war. Prairie
had voted for peace and got war, but it managed to make the
transition. Most of the Socialists ceased to be Socialists; only one
or two remained to argue that a nation could remain at peace
through pacifism. The Germans made the difficult shift from cordial well-wishers to enemies of the Fatherland; two or three would
have been hostile to their adopted country had they dared, but
all went steadily about their work. A few other citizens of Prairie,
stubborn individualists, opposed the Government, advancing private theories as to the cause of the conflict. But most of the people
drew together in fierce and intolerant loyalty. The town broke out
in flags immediately; within a week money had been raised by
subscription for a municipal flag and pole to be placed in the center
of Main Street. Four boys went to Oklahoma City and enlisted that
first week; before the end of April twenty-one had joined the
colors.

Then Congress passed the conscription act, calling up men
between twenty-one and thirty-one. The people generally were in
favor of the measure; it fitted their ideas of compelling everyone to
do his part. But it was a tense time that June 5 when the young
men registered, and the town was openly in tears when their numbers were drawn. Prairie had never traveled that road before.

The first Prairie soldier set foot on the soil of France in June.
He was a little fellow, small for his age, sixteen years old when he
had left high school with the hard-won consent of his parents to
enlist. In the trenches the next winter he wrote his mother that he
cried constantly with the cold, but he won a decoration before the

war was over. Three others were in France by the end of the year, forty-six in training camps at home. Their parents usually managed to send them away bravely, but beyond that nobody attempted to control his grief. The community had never become conditioned to that kind of loss.

The letters the boys wrote home were shared with the neighbors through the columns of the *News*. These communications were surprisingly articulate; and the mind of young Prairie, thus revealed in cross section, came out clear, poised, healthy. There was a lively interest in crops and farming practices, people and customs, cities and physical features, of places filled with the glamour of another world. During the training process there was a naïve and unashamed patriotism — "My blood will help protect those who are dear to me," "My heart swells with pride, and a lump comes in my throat . . ." Later, after the experience of battle, there was an overmastering stress and horror, but "I'd have been here sooner if I'd known what I know now." Prairie's knowledge of geography, its sense of the reality of far places, increased with these experiences of its young men. Everybody was taking a daily Oklahoma newspaper now, grasping at headlines, learning to trace positions on an unfamiliar map.

The Government meanwhile was creating machinery for carrying the war spirit to the grass roots by a hierarchy of volunteer workers organized in Councils of Defense. At the head was the National Council, composed of six members of the President's cabinet. Six days after war was declared, this body issued a call to the states to organize. The governor of Oklahoma appointed the State Council in June; the State Council organized the County Councils during July and August; and the County Councils formed local councils in the school districts the following February. This vast network relayed propaganda, calls for funds, and other Government measures down to the people, and acted on its own initiative in holding local communities in line with the war effort. Oklahoma's machinery functioned with a smoothness and dispatch that won the highest praise of the Washington office, at the same time that its fanatical zeal, its disregard of traditional American rights, brought dismay to those more liberal-minded leaders.

But Prairie — and Oklahoma — did not wait for this organization. Its reaction to the war was intensely personal: to support it was to back up son, nephew, neighbor's boy, any individual boy, who had grown up on its streets; to evade this support was to imperil their lives, and threaten the existence of the community. Nobody could be allowed to repudiate his obligation.

The First Liberty Loan drive was carried on early in June, with Banker Strickland in charge of the sales, and the *News* cooperating with emotional appeals. No one in the community had ever owned, or even seen, a Government bond, but under this sense of personal responsibility the people came to the bank and oversubscribed the township quota of $15,000. This left too much latitude for "slackers"; Prairie resolved that next time everybody should contribute.

The Red Cross drive began Sunday afternoon, June 15, by a mass meeting at the opera house. Arthur Goodwin presided, and three men from the county seat addressed the assembly. The community agreed to raise $2,200 of the county's $45,000, and five men were appointed to make a personal canvass.

The solicitors soon collected $3,003. They found only three "traitors" who refused to contribute: T. V. Gibson, a wealthy and penurious farmer, who ordered them off his place; George Hadley, who shook his fist and shouted, "Damn the President"; and Jacob Leutze, a rich German, who retreated into an obstinate "Nein." "The committee ought to've killed 'em," "They ought to be rode out of this country on a rail," "The old devils; they ought to be in jail," was the community comment. But since the quota was already oversubscribed they were not molested.

It was a concrete appeal that caused Prairie to pour its money into the Red Cross — "Think of *our* boys wounded, suffering, perhaps dying because we fail to provide for them." A similar directness brought the women to the work room to knit, sew, and fold bandages. And indignation against "traitors" in the community mounted to ferocity when an underprivileged tenant class in the hills of eastern Oklahoma rose in a brief revolt against conscription. The *News* declared that any Prairie citizen "who stands around and whines that the war should have been avoided is a traitor. If you have a man like that in your employ, fire him. If you have your farm rented to such a contemptible scoundrel, put him off and rent it to a good American."

Widespread, and probably justifiable, fear of sabotage by the I.W.W. in the oil fields around Tulsa threw Prairie into a panic of suspicion that summer. Everybody had a story to tell about the finding of ground glass in canned fruit or poison in bottled soft drinks. Every stranger was a potential spy. A too insistent peddler of furniture varnish frightened the housewives. A three-year-old child cried out in terror when she saw some boys coming back from hunting rabbits — "Look at those men with guns! Do you suppose they are Germans?"

The Second Liberty Loan drive came in the fall, with a township quota of $25,000. Gibson remained away from town, but the talk spread along the street on Saturday that he had never subscribed to any war fund. On Sunday night a group of grim, silent men went to his farm and called him out; and while he stood by helplessly they smeared yellow paint on his car and his barn. "Better see Strickland about your bonds tomorrow," they said in parting. "If you make us mad, we might show you what we think about traitors." The next day he "voluntarily" called on the banker and signed up for eight hundred dollars' worth of bonds. Again the quota was oversubscribed.

In December one hundred and ten men of the community joined the home guard, a volunteer organization authorized by the governor to act in conjunction with the County Councils of Defense. They assembled with their rifles and shotguns and laboriously worked out military evolutions from a manual they read; and they were sternly resolved to stamp out every spark of incipient disloyalty at Prairie. That month the Red Cross roll call was held, with emphasis not on contributions but on dollar memberships. The solicitors encountered three or four refusals. George Hadley again raved, "I wish somebody'd shoot that damned Wilson; I'd just as live do it myself." After the holidays two officers of the home guard were called to the county seat by the County Council of Defense to report the names of all who had refused to contribute. Out of this report grew the arrest of Hadley on a Federal warrant charging him with seditious utterances. The testimony at his trial showed that his greatest crime was in "shooting off his mouth too much," as his neighbors expressed it. He was found guilty and fined one dollar. He came back strangely meek, and Prairie, having won, was willing to drop the episode.

In February the local councils of defense were formed in the school districts. Their first duty was the circulation of a "loyalty pledge" sent out by the State Council. Three hundred persons in the Prairie community undertook this obligation to report "any dis-

loyal act or utterance that I may at any time know of. I will stamp
out the enemies at home whose every act or word means more
American graves in France."

It was also in February that word came of the sinking of the
troop transport, *Tuscania*. The people waited tensely; no Prairie
boy was on board, but four were there whom the people knew
well, from surrounding towns. Three were eventually reported
safe; one was lost, the first county casualty in the war. The people
felt in anguish that this was the beginning of a lengthening list.
More than one hundred drove down in their cars to attend a military funeral in his honor at the county seat.

Prairie never tired of war speeches; orators sent out by the
County Council of Defense always found a packed audience at the
opera house, swept by waves of patriotic emotion, wild with rage
at atrocity stories, breaking into tears at the sound of the national
anthem. When the German drive began that spring, with the threat
to Paris and the implied threat to Prairie, the town was ready to go
en masse. "It looks as though we went in too late; they'll break
through before we get there," beat in frantic repetition.

The Third Liberty Loan Drive came during those anxious days.
The township quota of $20,000 was apportioned by a committee
at the rate of 2½ per cent of the assessed value of each person's
property. It was again oversubscribed, with two or three failing
to participate. The next month a Red Cross drive began by special
sermons in all the churches. Reports reached the school district
council that the German minister intended to ignore the order.
"They say he never does preach on patriotic subjects," ran the
excited rumor. The council investigated, found the report un-
founded, and pronounced the minister "a loyal American," scru-
pulous in patriotic observances.

It was in this mood, and with the German drive in France still
gaining momentum, and with fifteen Prairie boys overseas, that
the community entered an intensive War Savings campaign. On
the afternoon of Friday, June 28, Prairie stopped in its toil to a
simultaneous blast of thresher whistles, and sweaty men with dust-
encrusted clothes converged upon their schoolhouses. Each person
was expected to make a pledge equal to 5 per cent of his property.
The Prairie district, town and surrounding farms, raised five thousand dollars above its allotment, but two of the rural districts fell

seriously behind, and the township thereby failed for the first time to raise its quota. Such a dereliction was not to be borne.

In one of the offending districts Jacob Leutze and two or three non-Germans had opposed the drive — "Nobody's goin' to tell me how much to take." The councils of defense worked quickly. Four posts were driven in the center of Main Street, woven wire was stapled on to form a small pen, and a cot was placed inside. In this "slacker cage" Jacob Leutze was confined through Saturday night; the next morning, shrinking from daylight and hostile stares, he was ready to make his pledge. The other "slackers" melted at the mere prospect of public humiliation, and the quota was raised.

All the German farmers were regarded with suspicion by super-patriots, but they conducted themselves so circumspectly that the responsible leaders of the community were convinced of their loyalty. But there was a general distaste for their culture. A German language class in high school was discontinued. The people humorously referred to sauerkraut as "liberty cabbage" and to an outbreak of German measles as "liberty measles." In August, 1918 under orders from the State Council of Defense the Evangelical church discontinued its German services, and the telephone exchange forbade the use of the language over its wires.

It was also in August that young Albert Koch, home on furlough, visiting in the home of Jacob Leutze found a framed picture of the Kaiser in an upstairs room. "I will take this," he said speaking easily in German. "I will send you a picture of President Wilson to put in its place. And I will find out what you do with it. You come along to town and see what I do with this one." And the young soldier burned it publicly in the middle of Main Street.

The people were furious. "The damned traitor. He ought to be made to kneel down and kiss the flag, like they made that son of a gun do out in western Oklahoma." But they were restrained by the fact that young Koch had the matter so efficiently in hand. Leutze's son, moreover, had recently registered, with others just come twenty-one; "I want to get a crack at that Kaiser," he had said when he submitted his questionnaire. "We'll let the old devil go this time," was the decision. "Mebbe he'll change his tune when his boy gits in."

Living under this strain Prairie had no heart to rejoice over the rocketing price of farm products. An immense crop of wheat was raised in 1917; the price stood at two dollars in harvest, reached $2.42 by the middle of August, with most of the farmers holding for still higher profits. Hogs — for the few who still raised hogs — rose from $9.20 a hundred at the beginning of 1917 to $16.30 the following October. Cattle brought as much as nine cents a pound. Before the end of 1917 butterfat reached 46 cents a pound, eggs 42 cents a dozen. But feed was scarce because of summer drought. The farmers rushed their live stock to market and concentrated more than ever on wheat. In 1917 the price of threshing rose from the usual nine cents a bushel to fifteen cents. The farmers began individually or in partnerships to buy small machines with tractors as the motive power to thresh their own grain; and the tractors were then used for the fall plowing. They flocked to tractor demonstrations in Enid and predicted a new era in power farming.

At the same time the community began to feel the force of measures taken by the Government through its policy of food control. The first orders came from the office of Food Administrator Hoover at Washington, but soon there was another hierarchy of volunteer workers, paralleling the network of defense councils, and with interlocking personnel. "Food Will Win the War" became the popular slogan, relayed from Washington to every Prairie kitchen and farm.

First, cards were distributed through the postoffice for housewives to sign, pledging themselves to conserve food. Then families were urged to observe "meatless days" and butchers were ordered to restrict their sales. In order to stimulate egg production, the farmers were forbidden to sell hens. Sugar became very scarce and the price reached 12½ cents a pound; an irregular rationing system was introduced in an attempt to cut the per capita consumption to three pounds a month.

The eating habits and the pocketbooks of Prairie were more directly affected by the wheat policy of the Food Administration — a policy based on the scarcity of this grain, the needs of Europe, and a reasonable system of price control.

In August, 1917, with most of the recent crop still in the hands of the growers, the price was forced down to about two dollars, where it remained during the remainder of the war. The farmers were as angry at "Dictator Hoover" as though they had never joined together to "Damn the Kaiser!" Many held their wheat, hoping the order would be relaxed. But nobody reduced his acreage; in spite of his grumbling, every farmer knew in his heart that a two dollar price was a sufficient incentive.

The following winter the Food Administration set two "wheatless days" a week, but a good many families continued to eat as usual. In February the voluntary method was abandoned; every purchaser of white flour was required to purchase an equal amount of corn meal, rolled oats, or other wheat substitute. This order was evaded by feeding the substitute to the chickens. In April a rationing system was attempted, with the per capita consumption limited to six pounds a month and grocers required to keep a record of sales. But such machinery was inadequate for real control, and violations of food regulations were carried on privately, safe from the community pressure that enforced compliance with other war measures.

A large store of desperately needed wheat remained in the granaries. In April the Prairie food administrator relayed an order through the *News:* "Any farmer holding wheat in excess of seed needs for 1918 is respectfully advised to sell by May 1. To do so will save you expense as well as humiliation." Nobody wanted his wheat seized and forcibly hauled to market. The roads were filled with loaded wagons as the hoarded grain poured into town from all directions.

The Prairie fields produced bountifully of the precious crop in the 1918 harvest. The State Council of Defense and the State Food Administrator tried to fix the maximum threshing price at seventeen cents, but it eventually reached twenty. Several more farmers bought "vest pocket" threshers. The wheat was hauled to town immediately, two hundred loads a day, thirty wagons lined up at one time waiting to unload.

But more than on their level wheat fields the eyes of Prairie were fixed on a confusion of streams and forests and bloody trenches where home town boys were locked in deadly combat with the enemy.

"We have lived through things almost untellable," wrote young Gordon Strickland after Château-Thierry, "and I have seen men brave beyond belief. We are resting now in a little village far from the battle lines, and how good it seems. The people here are wonderful to us. They give us credit for driving the Huns back from Paris, and I truly think we did.

"A few days ago a new regiment came up. Imagine how glad I was to see Warren Goodwin and Claude Abbott and Roy Zoellner. They are the first boys I have seen from home since I came over here. We had a wonderful visit talking over old times. Then they left for the front, and it made me so sad to know what they are facing that I wished I hadn't seen them at all. But I know they will be equal to it. . . ."

The letter reached the Stricklands in October, just as the banker was making his organization for the Fourth Liberty Loan. It was published in the *News*, and leading business men and farmers paid for a full page advertisement:

READ GORDON STRICKLAND'S LETTER
AND BUY BONDS

Before the drive was over Roy Zoellner's mother had received a telegram that her son had been killed at Saint-Mihiel. The chance meeting of Prairie boys in that far-off French village was filled with tragic meaning. At almost the same time Albert Koch died of influenza in training camp.

Young Koch's body was shipped back home for burial. Every business house in town was closed as the whole community attended the funeral. The little German church was filled, and several times as many people stood outside. A recently organized troop of boy scouts served as pall bearers; the feeble Old Soldiers, the home guard, the women of the Red Cross, the mothers of boys in service all had special places in the procession. The heart-broken mother had requested that the service be conducted in German — "so she can unterstand," explained her husband. Nobody objected. And to the people listening, the hateful alien accents were filled with the thought of home and love and kindly soil. One of the other ministers spoke briefly in English at the close.

"Albert was a good soldier," he said. "He grew up in this community, steady, dependable, strong; and when the call came he was willing to give his life to defend it. His death brings sorrow to us all, but we are honored by his devotion. We sympathize with his father and mother, his brothers and sisters. We know that Prairie's sacrifices are just beginning, that before this war is over other homes will be bereaved. We are resolved to bear our losses unflinchingly and carry on to the end."

The whole congregation, men and women, wept openly.

The news of young Koch's death had caused the bond campaign to be postponed until the day after the funeral. The township quota was $40,659.68 — a 5 per cent levy on the property valuation. Nearly $30,000 was taken the first day. When the drive closed, October 19, the amount had been raised, and while a few men had failed to take their full allotment, there was no "100 per cent slacker" in the township.

By this time a new calamity had struck. The "Spanish flu" came suddenly without warning the same week the Koch boy died in camp; probably the crowded church spread the contagion further. The mayor closed the school, the churches, the moving picture theatre, every public gathering. The people attempted, according to their kindly custom, to take care of their neighbors who were ill; but these volunteer nurses were stricken with frightening suddenness. After three weeks the epidemic had apparently run its course, and the ban was lifted on public meetings. There were seven new graves in the cemetery — mothers with new-born infants, strong young farmers, radiant girls. There were as many additional deaths at recurrent waves of the epidemic during the winter. Prairie had never known such a loss of the beautiful, the young, the useful. The suspicion grew that German spies in some way were spreading the germs. But just then the war came to a sudden and dramatic end.

False news of the armistice came during the last funeral of the influenza epidemic. The town was sad that day. The victim of the disease was beloved of the community — a girl of twenty-two, in the full glory of her youth and promise. By common consent the stores closed again. But the joyful news spread from house to house, even to the house of death where some close friends stood in the yard, obedient to the ban on public gatherings. A wave of excitement rose against the weight of grief. But Prairie was not in mood for demonstration, and the moment passed.

When the real news came, Prairie was expecting it. In the night the fire whistle blew its signal that the guns had stopped. People lay in their beds, relaxed from the strain of nineteen months, trying to imagine young, tired soldiers climbing out of bloody trenches, a sky no longer hideous, an atmosphere purified of the sounds of death. All that day people drifted down to Main Street, shaking hands, frankly shedding tears, exchanging news of sons.

"The casualty lists are a month old. I pray that he's safe."

"My boy was all right October 17. He said, 'We've got the Kaiser on the run.'"

"My boy is to report to the county seat tomorrow. I doubt if they'll even take him now."

"Do you know we have 117 boys in the service? And fifty of them are overseas."

"Wherever they are, they're all happy today."

It was not until evening that the noise started. Then anvils were fired, automobiles dashed through the streets with tin cans dragging, everybody shouted and sang. Far into the night the din lasted. It was the happiest day Prairie had ever known.

In the spring of 1921 the body of Roy Zoellner was brought back from France. He was buried beside his father, a young Strip homesteader who had died soon after settling on his claim. It was "a long, long trail" that led from a childhood on those virgin prairies to the battlefields of France and back again to the quiet cemetery, and the long procession of friends and neighbors felt that at last the end was peace. But just at this time the tension of the war years snapped into hysteria, and soon a sheeted terror roamed the countryside.

XIX
THE SHEETED TERROR

In 1921 the community was swept by a mawkish pseudo-patriotism, an insane fear of minority groups, a savage lust for violence. There were several causes of this emotional instability. Returned soldiers, already unstrung by their experiences, found no place in the economic pattern. The Eighteenth Amendment stimulated illicit liquor manufacture at Prairie, thus increasing the drinking and lawlessness of the "wets," the disapproval and intolerance of the "drys." There was a period of hard times as agriculture shifted back to a peace footing; the less successful failed and became bitter and envious, the more prosperous held to their property in grim anger against "subversive" elements. Most of all, the war had taught suspicion and violence, which the community now turned upon itself.

In a deeper sense the emotional excesses at Prairie were part of a larger psychic phenomenon that was eventually to convulse the world. Only a year later the Fascists were to march on Rome; only twelve years later with infinitely greater stress of soul the Nazis were to take over the destinies of the German people; and in between in other lands were many intermediate manifestations of the same tortured spirit. There was the fierce nationalism — 100 per cent Americanism, the Nordic race, the heirs of the Romans — the linking of bands in violence, even the puerile pleasure in fantastic garb. But in Prairie the terror ran its course harmlessly, and the community returned to sanity, ashamed of its aberration.

Nobody except the members knew just when the Ku Klux Klan began to work in the community. There was evidence of class tension the spring after the war ended. With the price of wheat still soaring, the farmers banded together and set four dollars as the maximum wage for the long harvest day. When June came, the town was flooded with young unemployed men waiting for the

wheat to ripen; they also banded together — to demand fifty cents
an hour and a ten-hour day. The farmers were outraged at this
"hold-up," but in some instances at least they paid a six-dollar
wage, while the ten-hour day was forgotten. The next year they
learned of a similar controversy between white farmers and Negro
pickers in the cotton-growing sections of the county; and when
they visited the county seat that winter, they noticed such hostility between the races on the streets and in the stores that only a
spark was lacking to sweep the city with fire and blood. Fortunately that spark was never struck.

These incidents may not have been connected with the rise of
the Ku Klux Klan. But that same winter of 1920–21 the high school
history teacher at Prairie was puzzled over a condition that later
was shown to be of Klan origin. Any innocent question would ig-
nite an anti-Catholic spirit as violent as it was inexplicable. It was
of course the Presidential election year; and one day she asked
her students to explain the election procedure. They answered:
"If a Catholic ever gets to be President, the old Pope will come to
Washington to live," "Old Woodrow Wilson is a Catholic," "His
son-in-law, old McAdoo, is a Catholic, too."

But there was no open demonstration until the fall of '21. It
occurred in the Christian church. The minister was completely out
of character for that level-headed, reason-loving group, for he was
preaching the second coming of Christ with fanatical fervor, and
he was unquestionably a member of the Klan. As he preached,
there was a sudden roar of arriving cars, and one hundred and
fifty sheeted citizens of the Invisible Empire entered the church
and marched down to the front. They carried warning banners:
"BE ONE HUNDRED PER CENT AMERICANS," "TAKE
YOUR OWN WIFE JOY RIDING," "BOOTLEGGERS, GET
OUT."

The congregation sprang to its feet and began to sing "America" with emotional ardor. The leader then spoke to the minister,
"We want to congratulate you for the good work you are doing
in this community. We are back of you in this county fifteen hundred strong. We are protecting American womanhood and American churches, and the bootleggers must get out."

And they turned and left as suddenly as they had come, while
the congregation broke into wild cheering. The minister then said
he had been "agreeably and pleasantly interrupted," and he drove

home the point of his sermon by showing that the coming of Christ would be as sudden and dramatic.

The Klansmen drove rapidly away. Apparently they had come from the county seat. It developed, in fact, as a rather common practice for Klan groups to stage their demonstrations away from home in order to keep up the fiction of anonymity. But it was fairly evident who the members in the community were.

Another year passed before the Klan spirit broke out again in public. Then the winter of 1922–23 was an emotional orgy of parades and initiations, of "Americanism" and hate, of prejudice and fear. It began by an anonymous notice in the News announcing a demonstration on Main Street for the evening of October 27. Before dark people began to assemble from the community and surrounding towns; soon a solid row of parked cars lined each curb of the half-mile-long street, and the largest crowd that the town had ever seen jammed the sidewalks. On the stroke of nine they came, riding in their cars, 215 strong, carrying an American flag at the head of the procession. As they drove down the street they spoke only once, when a man in the lead car paused to rebuke some by-standers who had failed to remove their hats as the flag passed by. They defiled into a pasture, where the watching thousands saw a cross burst into flame, and sheeted figures moving about in ghostly ritual. The observers were not close enough to hear the words, but their import was scarcely secret; everybody seemed to know that thirty-five new members were being initiated. When the ceremony was ended and the fire died down, the celebrants departed as silently as they had come.

The Klan issue entered largely into the regular state election a few days later. The sheriff of the county, who had made an excellent record as an honest and capable official, was running for re-election on the Republican ticket. He came out squarely against invisible government. "On two separate occasions the Klan has threatened me with political extinction if I refuse to support them. They want to get all the enforcement officers on their side so they can violate the law with impunity. But I don't think the people of this county believe in law enforcement by a masked band at midnight. If they do, I'm not their man." Prairie — its electorate increased by woman suffrage — voted against him 223 to 82, and he was overwhelmingly defeated. Other anti-Klan candidates in the county fared about the same.

The election for governor was complicated by other issues. The Farmer-Labor Reconstruction League had been organized by discontented farmers, members of labor unions, and ex-Socialists, uniting on a radical program of state ownership or regulation of industry and marketing. It had captured the state Democratic party by the nomination of its candidate John C. (Jack) Walton for governor. Walton traveled about with a jazz orchestra, arousing the enthusiasm of the underprivileged, and attempting to rally the anti-Klan forces to his support. Catholics and other groups subjected to Klan pressure did vote for him, but some of the Prairie Klansmen seemed to feel that his hostility was not very deep, while conservatives of anti-Klan convictions regarded him as a dangerous demagogue. The township gave him 121 votes to 186 for his Republican opponent, but he was elected by the support of other sections.

By this time the Klan had so completely captured the Masonic organization in Prairie that the lodge became the disseminator of its doctrines. Theoretically it opposed Negroes, Jews, and Catholics, but Prairie paid no attention to the Negro question, regarded the Jews at the county seat with tolerant friendliness, and concentrated all its venom on the Catholics. The superintendent of schools, himself a Mason, had become a convert to Klan doctrines or else found it expedient to bow to the storm. When the history teacher attempted to present medieval life and the Protestant Reformation objectively to her class in European history, she was spied upon by her students and browbeaten by the Masons as an emissary of the Vatican. She was even forbidden to use the *Literary Digest* in her current events classes, because the Klan believed one of its editors to be a Catholic. Only her own Protestant background saved her from dismissal, but at the end of the term she resigned in disgust and left the community; and the school became in effect a Klan organization.

Irish children on the playground were taunted by "Cat-licker! Cat-licker! Better get the old priest to forgive your sins." No adult Catholic was openly molested, but one woman was privately informed by her Klan brother-in-law,

"You've got no business to vote, and we're goin' to fix it so you can't. And we're goin' to hang every one of you before this is over."

The Catholics drew together in genuine apprehension. They knew that at the county seat members of their faith who had been in business for years were being driven out of town by organized boycotts. They rallied their fortitude and that of their unhappy children by the deeds of the martyrs. But it was not a wholesome experience for these people who had entered so freely into the building of the community, to feel themselves a persecuted minority; it was not good for their children to be compelled by force of numbers to restrain their natural Irish tendency to stand up and fight.

A few non-Catholics stood out against the rising tide of fanaticism, people of intelligence and culture, who valued tolerance as a spiritual quality. But their words — and they kept still for the most part — were snowflakes falling on molten lava. Terrible stories were circulated, of "escaped nuns," of underground fortifications built in the basement of the Catholic church at the county seat, of shipments of coffins which proved to be filled with rifles. Lurid periodicals, inciting to racial and religious hatred by every pornographic device, lay on the tables of decent citizens, and they were avidly read and believed.

The Klansmen in fact *were* decent citizens. A few were men who had suffered personal disappointment — a young soldier who had come back to find his wife untrue, a business man who had failed, a farmer driven to bankruptcy. But in general they were normal and healthy people, kindly disposed, moderately prosperous, secure in their family life. But Prairie had lacked educational opportunities; now in a crisis it lacked intellectual balance.

Only Kenneth Martin, using the top sergeant's language he had learned in France, carried on a one-man crusade against the Klan. Ken, the son of Dick Martin, had gone away a quiet boy, brought up in the Methodist church, respectful, courteous; he had come back bitter, disillusioned, unafraid of man or devil. Bill O'Hagan had been in his unit, and he had seen Bill under fire. It was Bill against the world for him, and he attacked the Klan openly, profanely, and with devastating sarcasm.

"We are fighting for American principles," said a supporter.

"Fighting? Fighting? Where the hell did *you* learn about fighting?" queried Ken. "I thought you stayed at home and bought a farm with two dollar wheat. Or can't you fight unless you're wrapped up in a bed sheet?"

A dangerous muttering spread through the community that Ken should be "run out of town." The fact that he sometimes patronized the bootleggers would serve as the excuse. But the matter somehow never quite came to a head.

The winter of 1923–24 was given over even more than previous years to emotional excesses. The Klan by this time had captured the Baptist church. The pastor of a big church at the county seat came and conducted a two-weeks' series of revival meetings. On the two Sundays he gave community lectures on "Under the Shadow of the Vatican" and "Who are the Ku Klux? — An Eye Opener on Americanism," and for an hour and twenty minutes he spoke to an audience crowded to the limit of the aisles, breathless, flushed, breaking into wild applause. When his meetings closed, the Klan gave a twenty-five dollar contribution to the two hundred dollar collection to pay for his services, and his converts seemed to be in some doubt as to whether they had embraced Christianity or the doctrines of the Invisible Empire.

It was difficult to go to church without making ambiguous commitments. A speaker was likely at any time to ask 100 per cent Americans to stand; if they rose they were Klansmen, if they remained seated they were somewhat less than Americans. Only the Evangelical church was unaffected by the division in the community. Lacking the traditional American background, the Germans failed to kindle at the catchwords, "Constitution," "Liberty," "Americanism," "Womanhood," just as they failed to be disturbed by this travesty on the American spirit. They were not subjected to outside pressure; because of their alien ancestry, they were not desired as members, while at the same time their Protestantism and their steady character placed them above suspicion.

The Methodist membership was strongly Klan. There were individual Methodists who disapproved it, just as there were individual Masons, Baptists, and members of the Christian church who stood out against the majority, but the church itself was saved from enlisting in the cause only by the opposition of its pastor.

This minister had served the congregation for two years before the Klan appeared, and had been especially well liked. He was a Mason, but he had become lax in his attendance through the press of other duties. His first warning came in a friendly inquiry from one of his stewards, "Why don't you come to lodge any more?" "Just too busy," he answered; "the days are too short as it is." "I think it would be best for you to start coming again," said the steward, putting somehow a mysterious significance into the com-

monplace words. From that time on, the minister noticed a cool-
ness in his congregation. Dick Martin, a Methodist pillar for many
years, defended him, but the Martin family stood almost alone.

He tried holding public meetings where he urged the exercise
of tolerance toward those of other races and religious beliefs, and
the orderly processes of law against any subversive elements. But
his audience became so angry that a few hot-bloods actually advocated riding him out of town on a rail. Again as in the case of
Kenneth Martin the suggestion was not followed.

Apparently he had been warned that something was astir when
he faced his people one Sunday morning in the fall of '23. As usual
he announced the evening service, and then he remarked so quietly
that the words were scarcely noticed, "I hope I shall be able to *see*
all the congregation." When the evening came, the Methodists
were out in surprisingly good attendance. Just before the service
started, the Baptist pastor and all his church came in and seated
themselves in the crowded room. The atmosphere fairly snapped
with tension. But the minister went through the service unruffled,
and again he spoke of tolerance in general terms as a desirable
Christian virtue. Just at the close, the door opened and ten or
twelve sheeted figures marched slowly up the aisle, and ranged
themselves along the chancel rail. A breathless hush settled on the
congregation. Then the leader spoke, apparently reciting from
memory.

"The Ku Klux Klan is a white man's organization, exalting the
Caucasian race and teaching the doctrine of White Supremacy.
This distinction between the races is clearly taught in the Bible.
Our country was established by whites and for whites, and any
attempt to wrest this control away from the whites is a violation
of the divine law and the constitution of the United States. We are
not enemies of colored and mongrel races, but we demand that
they respect the rights of the white race in whose country
they are permitted to reside. If they fail in this respect, they
must be forcibly reminded to seek a country more agreeable
to them.

"The Ku Klux Klan is a Gentile organization. We do not hate
the Jew. He is interested in his own things and we are exercising
the same privilege of banding our own kind together to realize the
highest and best for ourselves.

"The Ku Klux Klan is an American organization. We restrict

our membership to native-born American citizens. The aliens who
have been flooding our shores come not for love of America, but
to advance themselves. They obey the mandates of foreign governments to which they are subject.

"The Ku Klux Klan is a Protestant organization. We confine
our membership to those who accept the tenets of true Christianity, which is essentially Protestant. Our forefathers founded this
as a Protestant country, and it is our purpose to re-establish and
maintain it as such.

"We believe in the Declaration of Independence and the Constitution of the United States. We magnify the Bible, we teach the
worship of God, we honor the Christ as the Klansman's only cri-
terion of character. This is what we believe."

The last sentence rang out as a challenge over the hushed
church. Dick Martin was sitting near the front as always. He half
rose from his seat and shouted,

"Well, if that's what you believe, why don't you take off that
bed sheet and show us your face?"

The town marshal, a leading Baptist, was sitting just behind.
He put a strong hand on Martin's shoulder. "Sit down," he whispered, forcing him back in his seat.

The minister had stepped to the front until he was almost
touching the robed figures. "I do not like to accuse anyone un-
justly," he said clearly; "we have had too much of that. If any of
us have made mistakes, we know the source that will correct us
and make us right. Will you kneel with me at this altar while we
pray about it?"

The Klansmen knelt. There was nothing else to do. They were
trapped as completely as they had ever trapped their opponents
into removing their hats or rising to show their "Americanism."
And the minister prayed for mutual tolerance, for neighborly understanding, for humility of intellect. Then the sheeted figures
filed silently from the church.

"I wish he'd 'a' called on them to pray," whispered Dick Martin. "Then they would 'a' got tangled up. They claim to be so all-
fired pious."

That was the last time the Klan troubled that minister. But the
end of the "conference year" — to use the Methodist phrase —
came soon after, and he was transferred by Methodist sleight-of-
hand to another place. His successor ignored the issue, but the

church in spite of the known affiliation of a majority of its members, remained free from Klan domination.

The winter was filled with marching and fiery crosses, with trips to other towns, with gatherings of many towns at Prairie, with public lectures by high Klan potentates. The whole state was convulsed by a fight that culminated in the governor's impeachment and removal from office — martial law, dispersion of the legislature by the National Guard, loosing of convicts, open battles for spoils. The controversy was not entirely between Klan and anti-Klan, but it was used by demagogues of both sides to incite the people to violent partisanship. To Prairie every incident of the struggle revealed the Catholics' nefarious schemes to take over the government.

The Great Fear cast its shadow over everything. Just then dollar bills were coming into circulation to replace the heavy silver "cart wheels" Prairie had always used. Somebody "discovered" a cross and a picture of the pope diabolically concealed in the scrolls of the engraving, and from that time the currency was handled with a distaste never shown to money before.

Before the election of 1924 the Catholics quietly passed each other printed cards listing the names of Klan candidates, Republican or Democrat, with the notation, "Inform Yourself and Vote Accordingly." And lectures and processions multiplied on the other side. The Klan carried everything at Prairie, and its partisans had the satisfaction of seeing most of their candidates elected. Then somehow the tension relaxed. The Klan probably maintained its organization in secret for some time longer, but the fear it had invoked was gone.

"This will poison men's minds for generations," B. F. Abbott, who objected to the Klan on intellectual grounds, had said at the height of the terror. He proved to be a poor prophet. For two or three years a recurrence always seemed possible; then it passed completely from the public mind. Today, Prairie prefers to forget that it ever set the tempo of its life to the parade of sheeted figures on its streets.

"On the whole, I think it was a good thing," says a thoughtful Catholic. "It cleared the atmosphere and caused people of different religious beliefs to examine more closely their relation to each other. And ever since that time they have been more ready to co-operate in community building."

Probably this estimate is too optimistic. But certainly it is true, whether or not it accomplished good, that the disturbance passed with a minimum of harm. Looking back it seems incredible that feelings could have been stirred to such a pitch without violence, that such fanaticism could have passed without a trace. The answer must be found in the friendly years that Prairie's people had lived together, the affection that made it hard to lift one's hand against one's neighbor, or to believe that he could be an enemy. In the abstract Prairie had the credulity of the uneducated, but in a concrete situation it had the healthy-mindedness of a people that had lived and built together in security and peace. The war had been an agony that passed; the Klan was a fever that subsided. Prairie's answer to both was "Never Again."

XX

NEVER AGAIN

"THEY'RE COMING HOME AGAIN" was the headline that streamed across the whole front page of the *News* the third week after the Armistice. "Corporal Chester Cobb is the first soldier boy to strike glad hands with home folks." Chester had worked up from the ranks to officers' training and was close to his commission; he had been given the alternative of remaining. "But what do I want with a commission now? I'd as lief have one of those tin crowns that are falling off of the kings' heads over in Europe." Before "Back to Normalcy" was ever coined as a vote-catching slogan, it voiced Prairie's deepest convictions.

The civilian war machinery fell apart almost as soon as the enemy's lines crumbled. The drive for funds for United War Work had been scheduled to start the day the Armistice was signed; and a circular telegram was sent out November 13 by the State Council of Defense authorizing "drastic action" against "any citizen unwilling to subscribe." But Prairie was too happy for "drastic action" against anybody; the quota of twenty-five hundred dollars was over-subscribed in the spirit of a voluntary thank offering. The Red Cross continued to function until January, when the women were notified to discontinue their work. No drive was made when the Fifth, or Victory, Loan was floated in April; the bank took the entire quota. Most of the people sold their liberty bonds (at a ruinous discount) and cashed their war savings stamps almost immediately. But they responded generously and uncritically to any call for funds, whether for the Salvation Army at Oklahoma City or the Near East Relief.

The feeling against the Germans changed to sympathy almost as soon as the rigorous terms of the Armistice were known. Warren Goodwin returned from the Army of Occupation with such a kindly memory of the home in which he had been quartered that for many years letters regularly passed back and forth between this elderly

German couple and the friendly boy who was their "enemy." When
a family of immigrants straight from Germany settled in the community — the father a frail man broken by wounds and four years
of war, come he said to find a place where his sons might grow up
in peace — the people helped them over the hard places as generously as they had once helped another kind of pioneer driving a
covered wagon over a rough trail.

The German language was used as freely in the Evangelical
church as though it had never been disapproved, but it was gradually discontinued with the passing of the older generation. The first
of the young Germans to enter high school graduated in 1920;
soon they were graduating in numbers and entering fully into
community life with no barrier of language or sentiment. Their
strength and dependability thus became an integral part of Prairie's social structure.

But other effects of the war were not so easily erased. The soldiers began to come back from France in January; before the end
of 1919 they had all returned. They were given public receptions
at the schoolhouse, and picnics and parties by their friends and
relatives. A good many arrived in time for harvest and went to
work in their fathers' fields as gratefully as though the past months
had been an evil dream. A few went back to high school to resume
their interrupted studies. Several married as soon as they returned
— girls who had written to them, knitted for them, made candy for
them throughout their service. But they were nervous and fidgety,
strangers to their own families. More than one stayed away from
town to escape the silly question, "Did you kill anybody?"

It was not only they who had changed; they had come back
to a changed community. Economically it was geared to two dollar
wheat. With the removal of artificial regulations at the end of the
war, the price rose even higher. A fine crop in 1919 found a $2.15
market, but a good many farmers held it and sold it in April for
$2.60. The next year's crop struck a $2.40 market. By this time the
farmers had their own elevator.

The Farmers' Co-operative Elevator Company was incorpo-
rated with a capitalization of ten thousand dollars. Its shares were
sold only to producers of farm products, and its officers and directors were the most substantial farmers of the community. The company purchased one of the privately owned elevators, employed an
experienced manager, and began buying wheat in the 1920 har-

vest. During the first twelve months it bought more than 300,000 bushels. It had the complete confidence of the farmers and the cordial co-operation of the business men. But alongside the "Farmers' Elevator," privately owned elevators continued to function in healthy competition.

Although the war years had increased the tendency toward wheat farming, other prices were correspondingly high. A few farmers still raised hogs. Through Government action the price was forced down from twenty to eleven cents just before the war ended; then it rose again, reaching an all-time high of $22.25 a hundred the following August. About fifty carloads, or 2,100 head, of cattle were shipped out annually. Farmers were buying blooded Herefords, paying $800 for a young bull, $435 for a cow, $100 for a bull calf. With herds too small for the increased beef production to be apparent, the main profit in these fancy cattle lay in selling to other farmers. Although butterfat at one time reached 71 cents a pound, the number of dairy herds was decreasing. Eggs reached 65 cents a dozen one December day in 1919, but the community had almost ceased to raise poultry. With a wheat crop running into thousands of dollars, the weekly cream check or egg check looked like small change. Aside from wheat pasture, the farmers even bought much of their feed from supplies shipped in and sold at the elevators.

The farmers worked to the limit of human endurance during harvest, were moderately busy at plowing and sowing through the summer and early fall, and spent the rest of the year in almost complete leisure. At harvest time the towns and highways were filled with young men — farm boys for the most part, well-mannered and industrious — who had come for work. The farmers came to town and employed as many as they needed. In some of the surrounding cities they were ordered out of town or even thrown in jail for the crime of seeking work. But Prairie was not so cruel; they slept in the alleys unmolested, and if they were driven to ask for food they always obtained it from kitchen doors or from a fund set aside by the town officials. They might have been Prairie boys away from home; Prairie boys in fact did join the migration as the harvest moved northward.

The price of threshing went up to twenty-five cents a bushel in 1919, thirty cents in 1920. The latter year two farmers went together and purchased a "combination harvester-thresher" for eighteen hundred dollars. Crowds went out from town to watch it work. It was an impressive sight as it moved across the field, cutting, threshing, and scattering the straw as it came. It was pulled by a tractor, and a team drew a wagon alongside to catch the grain. The owners computed the cost of gasoline and oil, credited it with the saving of threshing bill, twine, and shockers' wages on their 250 acres and 4,980 bushels, and found they had saved $1,724 — almost enough to pay for the machine the first year. Best of all was the relief in knowing the grain was garnered and safe. Owners of the small threshing outfits began to regret their purchases; the "combine" had proved the better machine.

All the farmers were interested in tractors. Through demonstrations and newspaper advertising the Prairie dealers — Goodwin and Sons, J. Q. Walker, Joe Spragg — worked to convert them to the gospel of power farming. "It takes four hours a day to care for your horses; a tractor can be serviced in half an hour. It takes forty acres of feed for an eight-horse farm — wasted land that would grow sixteen hundred dollars' worth of wheat." The use of motor trucks came a little more slowly, but several farmers purchased them in the early '20's. A buggy was seldom seen any more on the highway, and a generation was growing up that knew only automobiles. An old settler attempted to tell his grandson the story of the Run. The child listened, his eyes shining; then he commented admiringly, "Gee! It must've took lots of gas."

The size of farm had not increased materially since 1910, but the prices had shot up as high as $13,000, $15,000, or even $17,000 for a good quarter. For the first time there was a definite movement back North towards the old home. Only a few farmers paid off mortgages during the era of lush prices; 51 per cent had held their land clear in 1910, only 53 per cent in 1920.

Several prosperous farmers leased their land and moved to town — either to Prairie or to Enid. And business men still purchased land as an investment. Thus the number of tenants increased from 38 per cent in 1910 to 41 in 1920, and 46 per cent in 1925. A few young tenants bought farms and paid for them outright during the peak prices of 1917–20. Others subject to military induction were forced to sell their live stock and equipment and leave the farm. When the soldiers returned, the farms were all taken; from that time on there was always a surplus of prospective tenants.

There was one large scale owner. S. W. Brown had died the first year of the war; his son, Merritt Brown, disposed of the hardware and implement business, and concentrated on the management of the ten quarters of farm land he had inherited. He lived on one of the farms, and managed the others with hired labor, paying twenty-five dollars a month. With his profits he bought more farms, or if he saw a chance for a profitable sale he sold and reinvested.

The state had appraised and sold the school land in 1915, giving the lessees the preference right to purchase. Purchasers were required to pay 5 per cent cash, and the remainder in forty annual payments with 5 per cent interest. Under this tenure the land changed hands like any other land subject to a mortgage.

The farm population of the two townships declined from 1126 in 1910 to 889 in 1920 — a decrease of 21 per cent. The decline was due to slightly larger farms and much smaller families. A special circumstance was that there were middle-aged pioneers still living on their original homesteads whose children had grown up and scattered.

Into this unfamiliar pattern of huge farm incomes, one-crop agriculture and its attendant leisure, motor transportation and increasing use of power machinery the soldiers returned from camp and battlefield. There was no place for them in the new economy; and if they went to the cities they found inflated wages, extravagant living standards — and no employment. Some were assisted by their fathers in farming or business ventures; others fretted away several years before they overcame the handicap of their military service.

A bonus seemed the easiest solution. Everybody had made money while they were gone, they reasoned; why should not they who had done the hardest and most dangerous work be given equality of compensation? In the spring of 1920 they organized a post of the American Legion, and within two years they were using all the strength of this machinery to agitate the measure. The question was twice submitted to the people of Oklahoma — in 1922 and 1923. Prairie Township voted against it 161 to 135 the first time, supported it 111 to 82 the next year. But it did not carry the state and the ex-service men had to await national action. When adjusted compensation finally came, it had no noticeable influence upon the economic status of the beneficiaries.

But before the people voted on the bonus, the whole community was in financial difficulties. It had never occurred to anyone at Prairie that the rocketing prices of the war years would not be permanent. Most farmers held their 1920 wheat crop, expecting an advance over the harvest price of $2.40. But the market dropped suddenly, and then "bobbed up and down like a frog in a rain barrel." Most of the grain was sold in April — eighty or ninety loads being marketed daily at an average price of about $1.18. The farmers met in May and agreed to reduce harvest wages from six to two dollars a day. Wheat dropped still more during the following years, reaching a low of 82 cents a bushel in '23. But the prices of other farm products dropped correspondingly; hence the trend towards mechanized wheat farming continued unchecked by the depression.

Several farmers went into voluntary bankruptcy during 1921–23. One was an ambitious young fellow on a rented farm who had invested unwisely in registered cattle. Another had spent his money as it came, buying a tractor and other machinery on future expectations. A third had begun on too small a margin, paying $11,000 — of which too much was mortgage — for his farm, and buying his equipment on credit. The Prairie merchants, who were their creditors, blamed them bitterly for "dodging their honest debts." They, too, were close to failure; a few, barely solvent, closed out their business and moved away. The bank deposits declined steadily from $276,000 at the beginning of the 1920 harvest to $157,000 at the same time in '24; after that, the worst was over. But it is significant that the period of the Ku Klux Klan exactly paralleled — almost to the month — these years of agricultural and business depression.

Even at the worst, however, the hard times had been mitigated somewhat by oil money. The wildcat drilling around Prairie had never slacked. The crews lived in town, boarding at the hotel, filling the houses, and their pay checks on Tulsa banks contributed materially to the support of the community. The lease money also, although it averaged only about a dollar an acre, brought about $50,000 annually to the community. The progress at the wells was mostly a succession of misfortunes: a drill lost, a water pipe broken, a bit bent on a resistant formation, a dry hole with the casing pulled and the test abandoned. The promoters were working on a financial margin too small for effective drilling; but Prairie knew that most of Oklahoma's great fields had been discovered and most of its spectacular oil fortunes made by such shoestring operators. The conviction grew that the town was "setting right on the dome of the biggest oil pool in the state."

From 1923 on, it was apparent that the major companies were becoming interested. Geologists put up at the hotel while they went out on mysterious explorations. Core drillers worked out from the town in all directions, sinking their shallow tests into the fields and sampling the rock; two crews of rival companies refused to speak to each other, even to visit the same pool hall, lest they be blamed for any "leak" of information. The promoters began to sell their blocks of leases; names to conjure with — Champlin, Slick, Roxana, Sinclair, Marland — came in as owners. Taller derricks were erected, and great rotary drills began grinding straight down to the place where the structure maps marked the possible location of the oil "sand."

The town needed the support of this industry. The shrinkage of farm population had decreased the number of its customers; the concentration on one crop had lessened its importance as a market; and most ominous of all, the use of the automobile had encouraged people to trade in the cities. The only offset came from the sale of tractors and combines, the multiplication of garages and filling stations. But this did not balance the loss; by 1920 Prairie was speaking nostalgically of the "old-fashioned Saturdays" when farmers from a wide radius had flocked to town to buy and sell. The census that year showed a population of 434, a loss of 10 per cent for the decade, but there had been a far greater loss in the volume of trade.

The business leaders revived the Commercial Club, and initiated projects to bring people to town. There were free moving pictures at the theatre on Saturday. There were "trades' days" with advertised bargains in merchandise, special prices on farm products, and substantial prizes distributed by lottery. There were auction days on which "Colonel" Eaton was employed by the business men to hold a free sale of all property offered, from a business house to a calf or an old washing machine.

The people came for all these special inducements. They came from a radius of twenty or twenty-five miles. Then the next day Prairie's own farm constituents traveled an equal distance to take the bait offered by some rival town. It might have been good busi-

ness to strew the highway with tacks. But Prairie was nothing if
not public spirited. The Commercial Club worked hard to obtain
through highways.

The old system of township supervision of citizen labor furnished good training in practical democracy, but it was inadequate
to construct drained and graded roads. Many miles of newspaper
type had been set in evangelistic exhortations to farmers to join
the "Good Roads Movement," but improvement waited until the
owner of the first automobile discovered that bad roads compelled
him to stay at home when he ardently wished to be elsewhere. In
1909 Prairie had no words to express its disgust at a scheme of
"dudes" in the county seat to bond the county $150,000 for a
through highway; in 1924 Prairie votes went to swell the majori-
ties when the two counties voted a million dollars each in bonds
for hard surfaced roads radiating from the county seats.

Traffic was congested on these highways and serious accidents involving maiming or death had become a factor in community experience. But there was nothing like the lure of the open
road. In the summer farmers and town dwellers flocked to the
mountains of Colorado, where the highways were crawling with
Fords bearing Oklahoma licenses. They made trips back to the old
home, they attended the state fair in Oklahoma City, Eighty-
Niners' Day at Guthrie, the anniversary of the Strip Opening at
Enid.

But the lengthened radius of automobile travel that was shifting the economic center from the town to Enid or the county seat
had shifted the social center of the rural districts to the town. A
statistically inclined person counted ninety-six cars parked in
Prairie one Saturday afternoon of a good picture show. And there
were lyceum courses in winter, Chautauquas in summer, and always school programs and athletic contests.

The school still headed the list of entertainments. Nobody —
except B. F. Abbott — worried over declining educational standards. Although the district taxed itself to the constitutional limit
of fifteen mills, its salaries in the war and post-war inflation years
were no longer sufficient to employ capable teachers. But the
young people who graduated during those years were the school's
most successful alumni. A number were sent to college, where they
attained social and athletic leadership, and graduated into the
professions, or business administration, or technical phases of the

oil industry. None of this ambitious group ever came back to Prairie.

In 1924 Prairie began for the first time in its history to prepare its young people for life in the community. The school managed to obtain a capable superintendent that year, and a wide-awake young married couple was employed to teach vocational agriculture and home economics. The boys and the farmers worked in close co-operation, holding poultry shows, demonstrating terracing and stock judging, testing soil, making ponds. The housewives supported the girls almost as actively in their sewing and food exhibits. And when members of the 4-H Clubs organized that winter won high state honors in poultry and live stock judging and domestic arts, the people were as proud as they had ever been of athletic or literary triumphs. Out of this group came two boys who went on and graduated from the state agricultural college and returned to Prairie to farm their fathers' land. During this same period the state itself achieved the national leadership, which it still holds, in boys' and girls' work; it was no accident that the sons and grandsons of the men who had brought the prairies under cultivation, the daughters and granddaughters of the women who had put white curtains at the windows of their dug-outs and rag carpets on their earthen floors, should excel in agricultural and homemaking techniques.

It was the friendly contact established between the agriculture class and the farmers that winter that induced three outlying districts to join the Prairie school. The consolidated district now comprised thirty-six square miles lying equally on both sides of the county line. The big white boxes where rural life had once centered so actively were advertised and sold, and motor buses were purchased to convey the children to school in town. Once again the centralization of the mechanical age triumphed over localism.

The Prairie churches also drew their members from this wider radius. But attendance was somewhat languid: Sunday work was becoming general through the influence of the oil field's seven day week, and some of the unrighteous even drove to the cities for Sunday moving pictures. Prairie had never been a moral community except for a few years just before the war; now the more serious-minded deplored a growing laxity of conduct. The change was due to the recklessness unleashed by the war, the economic instability — whether from swollen incomes or ruin and unemployment — and the faster tempo set by motor transportation and mechanical agriculture; and there was a further complication from a special development of the prohibition policy.

The Prairie people had found prohibition a practical, if not perfect, solution of a concrete community problem. They regretted the occasional epidemics of drunkenness when the town bootleggers received their rail shipments, and they rejoiced when in 1917 the United States Supreme Court upheld the Webb-Kenyon Act, outlawing such invasion of "dry" territory. They were disappointed when the law was negatived almost as soon as passed by the development of motor transportation. They turned then to national prohibition. They were entirely unprepared for the development that followed the passage of the Eighteenth Amendment.

Liquor manufacture, outlawed in the great distilleries, moved to Prairie. Stills were found everywhere — in vacant houses, in ravines, in straw stacks — especially in the timbered hills on the east side of the township. Many were confiscated by the sheriff, but it was seldom possible to establish the ownership in a court of law. Everybody knew the owners; most of them were of pioneer stock — improvident farmers living in the hills or shiftless laborers in town. They made no profit from their illicit industry — they drank up too much of their product — and the women's societies of the churches were perpetually busy making over clothes for their neglected children.

Their customers, however, came from all classes of the population. In 1923 there was so much drunkenness that it became necessary to rebuild the town jail, which had fallen into disrepair soon after the saloons closed. Two deaths had already occurred — one a murder committed in a brawl at one of the stills, the other of a helpless alcoholic of good family who had wandered off and frozen to death in a drunken coma. Even high school youths were seen intoxicated — a new worry for Prairie which had not seen young boys under the influence of liquor since the old wide-open days.

During this same period Prairie was exposed to the first arguments it had ever heard from a respectable source against the prohibition policy. The intellectuals of the East had paid no attention when an obscure pioneer society chose to experiment with a strange law, but the Eighteenth Amendment was a direct challenge. Every magazine lying in a Prairie living room was filled with their arguments — subtle, clever, barbed with innuendo. The people had no defense. They began to doubt their own convictions, or to uphold them with a growing sense of impotence. Out of this frustration over a liquor traffic they could not destroy and an argument they could not answer, came much of the strength of the Ku Klux Klan.

They showed the same craving for a "Return to Normalcy" through political reaction. Both sexes now expressed themselves through the ballot, for a woman's suffrage amendment to the constitution had carried Oklahoma in 1918. And they expressed themselves definitely and decisively against every form of international co-operation. From the election of 1920 when the township voted for Harding 145 to 95, through every pool hall conversation or woman's club discussion of succeeding years on League of Nations, World Court, war debts, treaty, commitment, or diplomatic relationship their reasoning was very simple and very clear. They would erase all outlying portions of the map, and stop their ears so that never again would the echoes of a world at conflict disturb their peace.

But they could not erase the war experiences from their memories. A top-heavy economy, mad pursuit of pleasure, restlessness, moral laxity — none of these was new to Prairie, but somehow the glory had been lost. It was significant that except for the labored repetition of hymns in church Prairie never sang any more. There was no more singing as the mocking birds sang because the day was fair and life was new. That stopped in the agony of the war years, and it was never heard again. But the people still strained toward the future. This time they saw it as a gilded future, shining and splendid with the gift of oil.

"THE HADLEY well just blew in. A gusher. Shooting over the top of the derrick." The big news traveled with the speed of light along Main Street, it spread from house to house by back-yard telegraphy, the excitement spilling over in delirious attempts at jokes.

"Better take your wash off of the line. Next thing you know it'll be all spattered with oil."

"I've got the car here. Let's go. Next time I fill the tank I reckon it'll be with our own gas."

All over town was the roar of starting motors. The street was empty. The houses were deserted. Everyone was on his way to the well. It was a hot June day in '27.

This was not the first time such word had come to town. For six months now, one or another of the drilling wells had thrown the community into excitement, flowing oil to the top of the hole, bringing important-looking men in long cars, causing leases to change hands for as much as one hundred dollars an acre. But the drills went on down; Prairie was oil wise enough to know that they were grinding their way through lesser formations to the fabulous Wilcox sand. For the past three weeks the tension about the Hadley well had been tightening; the uncommunicative caution of the driller, the watchfulness of visiting officials showed that something big was at hand. The depth was approaching six thousand feet. A massive "control head" had been securely screwed down over the top; it had a complicated system of valves and pipes leading to a battery of tanks men were feverishly building, and for these three weeks oil had been "flowing by heads" (intermittently, with the accumulation of gas), running about three hundred barrels a day. The real strike had been expected hourly. Now it had come.

The wheat stubble all about the derrick was black with cars. People were springing out and making for the well on the run.

("Don't step in that oil, Mrs. Weaver; you'll ruin your shoes."
"What do I care about shoes? I can buy a million pairs with what
we're makin' out of this.") George Hadley was standing about,
trying to pull his face into casual lines. Mrs. Hadley, her arms
wrapped in her apron, was frankly beatific. The oil was *not* spout-
ing over the top of the derrick; it had been held in successfully
by the control head, and it was rapidly filling the tanks.

"Man! At that rate she'll run more'n three thousand barrels
a day."

"Where's the tools?"

"They're still down in the hole. If they had 'em out, no tellin'
what she'd flow."

Some of the spectators were prosperous-looking men with
good clothes protected by overalls. There were company executives, oil scouts, geologists, newspaper reporters. The news that
meant so much to Prairie was going on the wires all over the Mid-
Continent field. The leading newspaper in the state predicted a
second Seminole.

Before the day was over, Prairie was a boom town. The
streets were blocked with strangers, the restaurants were filled
with hungry oil men, every available room was taken. Workmen
were swarming over the wheatfield, rushing the completion of
more tanks, building a pump station and laying a pipe line to
carry the oil to a refinery. Almost immediately an "off-set" was
projected on the adjoining farm, and the rig builders were raising a derrick there.

This new location was on Dick Martin's land. "This is the
way I understand the off-set business," old Dick explained to
his wife. "When they start to take the oil from under George's
farm, they drain me, too. And so the company that's got my land
leased has got to put a well down right away to keep that from
happening. And every time they bring in a well on George,
they'll have to drill a well on me. Looks like we got more'n we
expected when we settled on this claim in '89, don't it?"

What was happening to the Hadleys was enough to excite a
far more phlegmatic person than Dick Martin. Under the royalty clause of their lease, one-eighth of every barrel of oil that
poured into the tanks belonged to them; the price would run
more than five hundred dollars a day. And soon their farm
would be dotted with such wells. But their cows had to be

milked that night, and it was unthinkable to waste the cream. When Saturday came, they brought it in their old Ford to the produce dealer, a former farm neighbor they had known for thirty years. And they took their modest check as usual; there seemed to be nothing else to do.

"I guess this is the last cream we'll ever sell," said Mrs. Hadley. "We bought a house in Enid yesterday. Paid five thousand dollars for it. We always wanted to live in Enid."

As they walked up the street they were shadowed by an automobile dealer and a radio salesman. But they went to the bank and made out mineral deeds, dividing their royalty into eight equal parts for themselves and their six children. Their neighbors watched them with a certain awe — "It may happen to us next," was the unspoken thought.

The farmers whose land lay near the "discovery well" were even then being showered with the gifts of fortune. The day after the well came in, Dick Martin was offered eight hundred dollars an acre for his royalty. But the dealer's fountain pen went dry, and while he went for ink another agent raised the offer to one thousand dollars. Dick and his wife were ready to accept.

"A hundred and sixty thousand dollars ain't marbles," they reasoned.

"But you'd better hold out," argued their son and daughters, called into conference. "A year from now there will be wells all over the farm. You might be a millionaire."

"If that's the way you feel about it, you can have your share now," said Dick. "Me and your mother wants to sell. You can keep yours and git as rich as you want to." And there was another family division, Dick and his wife and each of their three children receiving equal portions. Then the elder couple went on with the sale. "Each of us gits $32,000," they said. "That's all we'll ever need. A million wouldn't do us a bit more good."

Other farmers sold one-half their royalties for a term of ten, fifteen, twenty years, and kept the remainder. "This may be all I'll ever git," they reasoned. "And it looks pretty good to me. But I'll keep half, and if my place gits in the big pay, I'll still have a sixteenth of all they find. And when the time runs out my farm'll be clear again."

Within a week six new locations had been made. The "Martin No. 1" was ready to "spud in" and start drilling; the others were in various stages of derrick construction. Heavy trucks of material lumbered over the dusty roads between Prairie and "the field." And investors from the county seat were buying lots on Main Street, tearing down wooden buildings, and erecting brick to rent to the new business firms they anticipated. One of the major lumber companies of the state was feverishly erecting a new yard in readiness for the building boom.

Truck drivers, pipe line crews, rig builders, drilling crews all needed a place to live: some found lodging in neighboring towns; some stayed in the county seat and drove thirty miles back and forth to their work. A newly organized Chamber of Commerce urged everyone to "build rent houses. This is our golden opportunity; if we fail to grasp it, some other town will be the oil center." But prospective builders met an obstacle in the tangled titles left by the almost forgotten lot sale of townsite days. Some, willing to take a chance, purchased tax titles and built flimsy little shacks or moved them in from declining oil fields.

Meanwhile the old residents were working feverishly to take the overflow: giving up rooms in their houses, or adding outside rooms crazily here and there; raising their garages to two stories, with an apartment overhead; building small houses on the back of their lots. Several built good new residences, and made the old house over into apartments. All day long the sound of hammering punctured the languid summer calm. "Hear that noise? That's Prairie growing," the people told each other.

The "oil people" were welcomed with the hospitality always accorded "new neighbors." Moving from place to place as they did, they were free from social controls; and they ran the gamut of human character. Some made their rented quarters in the homes of sober citizens veritable dens of prostitution and drunkenness; others entered into the community life with a spirit refined and broadened by more experience than Prairie had ever known.

Their way of life was different. In their speech they could strip from a quarter section its wheat land, farm home, farm family down to the naked oil prospect of "the Hadley lease," "the Martin lease." Their days ran from midnight to noon or from noon to midnight; the ministers calling on these new members of their congregations learned to knock softly lest they disturb the sleep of men who worked on "night tour." Conditioned to dwelling amidst squalid shacks and evil-smelling spray from wild wells, they kept down their blinds and lived all day long by electric light. They owned pampered dogs, loving them beyond reason, as the only substitute for flowers and lawn and settled hearth. They spent money lavishly, but they knew the sickening slack of unemployment; their tenure depended on chance and "company" caprice. Their children appeared in school one day, wise with travel, confused by many kinds of teaching; another day they were gone, on orders too sudden for them even to collect their books.

With their experience of life in many places, the "oil people" demanded modern conveniences. Prairie rose to the need. Less than three months after the strike, the town bonded itself $50,000 for a sewer system. "This is no mushroom town," said the *News*. "The Prairie Pool is one of the deepest in the world. It takes four to six months to drill a well, and it will take a good many years to exhaust the field." The oil editor of the leading daily in the state backed up this judgment; Prairie was making a steady growth that would be permanent.

The expression "Prairie Pool" or "the field," was a civic figure of speech, for so far there was only one producer. Then just before the end of the year "Martin No. 1" came in with a roar. "FIELD PROVEN BY SECOND BIG WELL," screamed the *News* headline. But not much oil flowed into the tanks. The drill went two feet deeper, *and struck salt water*. Its very wetness proved it a "dry hole." Every housewife knew that oil is lighter than water and rises to the top; thus when the drill tapped water it revealed the absence of oil. "Good thing you and me sold our royalty," said Old Man Martin to his wife.

The "Hadley No. 1" was still running twenty-five hundred barrels of oil every day through the pipe line to a distant refinery. It also produced daily two and a half million cubic feet of "wet" gas, only slightly lighter than gasoline; and a plant, looking very complex and complicated, had been built close by to condense this product into the highly volatile "natural gasoline" used to impart quick starting qualities to motor fuel. The "Hadley Lease" swarmed with people. There were rows of neat company bungalows with newly-sodded lawns for technicians and laborers in the gasoline plant. And an energetic promoter had laid out the shack town of "Hadley," where the "Tulsa General Store," the "Seminole Cafe," the "Borger Rooms," the "Three Sands Billiard Parlor" called the roll of dramatic oil strikes and revealed the adventitious character of the industry.

"The field" became a reality in January, when two more drills tapped the oil sand. Both wells were small producers — 614 and 281 barrels. Then the well on Henry Schultz's farm blew in with a greater production than the discovery well; it flowed more than four thousand barrels into the tanks the first day. Henry expressed a mild bewilderment.

"I paid fife tousand tollars for dat farm ven I come in 1907. Und I vorked and my voman vorked and all my kids vorked like de tefil. Now I sit pack und do notting, und I get fife tousand tollars efery veek."

There was another family division, and Henry built a brick house and came to Prairie to live.

The Schultz well accelerated all the activities that had been set in motion by the first strike. And transactions in five figures were whirling about in everybody's speech.

"Did you hear about the Peters farm? The lease ran out, and the heirs got a $30,000 bonus to renew. Too bad the old people didn't live to see this day."

"The Weavers done better than that. The company that had their lease wouldn't renew. The geologists said it was off of the oil structure. And 'Colonel' Eaton drove over to Tulsa the next day and leased it to a big oil man for $62,000. Bill Weaver gave him five thousand dollars and some of the royalty."

By this time the town had changed almost beyond recognition. There were ten lumber yards and eight supply houses handling oil field equipment. The railroad company had ballasted the track and built extra switches, and heavy freight trains were pulling in at all hours. A metallic embroidery of parked cars edged Main Street and the connecting streets and formed a solid strip of insertion down the center. More strangers than old residents were seen on the streets and in public gatherings. A new business man from Tulsa was president of the Chamber of Commerce. The *News* had added an oil editor to its force, and every issue recounted in technical terms the progress at each well. Every one of the new brick buildings was occupied by a business house.

The same week that the Schultz well came into production the town published an ordinance for paving Main Street. The contract

was let to a Tulsa firm for $50,000 to be paid in ten-year install-
ments by the lot owners. The work had scarcely started until the
people voted $25,000 in bonds to enlarge the water system. The
same day the voters gave a franchise to a gas company to supply
the town with gas from the field, and to an electric company to
take over and extend the services of the municipal light plant. In
July another contract was let for the paving of two additional
streets.

"These past twelve months have been the biggest year in our
history," ran the report of the Chamber of Commerce. "Thirteen
new bricks have gone up in the business district; fourteen fine
residences and twenty-five good rent houses have been built; and
dozens of small houses have been built or brought in from other
places. Over a quarter of a million dollars has been spent for
public improvements — sewers, water, and paving — and gas from
our own field has been brought to our dwellings." Six wells were
producing, including two which had just come in for 2,000 and
2,800 barrels a day; fifteen were drilling; and seven new locations
had been made.

Only Hugh Channing tried to strew tacks in the path of "progress." Hugh had sold his farm and invested in town property at
the coming of the railroad; he owned several small houses and a
good brick building on Main Street.

"They're all goin' crazy," he proclaimed loudly to everybody
and nobody. "Because the whole town's goin' in debt they think
they're rich. Course it makes it nice for the oil people to have modern houses and paving. All them things is nice if you don't have
to pay for 'em. They're just pilin' the cost on us fellows that's
got property."

But Old Man Channing's dissonant voice was scarcely heard
in the chorus of rejoicing when the new paving was completed.
The Chamber of Commerce employed an Oklahoma City carnival
company to advertise the town and the field by a "Pageant of
Progress." The celebration lasted through four hot August days.
There were dances by Cheyenne Indians, a terrapin derby, juggling acts, a barbecue — all free. Six hundred people came from the
county seat with banners and speeches and a plane circling overhead dropping congratulatory leaflets. Over fifteen hundred cars
were on the streets the last night when a queen was crowned and
the pavement was cleared for general dancing. A far cry from

that celebration thirty-seven years before, when Prairie "City" had
been a cross-roads store, and a group of pioneers no longer hungiy
had invited the whole county to a native grove to rejoice with
them over the first harvest. "Well, I'm glad I made that street
plenty wide," said Old Man Goodwin.

But this last celebration somehow lacked spontaneity. Running through everything was a sense of unreality. Prairie never
succeeded in directing the oil boom. Would it join those fabulous
names — Whiz Bang, Oilton, Seminole, Bowlegs, Borger — to become a chaos of oil-drenched soil, and hell and violence, and
millions staked and won? That depended on what yet lay beneath
the earth. Would it become a fair, strong city solidly built to endure into the future? That depended partly on the whims of fortune, more on the insight and long-range planning of its leaders.
But its newcomers were frankly transients, and its older settlers
were inadequate. Some of the latter even tried to shut out new
business firms in an attempt to monopolize the trade.

Always there was the sense of being moved by outside forces.
"What I would do with a million dollars" was the topic for discussion at a woman's missionary society. The pulses of every member
quickened as she let her imagination range. The wild speculative
spirit of the industry affected the thinking of all classes; sudden
wealth had struck with such caprice that individual effort seemed
futile. It all seemed like a gambling game in which the stakes were
high.

The few people — for the number was still small — who had
enjoyed the smiles of fortune were surprisingly unchanged. Virtually all of them first cleared their land of mortgages. Then there
was the almost invariable signing of mineral deeds to divide the
royalty among members of their family; this equalized the income
tax burden, but most of all it satisfied a fundamental sense of
family solidarity. Next there was the purchase of a sturdy, unpre-
tentious house in town — usually in Enid — which after years of
farming seemed the goal of desirable living. Then they bought a
better car and a few household conveniences. There was still the
problem of investment: most of them purchased some extra farms,
and they attempted so far as they could judge to buy conservative
stocks and bonds.

There were two or three instances where oil money gave un-
disciplined people their first large-scale opportunity for disorderly

living. The first well drilled on Bill Weaver's farm came in at 6,000 barrels; he was offered $800,000 for his royalty, but he held on, and soon four more wells were pouring gold into his shabby purse. He and his wife, who had quarreled and fought amicably for more than a generation, now had a stormy divorce trial and went their separate ways. Mrs. Weaver moved to the county seat, married again, and fattened her soul with diamond rings and houses and cars. Bill stayed on the farm, weaving a zig-zag trail from bawdy house to bootlegging den along the edge of the oil field, swindled, robbed, drugged, always the victim of marital and amatory adventures. The sons and daughters settled in various cities and entered a similar round of escapades.

George Hadley got the most satisfaction out of his oil money. Nobody had understood why through Populism and Socialism and lean year and good he had hungered and thirsted after money. But the answer was simple; he wanted to spend it on his family, to live in peace and comfort. Now he made wise investments, he learned to clip coupons, he lived simply, and for the first time in his life he indulged his natural generosity without the condemnation of his demanding wife. When he drove down from Enid to visit his old neighbors, he had mellowed until they scarcely knew him; and when the election came around in '28 he had become a stalwart Republican.

But not more than a dozen farms were covered with the orderly confusion of oil field activities. Probably fifty more farm families had received from twenty thousand to sixty thousand dollars each from the sale of royalty or the renewal of leases. Some moved to town and the money disappeared; more invested it in their farming operations or started out their sons and daughters. And the rest of the rural population — receiving smaller windfalls, or a dollar an acre, or nothing, according to the whims of chance — was still mainly dependent on farming.

The price of wheat had been more than a dollar a bushel most of the time since the harvest of 1924, and the average yield had been good. The harvesting, threshing, and marketing were one operation, as the combines marched across the field and trucks hauled the grain directly to the elevators. Then plows pulled by tractors began immediately to turn over the stubble. When the soil was in the right condition, many farmers with sons to work the shift plowed straight through the night; the sound of the motors could be heard in all directions through the quiet summer dark-ness. Horses were still seen on the farms, but a colt was a curiosity, and the price of work animals had gone down to forty or fifty dollars a head.

Some farmers had begun to raise sheep, keeping them through the winter on wheat pasture. But Prairie was no longer a live stock market. The farmers loaded their cattle and sheep — and their hogs, if any — into their trucks and drove to the stockyards at Oklahoma City. Even horses were hauled about from one farm to another; they rode along, looking bored by the long drive or mildly interested in the scenery, as accustomed as the people to motor transportation. Some cream and chickens and eggs were sold — always at good prices — to the Prairie produce dealers. In 1928 a hatchery was established in the town, and the farmers' wives began to raise their chickens without the drudgery of tending sitting hens or incubator.

The farm population went down another 15 per cent during the '20's. And there was a new development, presaging a greater decline in the future. Several farmers had come to town to live, leaving their machinery in sheds on the land, driving back and forth in their cars to plant and harvest their wheat. Some even kept cattle in their pastures and cared for them by the same long dis-tance method. Such "gentlemen farmers" might be semi-retired landowners or beginning tenants. A young man living in town and owning a combine, a tractor, and planting equipment might lease a quarter two miles east, an eighty a half mile north, and a quarter three miles west, and plant the whole to wheat. Landowners pre-ferred such all-wheat tenants to subsistence farmers, because the one-third rental brought in a larger cash income. By 1930 half the farmers were tenants; and a much larger portion of the land was under tenant culture as landowning farmers rented additional acreage. But farm ownership for the first time in the history of the community was almost stable; few owners were willing to sell land that might at any time begin to gush rivers of oil. When an oil-rich farmer or his son invested in land, he usually bought in some other locality.

Young men from the South no longer filled the town at harvest time, for the combine had displaced the shockers and the threshing crew. And even with the oil development, Prairie had serious un-employment, which passed almost unnoticed in the general prosperity. Most of the town building was done by outside contractors, who brought in their own crews. When laborers were needed in the oil field to dig ditches or build a plant Prairie's young men flocked there and the foreman selected the strongest and sturdiest by a "You," "You," "You," and a pointing finger.

In the fall of '28 the oil activity was slowed down by a state-wide policy of "proration." Overproduction had brought ruinous depression of the market; and the operators with the sanction of the Corporation Commission agreed on systematic limitation of output. The Prairie field at that time was producing 25,000 barrels a day from fourteen wells, fifteen more were drilling, and material for six new rigs stood on the railway siding ready to be hauled to location. By the next year there were thirty-two producing oil wells, "pinched back" to 20,000 barrels, ten gas wells, and five natural gasoline plants. About a thousand people were living in shacks and company bungalows scattered here and there over the leases, or in rooming houses in the town of "Hadley"; and the rural school had been enlarged to care for one hundred children.

Prairie had a slightly smaller population, but more school children. When the term closed in 1929 with 287 pupils enrolled in the grades and 108 in the high school, crowded forty-five or more in a room, the people voted thirty-five thousand dollars in bonds for a new building. They erected a combination gymnasium and auditorium flanked by classrooms and laboratories, and remodeled the old building for additional teaching space.

The high school students made the most of the oil money that was flooding the community. They drove to Enid for their class functions, holding their banquets in the finest hotel there. Staid citizens worried about their increasing wildness; liquor circulated freely on their chaperoned excursions, and several of the girls had taken up the new habit of smoking. But sixteen graduates were doing well in college, and four young alumni were themselves members of college faculties.

The people came in droves to the school games and entertainments; the Athletic Association collected almost a thousand dollars a year from gate receipts. They supported a semi-professional baseball team, the "Oilers," filling the grandstand in riotous hilarity through the hot Sunday afternoons. In the winter they attended wrestling matches and boxing matches. They made a speedway of the paved Main Street, until a special officer was employed to slow them down. They organized a golf club, and men and women took up the new game avidly. They seized upon bridge with fierce enthusiasm: there were bridge breakfasts and bridge luncheons and bridge dinners; even the woman's clubs virtually abandoned their study programs for the new craze.

Life had not been so fast and furious since the days of townsite promotion. People of early middle age who had grown up in the community and settled into its economic life, broke out in unrestrained wildness and dissipation. Drunkenness approached that of the old saloon days, not on the streets as formerly, but in the homes and at social gatherings. Organized criminal networks operating over a large area preyed upon the town, coming by night to rob the stores or seize parked automobiles, and spiriting the stolen property away to some undiscovered outlet. Not for twenty years had the people seen so many violent deaths; there were oil field accidents, automobile crashes, murder, suicide.

Other aspects of life were intensified. The town gained recognition throughout the state for the excellence of its amateur radio programs broadcast from the stations of surrounding cities. The reunions of the high school alumni kept alive a sense of historical continuity; when these young people came from positions of responsibility in the world outside, they brought a reassuring confidence in Prairie's creative achievements. Even more of an Old Home Week was the Decoration Day observance, with young married couples from many states coming to visit their parents and lay wreaths on family graves. For the first time, a man was employed to tend the cemetery, and it changed from a wilderness of tall grass and neglected graves to a beauty spot of smooth lawn and blooming flowers.

When the people read in their daily papers of a stock market crash on Wall Street they felt only a detached disdain for the unstable actions of Easterners. They were more concerned that fall of '29 over the slowing down of the oil field. A few new wells came in during the winter, but most of the reports became a succession of "Schultz No. 2 has gone on the pump," "Hadley No. 1 has dropped to forty barrels a day," "Peters No. 1 has been plugged back and abandoned as a dry hole," "Martin No. 2 has been plugged back to the Layton sand to be shot for a gasser." The "pool" had turned out to be disappointingly small; a ring of "dry holes" around the perimeter defined an area about three miles long and half as wide. Production had fallen off through natural decline and proration to 9,500 barrels. Before the end of the year the oil companies began to remove their employees to a spectacular new field at Oklahoma City.

These discouraging conditions were offset for a time by a showing of oil in a wildcat on the other side of town; hundreds of cars and several oil men in planes rushed to the place, and royalty changed hands for as much as $2,500 an acre. Prairie was in ecstasies over another "proven field," but nothing except drilling trouble ever developed there.

The town building continued, though at a slower pace, through 1930. But instead of the acute housing shortage of the three preceding years, several good buildings were vacant. The Federal census showed a population of 695, which represented a decline of probably two hundred. Before the end of the year the town lost several new businesses of the type depending mainly on the "oil people" — a men's clothing store, a dry cleaning establishment, a laundry, a restaurant, a soft drink place. The merchants again tried to lure customers to the town by free moving pictures, chances on a Ford car or a radio. Bank deposits, which had stood at $351,000 in the fall of '29 went down steadily during the following twelve months to $240,000; even the harvest passed without the usual increase. The wheat in fact was marketed at 61 to 67 cents a bushel, and other farm prices were falling. But the people still were not seriously alarmed as the shadow of the Great Depression moved ominously from the East across the country.

XXII

THE WEAKEST LINK

P RAIRIE's business had started languidly that December Monday; an unseasonable blizzard promised a dull day and an empty street. It was a woman who first discovered that something was amiss. Pale, trembling, almost crying she burst into the Goodwin store — "For God's sake, tell me. Is anything wrong with the bank?" Instantly Main Street was alarmed, with the few early morning customers joining the merchants who came running from their stores. A compact group gathered around the door of the Pioneer State Bank, reading and re-reading the brief notice.

BELIEVING IT TO BE TO THE BEST INTEREST OF THE DEPOSITORS WE HAVE PLACED THE AFFAIRS OF THIS BANK IN THE HANDS OF THE STATE BANKING DEPARTMENT, THIS FIFTEENTH DAY OF DECEMBER, 1930.

By order of the BOARD OF DIRECTORS.

That seemed to be all it said. The people peered around and under it as though some concealed meaning might be discovered there. Here was drama, exhilarating in spite of its personal implications. "I saw the light on in the bank all night Saturday night. I *knew* it was something like that." "I told my wife just this morning — " "That time the bank failed in Missouri — " "They say over in Arkansas — " Then as individual realization began to come — "How the devil am I goin' to pay my taxes?"

It was impossible, unthinkable. The Pioneer State Bank was more than a bank; it was a community institution. Only the old settlers remembered how, before the railroad came, when Prairie "City" had flung its first brave rows of shacks across the blistering prairie, young A. T. Strickland had come to town to establish a bank. In all the seasons since, while the lean young pioneers were growing into grizzled old-timers, while the raw new town was assuming the manners and acquiring the institutions of settled communities, through "green bugs" and drought, through good wheat years and oil years, it had stood there, warning the reckless, assisting the hard pressed, curbing the extravagant, building out of the scattered activities of individual initiative a solid structure of community credit.

If old A. T. was not exactly loved, he was respected. More than that, he was accepted. He had helped to shape the community. His family had grown up there. He was bound to the deep common life of the neighborhood by more than a generation of shared experience. Of course he had a few enemies — men who told bitter tales of financial exploitation and injustice and swore they would never deal with him again — but for the most part they were not believed. After all, there was something suspicious about a man who would drive to a distant town to transact his banking business; it implied that his credit was not good with his home town banker. The people had felt a deep personal pride in the stability of *their* bank — "the biggest financial institution in the county outside of the county seat," boasted the *News*.

It was therefore a shocked and incredulous crowd that gathered at the closed door in the swirling snow that December morning. Stronger than personal loss was a great loyalty to the grim old man whose life work had ended in failure. "It isn't old A. T.'s fault." "This hits him harder than any of us; the old man sure loved his bank." "I'd bet anything on old A. T.'s honesty. He just got in a tight place." Even the hopeful, "It'll be open again in a week. People've just been checkin' too heavy lately. But it's sound. We won't lose anything."

A dissenting voice came from the edge of the crowd, a voice profane and menacing. "Goddam them Stricklands. I'll tell you boys we ought to git our guns and round up the whole gang like we used to do horse thieves. They're a damn' sight lower than a horse thief." The others looked at Old Man Weaver with tolerant understanding. A few said, "That's so," but nobody followed his excited leadership. "Reckon most of what he had left was in the bank. Well, his oil money didn't do him any good. This puts him back just where he was before."

Slowly the town tried to resume its arrested life. Inconveniences, trivial or tragic, brought the loss home on every turn: a clerk saying, "Will you excuse me while I run over to the bank and get some change — oh, there isn't any bank — "; a bridge party canceled because when the flowers and refreshments arrived from the county seat there was no money to pay for them; a corpse carried back from the railway station because the pooled resources of the neighbors were insufficient to pay the transportation to the old home. Merchants looked at their Christmas stock sadly; there would be no Christmas buying in town that year. Would the school close? The school funds, like all others, had been deposited in the bank. The children discussed their prospects in voices shrill with hope and fear.

That night in the interest of economy the street lights were turned off; it was the first time the town had been in darkness since it burst into a white blaze with its first electricity. As the wild night closed down over the stormy day, every household group drew close together counting its losses and trying to reconstruct its future.

The widow of an oil field worker looked into a world suddenly grown menacing. "Bert always said we'd never be able to lay up anything, but he'd fix it so if anything happened to him, the children and I would be provided for. And just Saturday I deposited that insurance money. I felt as though Bert was still watching out for us. Now . . . Can I get work here? . . . Shall I write home? . . . I haven't enough in the house to . . ." In the next home a boy sat brooding in the unrelieved despair of inexperience. "Two hundred and seventy-nine dollars and thirty-four cents. I could have started next semester. And I always thought if I could manage one semester I could find work there to keep me going till I graduated. Now I'll have to wait . . . And I'll be so old . . ." A merchant checked and re-checked the same columns of figures. His neighbors called him wealthy; only the bank officials knew the extent of his indebtedness. "When the bank calls in its loans, that will be the end. And I'm still solvent; if I just had a little credit I could carry on." But the blow that had wiped out the savings of the community had destroyed its credit machinery.

And so in varying forms the same fear entered into every home. Every loss cut into the very life fabric of a people who could ill afford to lose.

The younger Stricklands had left town, but old A. T. and his wife remained and faced it all. They sat in their house behind drawn blinds, or walked furtively along the streets. Old friends sought them out, disregarding their own loss in sympathy for the man who perforce must carry such a heavy burden of self-reproach. Others came also, bitter, angry men who shook their clenched fists in his face and called him a scoundrel and a thief. He met friend and foe alike; he bowed his head and wept, and his old wife hung over him protecting.

Meanwhile the liquidator appointed by the state banking department had come to take over the bank. With characteristic suspicion of the expert, the people resented him as an intruder. When they had lost their means of living, why should some dude be drawing a fabulous salary merely for checking over the books? It was *their* money, wasn't it? Why not elect one of the home town people?

The depositors, men and women, held a mass meeting in the school auditorium. They chose a chairman and a secretary, and proceeded in a formal manner to consider the problem. Several of the most stable men in the community addressed the meeting — farmers, merchants, the manager of the Farmers' Elevator, the editor of the *News*.

"We've all got our money tied up here," spoke the aging voice of Arthur Goodwin, "and we want to get as much of it back as possible. And we'll get it all, if we can collect everything the bank has outstanding. But it has intangible assets that no stranger can ever discover. A note is not secured entirely by collateral, but by the good faith of the man that signed it. It takes a person that knows the community, to know when to foreclose or when to give a little more time. We want a man familiar with local conditions to liquidate this bank."

Somebody then suggested the name of Goodwin's son-in-law, Earl Peters; he was unanimously approved, and a committee was chosen to petition the state banking department for his appointment. But the officials at the capitol probably reasoned that such work required technical training. They did give the depositors the privilege of electing an advisory committee to work with the liquidator. Ten substantial farmers and business leaders were chosen by a second mass meeting; they rendered valuable assistance to the liquidator through their knowledge of local problems.

During these first days of community action, the people were drawn together as they had not been since their boys left for the training camps. Without waiting for Sunday the competing Protestant churches called their members together for a union meeting. Their usual Christmas programs with trees and presents could hardly be carried out — even the money for the children's "treats" had been lost, for the church collections had always been deposited in the bank — but brave new plans were made for a community observance. The women did most of the talking.

"I heard my children say there wouldn't be any Christmas this year," said a daughter of John Clark. "I must have given them the wrong idea of what Christmas is. I can remember — and so can a good many of you — when a school reader or a pencil or a pair of shoes was an acceptable Christmas present for a child. But we looked forward the whole year to Christmas because our parents took thought to make it a happy time. The one I remember best was in '96. Our parents had been to Hennessey and bought each of us a little pink cup and saucer — I've got mine yet. Mother made some molasses candy — we had a little sorghum that year — and filled our cups. When we came back from the program at the schoolhouse, we found the dishes all set out on the table with our names on them. And that was every single thing we got. But we were happy because our parents were happy. And yet I have heard them say that was the hardest year they ever had."

"We talk about hard times now, but we don't know anything about it," said the editor's wife. "Who in this neighborhood will have to put her baby to bed in a barn? And that's what Mary had to do."

"My mother did something about that hard," said Elizabeth King, smiling down at the faded, but still pretty woman. "I was born in a sod house myself, and so were some of the rest of you. And I can't see that it hurt us any." And she held her young head high. Prairie was proud when "Miss Beth" came home to visit her parents; she had won recognition throughout the state for her musical talents. As she stood there, beautiful, poised, vibrant with life, it was certain that her pioneer beginnings had not "hurt her any."

This spirit dominated the celebration that was held the next week at the school auditorium. And the Christmas issue of the *News* featured the reminiscences of men and women still hale and vigorous who knew the toil of creating a settlement in an untouched land. There were stories of "the time the mule balked and laid down in the quicksand," of how "we had no henhouse, and that hen laid an egg every day in a box I fixed under the bed," of "the time the rattlesnake crawled into the dug-out when my husband was away," of how "when the baby died George Hadley and

Bill Weaver made the coffin and we buried it on our claim." Thinking of these things the people reminded each other, "We built this community out of faith and grit and work, and we can build it up again."

This spiritual exultation carried them through a series of petty humiliations more annoying than the greater calamity — the return of checks they had mailed before the crash. They began to receive courteous notes from insurance companies to which they had yielded their savings, from mail order houses from which they had purchased some luxury —

"We are enclosing your check on the Pioneer State Bank, which has been returned to us unpaid. We regret that the failure of your bank makes it necessary for us to request payment by money order or registered mail. Kindly send the amount at once so that we may balance our books. . . ."

It was the last straw. How could they pay these bills again when they had neither cash nor credit?

The town reverted to barter: people who could not pay their rent tried to exchange goods or labor; those who had no money for groceries did the same; farmers and merchants, so far as they could, paid their employees in commodities. But taxes had to be paid in cash, and so did the wholesale houses and transportation companies; and underneath this makeshift system was the stark fear of those who knew themselves deeply indebted to the bank, with no cash to meet the day of reckoning.

Through the first shock of adjustment the community was sustained by the spiritual quality of its loyalty to A. T. Strickland; but this faith also began to fail. Ugly stories began to circulate and gain credence — stories of large sums of money saved out and protected by legal subterfuges, of the peoples' savings dissipated in private speculation, of manipulation of the books extending over a long period and almost diabolical in its planned cunning. People surrendered their confidence in the pioneer banker reluctantly — illogically they had trusted him simply because his face had long been familiar on their streets — but now a doubt more sinister than the economic menace began to cloud their courage.

When for the second time a crowd gathered before the door of the bank, its mood was angry and suspicious. It had been announced that a small dividend would be paid to the depositors;

but a deeper interest was aroused by the knowledge that the affairs
of the bank would be made public, and that the community would
soon know the full measure of its loss.

The door with its ominous notice was opened, and the crowd
pushed in. With mounting indignation they examined the statement of the bank's assets. Outwardly everything was in order —
no wonder the state examiner had been deceived in his periodical
inspections — but it was immediately apparent to these men who
knew their neighbors so well, that for many years the accounts had
been padded. "Well, I'll be blamed! Look where Clyde Jones bor-
ried ten thousand dollars. That's Dick Jones's boy, and the whole
family's shiftless. A. T., the son-of-a-gun, loaned that money to
hisself. Probly give the kid a little to sign the note and keep still."
"Look at the security on this note! How much would you give for
Ed Johnson's endorsement? All he's got is hound dogs."

Over the sullen muttering of the crowd the voice of Old Man
Weaver rang out with triumphant vindictiveness, "Didn't I tell
you? Remember what I said right at first? The old hypocrite —
goin' around cryin'. If you'd 'a' listened to me, he'd 'a' had sump'm
to cry about."

I told you so — words beloved of village oracles! The men
looked at the speaker with shamed respect. As he pushed impor-
tantly up to the window they fell silent. They heard his loud demand for "my money — all of it, damn you," and the courteous
reply of the official, "You haven't any deposit, Mr. Weaver. You
remember you had been checking pretty heavily before the bank
failed. You have overdrawn your account seven dollars."

The old man made an attempt to bluster — "I'll never pay it;
you're a crook, too, just like the Strickland outfit" — but he slunk
away, a discredited prophet. He was followed by the laughter of
the crowd, and it was not friendly laughter.

The men now discovered a new source of malicious satisfaction. They began to examine the list of depositors, to the discom-
fiture of boastful citizens who had achieved a temporary celebrity
by exaggerating their losses. They called across to embarrassed
neighbors, "How does this come, Charlie? I thought you told me
you lost four thousand dollars. Well, here it gives you a balance
of seventy-one cents. Course that's likely to happen; a man can't
be all the time countin' his money." There was something leveling
about the opened books, but it brought a surly individualism very

different from the spirit that at first had drawn them to stand together in a common poverty. The betrayal of their confidence by the veteran banker had poisoned the old neighborly relations.

The men returned to their homes with the meager dividends, that were so inadequate to meet their obligations. Indignantly they related to their families the frank revelations of the opened books. Most unsettling of all, they reported the indebtedness of stable mercantile houses, which in turn were known to carry large credit accounts of farmers. It became common knowledge that the bank would pull down in its fall many a fair-seeming business structure, and that substantial farmers of the community would be involved in the general ruin.

This knowledge prepared the people for the next development — a series of bankruptcies among the debtors of the bank. These new defaulters were not given the benefit of the strong community loyalty that had rallied to A. T.'s defense, for their neighbors now were watchful and suspicious. It was whispered that none of them had quit poor. Certain it was that valuable farms passed out of the reach of creditors by the legerdemain of family transactions; live stock, stored wheat, farm machinery were surreptitiously sold, and the money disappeared; merchandise was spirited away from shelves to family storerooms. Even young sons who had paid their way through college by borrowing money in their own names with their fathers' endorsement on the notes, threw this debt into the family hopper and emerged clear.

These transactions involved people who had been among the leaders of the community. There was James Alexander, who with his sons had branched out unwisely in farming operations; J. Q. Walker, who had extended too much credit to his customers; B. F. Abbott, who had an extravagant family. They had never intended to defraud anybody, but when they were faced with ruin they were unwilling to renounce their economic prestige and descend to the common level of poverty. In thus evading the provisions of the bankrupt law, however, they made their private affairs a matter of community interest. Their scale of living was jealously and closely scrutinized, and if they were betrayed into the purchase of some luxury the whispers rose to a chorus, "They bought that with our money — the money they saved out when they went bankrupt." The community began to break up into mutually hostile groups. People became cynical, and believed no man could be trusted; in bitterness of spirit they absented themselves from church and neighborhood gatherings because they were unwilling "to associate with thieves and crooks."

There was a general lowering of the standards of financial integrity — a tendency to follow the general example and take the easy way, to balance the relative advantages of honor and dishonor. Citizens began to cast about for ways by which the town might repudiate its bonded indebtedness, not altogether because taxes were cruelly hard to pay, but because repudiation seemed so easy and alluring.

Meanwhile the liquidator was uncovering evidence that he believed would send A. T. Strickland and possibly his sons to the penitentiary. But before the case came to trial the community received a second shock in the banker's suicide. The public never knew the contents of the note he left for his family, but the strength and the weakness of his life showed forth more clearly as his neighbors gathered about his coffin. He had not been intentionally a scoundrel. He had conducted his bank through all the years with a serious sense of community responsibility. He had loaned its money too freely, possibly through a sense of friendship, certainly through overconfidence in the permanence of the oil boom. This was not a crime. But alongside his sober trusteeship was a fierce, untamed streak of the gambler's nature. The lure of oil stock had been irresistible; as early as 1913 he had begun to use first his own money, then to a limited extent the bank's money, concealing the embezzlement by fictitious loans. This probably had not caused the crash, but it had contributed to its evil effects. As for his sons, they had been completely under his dominance; the cases against them were never brought to trial.

To a certain extent the death of the veteran banker cleared the moral atmosphere. Neighborly feelings flowed again in sympathy for the grim old pioneer who had helped to build the town; and for the younger men who had once eaten bread and jam in hospitable kitchens, and played on the high school football team. At the same time there was a stern sense of satisfaction entirely disassociated from the idea of revenge. With this vindication of justice a struggling faith in the old standards began to wake once more. But even so, the people's faith had proved to be credulity; their loyalty had made them dupes; the glory had faded from their courage.

XXIII
THE DEPRESSION YEARS

THERE were many reorganizations during those first months of
'31, immediately after the bank failure. As Abbott's drug store,
Walker's general merchandise, Spragg's big garage with its numerous employees, one of the grain elevators, and other established
firms were closed out by bankruptcy proceedings, names known
since the early days of the town were dramatically erased from
Main Street. In most cases their fixtures and stocks were acquired
by out-of-town purchasers and hauled away. They were followed
by an unstable succession of new ventures: an employee thrown
out of work by the failure of his firm, attempting to set up for himself; a farmer, at the end of his resources, casting about for something new; a young man, finding no employment, trying to create
opportunities through his own initiative.

"Now when things are at rock bottom is the time to start a new
business," urged the daily papers and the "fillers" of the *News*.
"Don't be afraid to invest in the future. The future is sure. Now
as never before, courage and resourcefulness will pay big dividends." But the young and the brave of Prairie who staked their
small capital on such faith, found it false. One after another gave
up the fight; only one or two managed to hold on.

The established firms were only slightly more fortunate. The
furniture store had not been pulled down by the crash, but its
continued survival was dependent mainly on its undertaking department. The drug business was carried on by a tawdry store that
had come with the oil boom. Its main income was from slot machines, always surrounded by men — unsuccessful men, whose
gambling instinct had been stimulated by financial uncertainty.
The "movie" theatre had closed with the bank failure; it was re-
opened with inferior pictures and a ten-cent admission charge,
and the people — especially the women and children — flocked
there, avid for this tinseled relief from actuality.

Goodwin and Sons had remained solvent, but the firm had lost heavily from bad debts. Now the business was completely reorganized. Arthur Goodwin retired, to devote his time to supervising his farm, sitting on a Main Street bench in the sunshine, taking a modest summer trip to the mountains. His sons separated, one keeping the dry goods and groceries and carrying on at the old stand, the other with his brother-in-law moving the hardware down the street and combining it with a garage and service station. They employed sons and daughters and daughters' husbands — all industrious young people, given to early marriage and dependability. "This is getting to be a one-family town," said the envious. But none of the Goodwins had ever sought to restrict its growth. They carried on their business quietly, serving the community and managing to support their branching families on its contracted income.

The *News* was in hard straits. The bank failure found its pages overflowing with Christmas advertising; then this source of revenue was suddenly and almost completely cut off. The editor gave notice that he would accept "eggs, fresh butchered meat, or what have you" on subscription, but most of the subscribers simply let the paper come without paying for it. To have dropped them would have been construed as an insult, as an implication that they were dishonest. But the editor too had extended himself unwisely in those golden days of the old boom, changing from hand press and hand set type to power press and linotype purchased on credit. Now forced to let his helpers go, he was too busy with mechanical and financial problems to gather news. The paper deteriorated until aside from its editorials it ceased to have any community significance. But its editorial voice still rang out bravely.

"The town that wins is the one that has the courage to launch out to new ventures. If the first one fails, try another. The world belongs to the man who dares, and the same thing is true of a town.

"Yesterday we heard one of our citizens grumbling about the cost of our schools, sewers, paving, and lights. ["That would be Old Man Channing," said the readers.] But those things are not an expense, but an investment; they are an insurance against the death of the town. This man has his own property insured against fire; he should be glad that we have the kind of leadership that creates these desirable living conditions, and thus insures him against the loss of population to larger towns."

But Channing knew that two of his houses stood vacant; in two others the tenants stranded by the bank crash were frankly waiting to pay till better times; and he had lowered the rental on all from thirty-five dollars a month to ten dollars. The exodus of "oil people" was gradual — one gasoline plant and the pumping wells in the field gave some employment, and there were sporadic bursts of wildcatting on the other side of town — but here one crew and there another was ordered to Oklahoma City, to East Texas, to Kansas. Many of them were reluctant to leave — "We like Prairie. It's such a friendly place, and such a progressive place. But we can't figure out a way to stay here." The old residents, spread out thinly over the enlarged area of the town, were left to pay its debts.

Channing, steady, unimaginative, honest, cut his personal expenses to the bone and paid his taxes — paving and all — as he would have met any other obligation. A few others did the same. But with their cash tied up in the bank it was an impossibility for many to pay, and the legislature, influenced by similar conditions throughout the state, began the practice of moratoriums. And as unpaid taxes piled up, many voluntarily abandoned the attempt to clear their property.

It was early in '33 that Arthur Goodwin, walking along the street, paused to watch Channing painstakingly painting a vacant house.

"I hate to see you working and spending money on that house, Hugh. You're going to lose it."

"Lose it! I don't owe a cent on it."

"Not in your own name, you don't. But you owe a share of the town's debt. We're letting our store building go. The boys and I figured it up. With paving along the side and front both, the taxes are more than it's worth. No use throwing good money after bad."

It was unthinkable. Goodwin's title had seemed as secure as the sturdy-looking building he had owned debt-free ever since he had placed it there on his corner lot in 1909. Was it possible for a public debt thus to absorb all one's private investment in house and land? Old Man Channing climbed down from the ladder and stood lost in thought. From that time on, he checked all but his own residence off his tax list. By this time most of the good buildings in town stood subject to the county's lien. As for the small oil field shacks, these were hauled away at night, leaving only the vacant lot as surety for the uncollectable assessment.

Meanwhile, in the months after the bank failure, embattled citizens met in the Odd Fellows' Hall to form a Taxpayers' Association of the township, with a hierarchy of delegates connecting with a county and a state organization. They received some promises from candidates for office in the election of 1932, and the cost of the state government was gradually shifted from the general property tax to other means of revenue. But most of Prairie's tax represented a debt for improvements that the people had purchased on credit and continued to enjoy.

An effort was made to scale down the cost of these and other modern conveniences. The people were making comparisons and discovering that they were paying more for utilities than the surrounding towns. In February of '31 — three months after the bank failure — a conspicuous summons on the front page of the *News* urged every citizen to attend a mass meeting in the school auditorium to find out how the town stood. "We discuss and wonder about these problems among ourselves — Let's Get Together and Find Out. If we ever needed the Co-operation of Every Man and Every Woman it is NOW."

Nearly everybody came. The mayor at that time was B. F. Abbott, then at the very height of his unpopularity over his somewhat-less-than-complete bankruptcy. He stayed away from the meeting, but a member of the council came and answered the people's questions. He explained the water situation: the uncertain supply which had necessitated the sinking of many wells, the expense of operation that precluded the reduction of rates. As for electricity, it was now apparent that the town had not driven a good bargain with the company that bought the municipal plant; but it was too late to correct the mistake. A sinister suspicion almost came into the open during the questioning, a suspicion that the mayor's influence had been purchased in making these contracts, but no evidence was ever adduced; apparently the town officials like the other citizens had simply been inexperienced. What was the bonded debt of the town? About $131,000, answered the official; this did not include the school indebtedness, which was shared by the surrounding country, and the paving, which was charged to the abutting property. All this for a town of about four hundred permanent residents.

An official of the gas company was present for questioning. He explained the poverty of his company that prevented the reduction of rates. The people still remember the blue light that blazed from the diamonds on his finger and in his tie. Apparently they had been too hasty in granting this franchise. A committee was also appointed to draft a petition to the telephone company. But the rates were not reduced. Fully two-thirds of the people then ordered their telephones disconnected — some because they were unable to pay the charge, others because with their neighbors off the line their own instruments were of little use. Not since 1903 had the community been so generally without this means of communication. Many of the people also sold their gas stoves, and began buying wood from "the jacks" — a fuel they had abandoned for coal when the railroad came through.

At the city election that spring the voters chose a complete set of new officers, men who had never been connected with the bank or any of the bankrupt firms; and the town settled down to grim retrenchment. And the people came out to the annual school meeting and retired Abbott, whose term on the board expired that year. A new faculty was employed, with drastic salary cuts. Latin and other subjects believed to be purely cultural were eliminated, a commercial department was established, and renewed emphasis was placed on agriculture and domestic arts. Athletics were retrenched, literary and musical events were eliminated, social activities were sharply curtailed; and young Prairie settled down to an unrelieved grind of hard study and good conduct.

But this did not provide for the graduates. The community was full of unattached young people fretting their lives away because society had no use for their strength and industry. Even college graduates came back home to enforced idleness and dependence. "There was something to be said for slavery," said one. "A good strong Negro field hand knew he was worth fifteen hundred dollars. It must have given him quite a feeling of self respect."

These young people even made the sinister discovery that high scholarship and superior skills were disqualifications, that executives were envious and afraid of their attainments. Even those who had prepared themselves to teach found it good practice to conceal college degrees and successful experience. Clearly the copy book maxims were lies.

Men and women at the height of their productive capacity —

employees of the closed business houses, oil workers left behind by "the company" — suffered the same bitterness of unemployment. They held their heads high, trying to conceal their plight, ashamed of their failure to measure up to the standards of the "success" dogma. Had they not always believed that people unable to hold or attain jobs were lazy or inefficient?

As accumulated savings were swept away or gradually consumed, self-respecting people were finally driven to ask for food. Those who were handicapped — by widowhood, illness, old age, even congenital improvidence — were the first. And Prairie always responded. The business men bore more than their share of the burden; the grocers in particular could not withhold food from a neighbor who was hungry. At the same time migrant families came through, working the town shamelessly with an unvarying story of a sick father and a tubercular mother and a haven they were trying to reach, gleaning more cash and canned goods and potatoes than Prairie's self supporting people ever saw in one pile. The people decided to systematize their giving.

At the beginning of 1932 the leading men of the community, farmers, business men, oil workers, met at the garage and formed an organization. They accepted donations, examined the status of applicants, and distributed relief in accordance with actual need. The cash they handled was small — not more than fifty dollars for the remainder of the winter — but it was supplemented by a sharing of food. They also created a clearing house for such meagre employment opportunities as they found. They assisted only people who had lived in the community thirty days — "If word gets around that we take care of our people, they'll all flock here unless we protect ourselves some way." And they notified the county commissioners that they would not participate in any county-wide plan of relief. "We don't want any of our money to go to niggers," they decided. "Let the towns that's got 'em take care of 'em." Thus nobody in the community actually starved. But rehabilitation of the town's economy was as far away as ever.

There was no prospect of relief from agriculture. There was an immense crop of wheat in '31, but the price was 36 cents in harvest, 29 cents by the middle of July. The next year's crop hit a 29-cent market, and the price dropped to 28 cents before the year was over. Cattle went down to $3.70 a hundred in '31; $2.75 in '32. As for the women's products, butterfat at one time reached a low of 11 cents a pound; chickens, six cents a pound; eggs, seven cents a dozen. Nobody could suggest a remedy except to keep on producing; but producing at a loss was more expensive than sitting still.

Most farmers who owned their land were still receiving a little money — usually a dollar an acre — from oil leases; but tenant farmers of course had no such resource. The few with producing wells on their land were still receiving royalties; but their income had dwindled, for production was declining, and the posted price of crude dropped as low as ten cents a barrel. And the large sums that had so recently come to farmers from royalty sales and lease bonuses had been largely swept away as the securities they had purchased had turned out to be worthless.

It was under these conditions that the liquidator attempted to convert the bank's assets into cash. Numerous loans had been made on farms, but now a farm worth $12,000 would hardly sell for enough to clear a $3,000 mortgage. Some of the bank's money had helped to build the new houses, safe investments if one accepted the thesis that the oil development would be permanent; now a house was an actual liability. Part of these debts were compromised for a fraction of their face value; in other cases there were foreclosures and auction sales with the banking department as the only bidder. Combines, tractors, cattle, grain in the bin, growing crops also were sold at public auction at calamitous prices.

When the affairs of the bank were finally wound up at the end of 1934 and the depositors received their last dividend, they found they had salvaged a total of 52½ per cent of their accounts. Even in ruin the Pioneer State Bank had proved itself more stable than anything else in Prairie's financial world. Houses and lots, stocks and bonds, farm land, oil wells, live stock, grain in the bin — the value of all these had plummeted to more disastrous depths. The bank after all had proved the safest custodian of the people's money.

More serious of course than the loss to the depositors was the ruin of the bank's debtors. Even those who had been able to circumvent the bankrupt law by hiding out their property lost the businesses that had filled their lives. And many of the more humble bankrupts were completely stripped. Behind the liquidator's routine sales of farm equipment lay many human tragedies — young men who had made a good start at farming sold out and reduced to day laborers. The real estate foreclosures had deprived others of their farms and houses; even two or three men who had staked their claims in the Runs were uprooted and thrown upon the mercy of society in their declining years.

The retrenched business of the town was still carried on without a local bank. People hid their money in their houses; and when it was necessary to transact banking business, they drove to a village eight miles away. Here a little bank was holding out steadily against the depression, though its deposits went down from $112,-000 at the close of '29 to $33,000 at the close of '32. Then came the spring of '33 and the collapse of everything. Following the example set by neighboring states and Eastern financial circles the governor of Oklahoma issued a proclamation closing all banks for the four days following the first of March.

The attenuated pages of the *News* that week carried only one advertisement — that of Goodwin's Dry Goods and Groceries. The quoted prices were eloquent of the ruinous deflation:

Tomatoes, corn, sauerkraut, green beans, No. 2 cans	3 for 25¢
Catsup, bottle	10¢
Pink salmon, pound tin	10¢
Cornmeal, 5 lb. bag	10¢
Navy beans, 10 lbs.	39¢
Beef roast, 3 lbs.	25¢
Hamburger meat, 2 lbs.	15¢
American cheese, 2 lbs.	25¢

Goodwin had published the advertisement more as a gallant gesture of good will toward the home town newspaper than from any hope of increasing his sales. Nothing was bought that week but the barest necessities. But strangely enough the very magnitude of the catastrophe brought a certain buoyancy of spirit. "We have absolutely hit the bottom," said Prairie. "The only direction we can go from here is up."

The people were looking desperately towards Washington, where a new President was at the helm and a new Congress had convened in extraordinary session. They had voted for Hoover — 336 to 109 was the township vote — in '28; although still holding a little grudge against the former Food Administrator, they had believed him to be "dry" and Smith "wet," there may have been some unexpressed prejudice left over from Klan days against

Smith's religion, and the bounty of oil had brought an expansive sense of well being that expressed itself in Republican votes. Then with the bank failure and the hard times had come a revulsion of sentiment and a hatred of "old Hoover" more personal and savage than Prairie had ever felt before for a political leader. And as the community struggled vainly to extricate itself from a system where the producer had an unsalable surplus, the consumer was starving, and the industrious and the capable were forced to sit with idle hands, it turned to Washington as its only hope. It had tried everything it knew; it was ready for a "New Deal."

XXIV
THE RULES ARE CHANGED

$\mathbf{F}$IRST came the NRA. This was a difficult place for Prairie to begin its recovery; its little business men struggling under crushing burdens could hardly carry the extra load of increased wages and decreased working hours for their employees. But they were willing to believe it would increase the purchasing power of their customers, while the drafting of codes held out the ultimate promise of easing the pressure. Listening over the radio they caught a rare vision of a whole great country united in prosperity through justice to its humblest citizens. They were willing to enlist in the crusade. At the same time the unemployed were waiting with almost desperate hope the day when the law would go into effect.

By the first week in August virtually every business house in town was displaying the Blue Eagle. This meant to employees a minimum wage of twelve dollars a week for not over forty hours of work. By general agreement the stores closed at six except for a nine o'clock closing on Saturdays. More important in immediate results, the oil companies broadened their employment base greatly by cutting down their twelve-hour shifts.

By this time unemployment of able-bodied men in Prairie had virtually disappeared — mainly through wildcatting operations by oil companies in an area twenty miles away. The merchants already saw an encouraging rise in the price of their goods. On the night of August 27 the people listened again to an earnest radio appeal to cast off short-sighted selfishness for the longer good. It was followed by a personal canvass by a committee of Prairie women seeking consumer support for the program through a boycott of "chiselers" who failed to observe NRA standards. Only six persons in town declined to sign, but the farm people were almost a unit in their refusal.

In spite of their temporary alliance with workingmen in the Industrial Legion of the '90's and the Socialist movement of prewar days, Prairie farmers had always been antagonistic toward the demands of labor. To them it was only good business for an employer to work his laborers as many hours for as small a wage as possible. That was the way they paid *their* hired hands. If a man didn't like it, he could quit, couldn't he? As for any obligation to buy from dealers who followed a certain code, didn't everybody have a right to buy where he could get his goods the cheapest? A man that wouldn't do that was a fool. Now in Enid, there was a man who would sell that same article for —

In the last analysis that was the philosophy of Prairie's town people, too. It was only their desperation that had made them willing at first to accept the NRA. Soon every consumer was a potential "chiseler," and every merchant was tempted to cut under his rivals to make a sale. When the Supreme Court declared the law unconstitutional, there were few regrets. It had cut straight across the ruthless individualism that underlay Prairie's economic thinking.

Meanwhile the farmers were working out their own system of relief through the newly created AAA. As applied to Prairie, this policy meant an increase of wheat prices through a systematic reduction of acreage. Farmers subscribing to the program were to be compensated from a processing tax collected at the mills and passed on to the consumers of wheat products.

The theory of crop reduction and Government aid to agriculture was not new. Before the days of the New Deal, Carl Williams, one time editor of the *Oklahoma Farmer-Stockman* and later member of the Federal Farm Board, had openly advocated plowing under every third row of cotton in the South, and Alexander Legg of the same Board had come to Enid to impress on the farmers the need for reducing the acreage of wheat. The struggle for Government intervention had been strongly expressed by all farm organizations, and a number of laws had been passed by Congress to ameliorate agricultural distress. But Prairie farmers, with their attention fixed on oil, had been largely unmoved by the agricultural clamor of the turbulent '20's; to them the AAA brought a revolutionary philosophy.

Before the acreage was actually reduced, the effect on the market was apparent — though a short crop in some parts of the United States may have been a contributing factor. Prairie seemed to come out of a nightmare as the price gradually rose from 29 cents that dark February of '33 to 59 cents at the beginning of harvest, 85 cents the first week in July, and 89 cents on July 15. It was in this hopeful atmosphere that the farmers met to take action on the program.

The county agricultural agent and men from the state agricultural college held many conferences with the farmers during July and August. A local organization, taking in the wheat growers of two townships, was formed at the schoolhouse the evening of August 30. Cars were parked close around the auditorium, and the room was filled with tanned, clear-eyed men, who went to work incisively to adapt the agriculture of the community to the policy of the AAA. Forty farmers signed contracts that night to reduce their acreage. These forty elected a delegate to a county meeting, which would choose a committee to apportion the county quota among the communities; and elected a committee of three to apportion the community quota among individual farms.

Other farmers signed up during succeeding weeks — altogether about 60 per cent of the wheat growers of the community. The quota finally fixed that year by the Government was a 15 per cent reduction — which meant that the entire planting of the two townships was reduced about 9 per cent. Most of the land withdrawn from planting was allowed to lie fallow — a practice that gave the country a ragged, unkempt appearance. The benefit payment — computed on the ratio of total American consumption to export sales — turned out to be 29 cents a bushel, paid on the average production of the unplanted land. Best of all was the effect on the price; the 1934 harvest began with an 80-cent market, which fluctuated between 74 and 91 cents during succeeding weeks.

This crop reduction was a desperate remedy for a desperate situation, but the people never accepted it in principle. It reversed the thinking of ten generations of frontier history, of which Oklahomans more than any other Americans were the spiritual heirs. Opening new land for agriculture had become the most sacred article in their creed. Ruthless exploitation of natural resources, robbing the Indians — all this was tolerated and even glorified in the name of "progress"; but to retire land from cultivation was abhorrent to their deepest convictions. "When you come right down to it, it's not right for a man to be paid for not working," was the general reaction.

Nature seemed to support their judgment. For some years the weather had been working up to a dry cycle, which reached a ter-

rible intensity during 1934–36. In the spring sky and plain were
shut off by curtains of dust, sometimes torn by the wind from
surrounding farms, sometimes brought from distant regions. Cars
drove with lights, visibility was limited to two or three blocks,
people huddled in their houses until the fury was over. In the summer the land lay desolate under blazing sun and fiery wind. Trees
died in great numbers along the creeks, their limbs standing out
gaunt above the tortured vegetation. Day after day through the
summer of '36 the thermometer mounted to 113, 114, even 115
degrees; people exercised their ingenuity to make cooling systems,
but several died from the heat.

Probably the drought was no more severe than that following
the Strip Opening; possibly it was little worse than the one beginning in 1910; but this time Prairie's own impressions were deepened by radio reports and news reel photographs and national concern over "the dust bowl." To a people living so close to nature it
seemed personal and purposeful, not to be explained by isothermal
curves and barometric pressures.

"God Almighty never meant for people to make food scarce,"
said the religious. "He gave us this country so we could produce.
And we grumbled about a 'surplus.' Before this is over, we may
find He's taken 'overproduction' into His own hands."

But in spite of such misgivings, the farmers voted overwhelmingly in the dust-choked spring of '35 to extend the AAA four more
seasons. And when the Supreme Court ruled against the law and
returned the processing tax to the millers early in '36, a way was
found to continue the program in the guise of "soil conservation"
with a Congressional subsidy.

Strangely enough the farmers were fairly prosperous during
the drought. There were enough scattered rains to carry the wheat
through the winters, and the crop was matured before the fierce
summers struck. Even in '36, when most of Oklahoma had a short
yield, Prairie's harvest was fairly good; and the price that year
went up to a dollar a bushel for the first time since '29. Corn, of
course, was out of the question, but a field of corn was now as
much of a curiosity as a horse and buggy. Then came rain — steady,
soaking rain — in the fall of '36, and the worst was over. The native
grass, which even the old-timers had believed to be completely
dead, eventually spread over the pastures; the surviving trees became green and dark once more. The year 1937 was more pros-

perous agriculturally — that is, aside from the farmers' oil incomes — than the boom years before the bank failure. Whatever its results from the standpoint of larger economic policy, the AAA certainly achieved in Prairie its immediate aim of pulling the farmers out of the depression.

Alongside the system of farm relief came the task of providing work for the unemployed. A beginning had been made during the last months of Hoover's administration under the Emergency Relief and Construction Act, which appropriated three hundred million dollars in RFC funds to be distributed to the states upon the call of the governors. The money was made available in the fall of 1932, when the county received a grant of $25,700. It was expended for "made work" on the roads — cutting weeds, shoveling the soil around culverts, any trivial employment. Then came the more extensive work relief program of the Roosevelt era, with the Federal government in charge of the work and paying most of the cost, and the local unit of government selecting the "project" and making a limited financial contribution.

The first project in Prairie got under way, employing twenty-five men, in the fall of '33. Like the "made work" of the previous year it served little purpose except employment. The town officials were only harassed small business men, not long range civic planners. Besides they had already constructed everything they needed or wanted back in the lush days before the depression. But casting about for something they could support they decided it would do no harm to grade the streets; and by avoiding labor saving machinery the job might be stretched out for a considerable period.

The Government agency had been hastily set up to meet a dire emergency. At first all applicants were employed without investigation. Young farmers, in desperate straits from the agricultural depression, came and worked during the slack season; it was some time before their names were removed from the rolls. No provision had been made for the discipline of loafers. Some of the men stood and talked for half an hour at a time between intervals of filling their shovels.

People watching coined a new vocabulary of scornful epithets for relief workers. But there were several facts they overlooked. It was they themselves who were to blame for the failure to draft a significant project. As for the drones, they had always been a charge upon the community, stealing, debauching the young, accepting the charity of the thrifty; public recognition of their status only made the condition more apparent. And some of the men never stopped their steady shoveling. The relief work, moreover, furnished several young men of recent high school classes the first gainful employment they had ever known. There was a veritable epidemic of marriages in the summer of '34, as this forgotten generation, for the first time precariously self supporting, began to form the normal human ties of hearth and home.

Four or five of these unwanted young men managed to qualify for enrollment in CCC camps. They were selected on the basis of family needs — widowed mother, invalid (or shiftless) father — and they were required to send most of their pay home. Prairie's general impression was that these camps were efficiently conducted, and that the boys returned home benefited by the training. Early in 1934 the Government began allocating funds to assist students through college by part time work, but none of Prairie's young people obtained an appointment. They would have been disillusioned if they had known that the small state college to which they applied selected its applicants on the basis of athletic qualifications, thus diverting the money to subsidize its football and basketball teams. Later the NYA was created, and a portion of the money was allocated to assist students through high school. This served no useful purpose in Prairie, where any boy or girl could defray high school expenses by mowing lawns, delivering papers, or taking care of babies. The policy merely confirmed the children of chronic relief clients in the habit of dependency, and the teachers to whom they were assigned were too busy to direct them in productive work.

In the fall of 1934 relief work was provided for the women through a sewing room sponsored by the county government. About ten women — young business women thrown out of work through the failure of Prairie firms, widows with children, elderly housewives — all worked together with one of their own number serving without additional pay as supervisor. Deft and efficient, co-operative and helpful, they worked with an enthusiasm learned in church sewing societies, and they turned out an imposing number of garments and warm comforts, which were distributed by the county to destitute families. Apparently most of these articles were wasted by recipients too shiftless to sew and patch for themselves; but the women who made them at least had the feeling that their labor was productive. The sewing room was discontinued in the spring because most of its workers had found re-employment opportunities.

A few other projects were sponsored by the town. Two provided necessary extensions to the water system, always a problem in time of drought. But in general Prairie was not a WPA town. Its people had learned economy too recently in too hard a school. They resisted the temptation to spend $989 and accept $66,788 for the construction of a lake that would have been a pleasant resort, and they rejected a proposal to build a stone and cement athletic stadium.

After the first winter the Federal administration was tightened to eliminate spurious applicants and to improve the quality of the work. This required a considerable hierarchy of non-relief personnel. Some of these supervisors were political appointees, though they were forbidden — and this rule was drastically enforced — to engage in political activity during their employment; many others, especially in positions requiring technical skills, were chosen solely on the basis of their qualifications. As a group they were honest and hard working, though too much of their time and energy was wasted in struggling against encircling meshes of red tape. The whole policy of the organization was enlightened and humane, calculated to give the humblest employee a sense of the importance of his work. All this was good in building up the morale of the workers, but it did tend to create a class of "career men" satisfied to remain permanently in the WPA.

In Prairie the need for work relief was not so apparent after the first two winters. All of the younger men were eventually absorbed by private industry. Others — some of them, men in the prime of life — removed to the county seat, frankly seeking larger relief opportunities. A few chronic WPA workers — virtual unemployables because of age or personal handicaps — hung on precariously, tightening their belts between projects. But a larger number than Prairie ever knew of its young and capable would have been unemployed except for the non-relief opportunities of the WPA and other Government agencies. And unemployed people who never accepted relief, felt their courage stiffened by the knowledge that in the last desperate extremity this recourse was available.

All in all, work relief in Prairie was a palliative for a grave economic ill. Its effectiveness could have been increased by more intelligent planning on the part of the local people, and less red tape and consequently fewer supervisors — but never less super-vision — on the part of the Federal agency. The tendency toward self perpetuation should have been cut back ruthlessly, and the value of the whole program would have been improved by curtail-ment.

Direct relief, even more than work relief, was administered on a scale so lavish as to defeat its purpose. Nothing could have been sounder than the theory back of the Federal program. The Govern-ment would buy surplus farm commodities at the cost of produc-tion and distribute them to the hungry and unclothed; this would end the anti-social practice of retiring land from cultivation, and it would break up the vicious circle of farmers producing at a loss because they had no market, and consumers starving because they could not buy. The supplies were given out, apparently with little investigation, to anybody who would ask for them. There were various methods of distribution: from trucks making monthly trips to Prairie, from the sewing room, from a warehouse at the county seat, and finally from the grocery stores by the use of food stamps. At the same time an extensive system of relief was carried on by the state and the counties through 1935–39.

The first trucks came to Prairie in 1934 to deliver meat pur-chased by the FERA. They were met by a greedy rabble, snatch-ing, scrambling over their portions. The community had always regarded its improvident citizens with easy tolerance; now seeing them together was enough to discredit the whole system of relief. "Look at that bunch of varmints; and they tax us to feed 'em." But on the edge of the unsavory crowd stood one whose presence twisted his neighbors' hearts — old Joe Spragg, long a leader of the town, reduced in his old age to this extremity.

There were more than one hundred old people in the com-munity, as the young settlers of '89 and the '90's reached their declining years at the same time; and many of these were in a state of pitiable destitution. Some were proud and thrifty couples who had provided adequately for their old age, only to see their investments swept away in the general debacle. More belonged to that restless class that had disposed of their farms in the early years, experimented with various forms of livelihood, and ended up penniless. A few had been completely shiftless. Whatever the cause of their indigence, the community for the first time had reached a maturity when the care of its aged dependents was a serious obligation.

The actual human problem was complicated by the naive cupidity of the Townsendites. Their grotesque plan to stimulate business by giving every elderly person two hundred dollars a month in spending money, swept the community with emotional fervor during 1936. It appealed to the gambling instincts of a people that had experienced the chances of the Runs, the excitement of townsite promotion, and the unpredictable luck of oil. Old people settling down for the first time in their restless lives to a prospect of no more glittering dreams were stimulated by this promise of a last fling. Younger people looked forward to future affluence. They advised the thrifty to spend their money as it came — "Might as well enjoy it now; the Townsend Plan'll take care of you when you're old." Such innocents were clay in the hands of demagogues. Some politicians campaigned actively on the Townsend platform; others skirted the edge in an attempt to win all classes; none dared openly to condemn it.

An initiative petition in harmony with the Federal Social Security Act was approved by Prairie — and Oklahoma — in the summer of '36. It provided for a maximum payment of thirty dollars a month — later raised to forty dollars — to the aged and to the dependent blind, and eighteen dollars for one child, twelve each for additional children, for the support of dependent children. Half the cost was to be borne by the Federal Government, half by the state.

After the passage of this law few of the old people claimed the privilege of sharing in the distribution of surplus commodities. Then in the spring of 1942 the food stamp plan tested earlier in other parts of the state was extended to the Prairie community. Every month the grocers received a circular listing the goods defined by the Government as "surplus"; and persons of low income were entitled to purchase orange stamps and receive free additional blue ones good for the purchase of these commodities at the stores. In Prairie, though many others were eligible, only recipients of old age assistance — and only about two-thirds of that group — applied for and received these stamps.

By this time except for cereals, which were always on the list, the existence of "surplus" commodities was a bureaucratic fiction.

One typical month during the winter of 1942–43 commodities listed as "surplus" sold in the Prairie stores at the following scarcity prices:

Irish potatoes	10 lbs. for 49¢
Sweet potatoes	4 lbs. for 25¢
Dry beans	3 lbs. for 25¢
Apples, each	10¢
Lettuce, small head	10¢

The system was not abandoned until the spring of 1943. Thus continued after the "surplus" had disappeared, it raised the price of the commodities for low income groups that did not accept relief. But it did enable the old people to stretch their grocery purchases without the slightest sense of degradation. The stamps were sent by mail, and only the grocers knew who the recipients were.

There are now (1943) thirty-one persons in the Prairie community receiving old age assistance. This constitutes about 2½ per cent of the population. (The average for the state as a whole, including cotton areas, hills and timber, and city slums, is 3.3 per cent.) The status of each applicant is investigated as carefully as is humanly possible by a case worker, and the payments are apportioned according to varying needs. The average is about $22.25 a month for each person. Two widowed mothers with dependent children are also receiving limited assistance.

In spite of careful investigation several undeserving names are on the rolls. Some old people, otherwise religious and honest, have refused to face the fact that by claiming assistance when it is not needed, they are taking actual food from the mouths of the destitute; and prosperous sons and daughters, formerly willing to provide for their parents, abandoned the obligation as soon as they could shift it to the public. Most of this has been due to the influence of Townsendism, which created the belief that universal pensions could be given without cost to anybody.

The old people live comfortably, if frugally, on their meagre allowances. Most of them have additional resources such as home ownership, gardens, gifts from sons and daughters, prolonged visits to relatives. They carry on their small affairs in pride and self respect, untroubled by any humiliating sense of dependence. There is no doubt that they are more fortunate than a previous generation, too often cast upon the grudging bounty of undutiful children.

Oklahoma's share of the cost is paid by a sales' tax of 2 per cent. This is of course an inequitable form of taxation, since it bears disproportionately upon the food and clothing of the poor, but it has a psychological value in bringing the cost of old age assistance home to a people still relying too much on Townsend magic. Many still feel aggrieved that the money does not appear miraculously and painlessly. Most of all, they resent the modest salaries paid to the overworked case workers, and the whole idea of investigating the status of applicants — "I think every old person should have a pension. Then we wouldn't need all these people prying into their business. Just mail every one a check every month." Thus Prairie, taught by Townsendism, continues to fly in the face of arithmetic.

Prairie tried another magic mathematical formula in the licensing of beer. The "Beer for Oklahoma League" ran "fillers" in the *News* before the people voted on the measure in the summer of '33. The arguments were very practical and statistical. In territorial days eight main Oklahoma counties had drunk 147,600 barrels of beer annually, with the saloons open only six days a week. That was 22 gallons per capita. Now in a seven-day week at drug stores, grocery stores, filling stations, and restaurants they would drink at least 44 gallons. Multiplying the population of Oklahoma by 44, with the tax of $2.50 a barrel, that would bring ten and a quarter million dollars in revenue to the state, besides the local license fees. But Prairie always needed a crusading motive; and other "fillers" carried impassioned speeches by a Missouri politician showing how the measure would prevent lawlessness, promote temperance, and advance Christianity. The "drys" were unorganized and impotent; all the publicity was in the hands of their opponents. The township voted for beer (and prosperity and Christianity) 151 to 84, and the first truck was unloaded in town the next day. The law limited it to an alcoholic content of 3.2 per cent.

The results were somewhat disappointing. At first Prairie did not like the new beverage, having been educated by prohibition to total abstinence or the hard liquor furnished by bootleggers; it gradually increased its consumption, but fell far short of its 44-gallon quota. The Brewing Industry Foundation itself claims a mere million dollars in state taxes and local licenses. As for the cause of temperance, nobody could notice any difference. Bootlegging continued on about the same scale as before the abnormal increase of the oil years. The method changed with the national repeal of the

Eighteenth Amendment; stills vanished from the creeks and vacant buildings, and rum runners brought in cargoes manufactured
legally in Missouri and Arkansas. In the summer of '36 the people
voted on a measure to repeal the prohibition article in the state
constitution. An attempt was made to join it, as the source of revenue, with the pending measure for old age assistance; but Prairie
— and Oklahoma — rejected repeal and voted the sales' tax.

Probably the soundest of all the "recovery" measures instituted
in Prairie was the establishment of a bank. In June of '34 the village bank to which the people had driven for three and one-half
years to conduct their business, was moved to the town in compliance with a recommendation of the State Banking Department
and the Federal Deposit Insurance Corporation. The community
was happier than it had been since the discovery of oil. The directors of the new institution were Enid capitalists; its policy was
impersonal, correct, conservative, very different from the old days
when a good customer's overdraft was paid without question, and
the bank rendered as many kinds of free service as a filling station.
But it was a great convenience. Its deposits were guaranteed by
the Federal Government under a law passed by that historic extra
session of Congress that created NRA and farm relief and work
relief. It had $162,000 on deposit at the close of the first harvest
after it was moved to Prairie, $356,000 after the harvest of '37.
These figures, however, are not comparable with those of pre-
depression days, for Prairie now had the only bank within a radius
of fifteen miles.

But the town did not revive with the bank and agricultural
recovery. Its debts were fixed and constant, while its property
values dropped to abysmal depths. In the struggle its real estate
titles fell into inextricable confusion.

A number of people lost their homes through mortgages to the
bank or private individuals. Half a dozen, about to be foreclosed,
were saved temporarily by the Home Owners' Loan Corporation,
created by that same productive Congress of '33. But Prairie real
estate values were now so ruinously deflated that the houses were
worth far less than the mortgage. The owners accordingly de-
faulted on their payments, and the HOLC itself was forced to foreclose. Then during 1939–40 the houses were sold to new home-
owners at an average of 62 per cent of the original note. The former
owners thus lost their entire equity, and the Government lost 38

per cent of its investment; but this property was at last on a stable basis, in the hands of people who made regular payments and continued to reduce their debt.

A far more serious condition arose through tax delinquency. After the early '30's most people managed to clear their residences, especially if they were off the paving; but nearly all the property on the paving — including almost the entire business area — remained delinquent, as did vacant lots and scattered buildings here and there throughout the town. Attempts to make compromise settlements with the bondholders all failed, and the debt ran on.

Finally in 1939 the county officials began to "run the town through the wringer." The delinquent property was offered for sale, subject to the accrued taxes and penalties. Nobody considered it worth redeeming; the county obtained title to the whole, and, as the landlord, collected rents from the former owners or their lessees. Then the property, now free of the county's tax lien, was again offered for sale. The people acted for each other, usually making a bid of fifty dollars, whether for a small residence or the largest brick building on Main Street. It was then a routine matter to deed it back to the original owner. In a few cases outside buyers appeared, and the owner lost his property or was forced to purchase it from the successful bidder.

All these transactions were carried on in an atmosphere of demoralizing uncertainty. It had not been good for sober citizens to use their property eight years with the sense that it was forfeit to the state. It was not good to gamble against the chances of the sale. And it was still not good to guess the status of their recovered possessions. The guessing was soon resolved into depressing certainty. The owner of the paving bonds challenged the right of the county to wipe his lien off the books, and he won his contention in the courts. The sword of Damocles thus hangs over every piece of property on the paving — except some half dozen lots that have been paid out. Families live in their houses and care for the shrubs in their yards, men carry on their business in buildings they erected and do not own, some even risk a few dollars to purchase a tenuous title to a house or a lot they need; but back of it all is the knowledge that today or tomorrow the blow may fall. And all business initiative is paralyzed by this unsettling fact.

XXV

THE DOLDRUMS

EPRESSION and "recovery" were all the same so far as Prairie's business was concerned; every year brought a further decline. New Chevrolets and Fords — sleek, perfect machines — reeled off the miles so smoothly that the town became little more than a way station on the road to the cities. The merchants carried only articles of daily need. Nearly every business man filled his empty time and his depleted income by two or three activities: one ran a store by day and the picture theatre at night; another drove a school bus, ran a produce house, and repaired shoes and radios; a third worked in the bank and sold combines outside banking hours. Trucks brought city goods and services to every door. The railroad, once the lifeline of the community, maintained a limited service only because it connected two main lines.

The editor of the town paper gave up his struggle to fill the gap between expensive equipment and restricted advertising. He was succeeded by an absentee owner who tried to manage a chain of small newspapers, entrusting the local work to a young, under-paid assistant. Thus the *News* tottered on a few more years, illiterate in expression, vacuous in content. Finally it suspended publication. There was general regret when its feeble life ended; and the voice of Prairie, once so strong and confident, was completely stilled.

The contracted firms huddled together in the middle block of Main Street; good brick buildings — the pride of the community in the growing years of 1909–14 or the sanguine days of oil — stood unoccupied, falling down through neglect. The town became a sea of weeds, every year engulfing more of the scattered islands of habitation. The census of 1940 showed a population of 382 — the smallest since 1907.

More than half of this reduced population was directly connected with agriculture. There were retired elderly couples and

elderly widows living off the rental of their land, "gentlemen farmers" driving out to their work, business men operating a farm as a
side line with hired labor and their own spare time.

Typical of this agricultural supremacy is the towering concrete
column of the Farmers' Elevator, built in time for the 1939 harvest
with money borrowed from the Federal Bank for Co-operatives,
and paid out in full at the end of 1941. Rising far above the town,
visible for many miles across the level farmland, it stands as a
symbol of the dominance of wheat. From its top can be seen the
massed bins, row on row, of the huge terminal elevators at Enid,
the center of the great network of co-operatives to which it belongs. Its management is a marvel of smooth-running efficiency,
and the volume of business it handles dwarfs by comparison all
other business of the town. Characteristically a number of the
"producers of farm products" who are the stockholders — even
some of the officers and directors — live within the town.

This direct participation of the town-dwellers in agriculture
is based on a land tenure reflecting the maturity of the community.
Less than one-fourth of the land is now (1943) in the hands of
farmers who acquired it in their own name and are still active.
About one-third is owned by retired elderly people or is held in
undivided estates by the heirs of deceased farmers; another one-
third has passed to the second generation of owners. A few farms
are owned by absentees, men who have never lived at Prairie, and
hold the land simply as an investment. The tendency to gather the
land into large holdings, so apparent in the first years of the century, has been largely reversed by this process of death and division. Only Merritt Brown still owns twelve quarters, and even his
land monopoly has been modified somewhat by the agricultural
needs of his sons.

About half the land in the community is cultivated by tenants,
but the majority of these are relatives — sons, sons-in-law, or grandsons — of the owner. Through all the decade of the Thirties an increasing number of young people found their economic opportunity through the death or retirement of the older generation of
farmers. At the same time the sons of landless families were largely
shut out. There are a few middle aged tenants — young men who
began before the First World War, and have become extensive
farmers without acquiring enough capital to purchase the land
they use.

Most of the active farmers who live on the land cultivate a half section or more; but the average agricultural unit, counting in the part time farmers, is 223 acres. The farm population of the two townships in 1940 was 674, a loss of 10 per cent for the decade. Altogether the community has only a little more than half the rural population it had in 1900, when the first census was taken after the Strip Opening. Old settlers driving along the familiar roads grieve over a vacant house falling into dilapidation, a hedge of tamarisks along the highway, a clump of lilacs in a wheat field, where the plow has obliterated all other traces of the family life that once grew so riotously on every quarter section. But they forget that the greatest loss in population came in the years following the turn of the century; and that the people who left the farms at that time were not forced out by poverty but tempted by affluence. The decade of the Thirties showed the smallest decline of all; and only in these last years is agriculture settling into a stability of tenure.

Most of the pioneers who resisted the rising land prices of the early 1900's continued to hold their farms; hence about 20 per cent of the land is still in the hands of the original homesteaders or their families. A few of these elderly people — especially in the Strip, for the four years' difference in settlement counts in the declining strength of the aged — still live on the farms they brought under cultivation. Whether active or retired, they love every foot of the soil with a brooding tenderness that no future American genera- tion will ever know — "Right here is where we camped the first night, and here — you can see the marks — is where we made our dug-out; we broke our first sod right over there; and this place has been our home ever since." Sharing their feelings is another generation of pioneers, people in the prime of life who were pres- ent as children at the great Runs and who have a lively recollection of all the experiences of settlement.

The past decade has seen a further decline of the local institu- tions that functioned so actively in those early days. The township government was abolished; the poll tax and the local road work were discontinued in favor of county and state maintenance. One rural school district after another voted to transfer its pupils to Prairie, not by consolidation, but more thriftily by paying only the per capita cost of their schooling. The total school area now comprises 130 square miles, a compact block of territory touching on every side similar areas centering in surrounding towns. Only one or two rural schools in the hill country to the east still stand out as the last strongholds of localism.

This extension of territory brought a new element into the school population, young second-generation Bohemians and Moravians whose parents had been settling for many years as large scale wheat farmers in the area west of town. A young Jezek grandson was the first to graduate, in 1934; by the end of the decade the Svobodas, the Kubiceks, the Walentas, and the Najvars were crowding the rolls. Strong, vital young people, eager for educational opportunities, they are respected by their classmates, but not yet entirely assimilated; and they have a rich social life of their own, centering about weddings and family celebrations, and dancing, music, and lectures in a huge barn-like "Bohemian Hall" standing on a hill in the midst of their settlement. But through the influence of the school their parents have come increasingly to town, where they stand talking in animated groups, filling the air with swishing consonants new to Prairie ears.

The people of all this expanded territory are united by the activities of the school. After six years of too much study — which hurt the parents far more than the children — it broke out again in athletics and entertainments and driving here and there. The current band craze struck in '37. The community could hardly contain its pride at the sight of its children twirling and prancing, turning and wheeling in complex evolutions down the wide pavement of Main Street. And as the light of civilization went out in Europe and horror piled on horror in Asia, they seemed so safe marching there in the sunlight while the town watched in affection and nobody in their whole world would do them harm. But there was time left over for study; the high school graduates of this period are the most literate the school has ever had.

The Prairie churches also draw their congregations from this same enlarged area. The Catholic church has been strengthened by the sturdy Christianity of the Czechs. The Protestant churches have shed their historic differences — the German language of the Evangelical congregation, the catch-words and arguments of the Christians, the revivalism of the Methodists — in favor of a modern religious concept growing out of Prairie experience. Only the Baptists hold to the "old time religion," conservative as ever, but neighborly as ever to sister churches. All the churches are served by able ministers, most of whom come only on Sunday from neighboring cities. Prairie listens irregularly to their sermons, its religion more a matter of courteous assent than vital conviction.

The community never lost its spontaneous friendliness — the close ties binding old settlers, the instant welcome to newcomers. There were few newcomers now, as oil activity declined and finally ceased entirely. Those few were scarcely strangers. The half century through which the whole fluid population of Oklahoma and the Southwest had swirled here and there in restless eddies, merging, separating, merging again, furnished a common basis of acquaintance.

Main Street was always full of parked cars as farmers drove in to buy a Sunday newspaper or attend the picture show or stand on the street to talk. One amusement and then another — golf, bridge, soft ball — ran its ephemeral course and then declined. There was usually a civic club — the name varied from time to time — with farmer and town members and regular nights of meeting to plan community activities. A group of women started a library. Living was unhurried and pleasant. But the town for the first time was living in the present rather than the future, and its hopeful spirit had given place to a mild feeling of futility.

Some of this dissatisfaction was expressed in the political campaign of 1936. The Republicans raised the bogy of "communism," and succeeded probably better than they had intended; for they frightened themselves and drove the whole community into a phobia of red. They appealed to the past, to the old days of untrammeled opportunity in taking to themselves the resources of a virgin land. But all except the older, the settled, the untouched people knew that those days were dead; the frontier was closed, its expanding values were gone forever; a way must be found to live with what they had. The New Deal had brought no solution; but it had brought amelioration. The people voted without enthusiasm for Roosevelt.

Followed more years of easy living, but of disillusionment with a "recovery" that always seemed artificial, of disgust with the shiftlessness of relief clients, of vexation over the ubiquity of Government activity. Matters came to a head in the wheat reduction program for the crop year of 1941.

The AAA still kept up the benefit payments; and its policy had been stiffened by a system of penalties levied upon acreage planted in excess of the quota. But a large proportion of the Prairie farmers ignored the limitation, trusting to the reduction of others to keep up the price, and to their own profits to absorb the penalty. In the spring of 1940 this penalty was raised from fifteen cents to a figure that worked out as forty-nine cents a bushel, computed on the normal yield of the excess acreage. Word of the change came just at the time that the county agent was assisting the farmers in their annual meetings to formulate their planting policy. He explained the new regulation, but many overlooked its significance and continued as usual to plant all their land to wheat.

Then came the harvest of 1941, and the penalty. The farmers were more angry than they had been since the decline of prices in 1930–32; and they worked up a hatred of Roosevelt as personal and bitter as they had felt for the much-maligned Hoover in depression years. The daily newspapers joined in the outcry, and carried stories — mainly apocryphal — of an actual yield so low on the allotted acreage at the current price of ninety-eight cents that the whole would not pay the penalty of forty-nine cents on the normal yield of the excess acreage. They brought pressure on Congress, and finally succeeded in having the penalty computed on the actual yield if it was lower than the normal.

From that time on, Prairie farmers observed the quota. The wheat acreage, still apportioned by a community committee, was cut more drastically, running from 33⅓ to 50 per cent in acreage reduction. Even so, the country was so full of wheat that in the lush harvest of 1942 the huge bins of the Farmers' Elevator and the smaller elevators were filled to capacity, and many thousand bushels were stored in vacant brick buildings along Main Street. The price that year averaged about one dollar a bushel, and the farmers received a payment of 13½ cents to bring it up to "parity," or the purchasing power of a bushel of wheat during the favorable years of 1910–14, and a soil conservation payment of 9.9 cents, both benefits being computed on the normal yield of the allotted acreage.

The farmers used the land withdrawn from wheat planting for the production of feed. Many planted alfalfa, which proved to be very profitable during the wet years that closed the decade. Others experimented with millet, and a small acreage was planted to legumes for soil building. A few returned to the early day practice of planting sorghums. But the bulk of the acreage was planted to oats and barley; those crops were more adapted to the familiar techniques of wheat farming, and required the same machinery except that they were cut with binders instead of combines.

With this feed on hand, farmers were almost forced to raise live stock. The number of cattle and sheep increased greatly, and hog raising became important for the first time in many years. Even chickens were numerous — in this case, not through pressure of AAA, but from the convenience of the Prairie hatchery.

But the farmers felt that wheat was potentially their most profitable crop. "The Government won't let us raise wheat," was their deepest grievance. Every spring an election by secret ballot was held at the Farmers' Elevator as to the continuance of the reduction program. It always carried the United States because of the support of wheat growers in other sections, but the Prairie farmers voted against it. As to how an artificial price structure could be maintained on a full acreage, they did not attempt to explain. Probably they would have been more nearly satisfied if all controls had been removed, and they had been driven to reduction by general economic laws.

There was of course the possibility of a good price for a full acreage through world recovery. But Prairie's people were fiercely isolationist. Newspaper correspondents reported the hideous travesty of social coherence that had engulfed the civilization of Germany. "Propaganda," they said, determined not to be fooled again. But they did receive propaganda. As early as 1934 circulars were coming to them through the mail — they never knew the origin — pointing out with convincing mildness the need of Hitlerism to deliver the world from Jewish dominance. And they were influenced to a certain extent by these arguments. When one free people after another fell before the might of military conquest, they temporized — "There hadn't ought to be any little, weak countries. They're always starting wars."

They heard over the radio of the Marco Polo bridge incident of July 7, 1937, which launched Japan's attack at the heart of China. Before the end of the month the Farmers' Elevator was advertising for "all your old tractors, steam engines, and heavy machinery." Boys scoured the alleys for scrap iron; shiftless citizens helped themselves to stoves — discarded or good — from their neighbors' outbuildings; others combed the town dump. The piled flat cars that left the station meant a windfall for the farmers, spending money for the boys, gleanings for a low income group.

Only a few religious women, trained in missionary tradition, protested against the traffic; and not a single one of these was willing to face the implications of a break with Japan.

The *Panay* incident occurred on December 12 of that same year. That week the young editor of a hectographed sheet published by the high school expressed his reaction under the heading, "NEUTRALITY WE HOPE":

"Can we blame Japan for bombing our ships? Has the United States any right to carry on trade with China, and expect Japan to respect our neutrality? Our four years in high school have been shadowed by foreign war. What does the future offer to those who will graduate this year? Possibly long suffering and separation from our loved ones instead of a chance to lead normal, happy lives. If we are to be brought up with war, let us be its worst enemy. We may be traitors and cowards if we dodge the call, but it is better to be a live coward than a dead hero."

And older people also were in favor of appeasement — "China might as well pass off the map. She can't govern herself anyhow." And as the cataclysm engulfed more and more of Europe, they became more belligerently pacifist. "That Roosevelt is just scheming to get us in. Germany's goin' to win anyhow; if he'd 'a' let things alone, it would've been over by this time." One measure of defense they were willing to accept — the policy of universal military training. "It will do the boys good. They might as well go and serve their year and get it over." But the war itself they dismissed with annoyance as something concocted by "them foreign countries" or "that Roosevelt" to disturb their ease.

XXVI

PEARL HARBOR

It was a typical fall day — that Sunday, the Seventh of December — warm and golden, too warm in fact for comfort. Gadabout Prairie had taken as usual to the open road, to visit a relative in Tulsa, to attend a picture show in Enid, to join a family celebration in Oklahoma City. But enough people remained at home to fill the school auditorium for the funeral of Old Man Hadley.

Prairie liked this community meeting place for its funerals; it was the only room large enough to hold the congregation. It was not too sad an occasion; rather a neighborhood gathering, where old friends, long separated, came from a distance to drop a tear or two for the dead and exchange gay greetings with the living. There was spiritual uplift in their tribute to the sturdy citizen of rash speech and warm heart, whose life had spanned the whole history of the community. There was a drawing together in love for the wild land they had settled, in pride for the institutions they had planted there. And even then, far beyond the level horizon, their outer defenses lay in ruins, where an enemy had struck against their peace.

In one of the houses a woman, who for some reason had not attended the funeral, was listening to the radio. Suddenly the program was switched off, and a voice came clear, unhurried, matter-of-fact, pronouncing incredible words — ". . . that the Japanese have attacked the island of Oahu . . . Hawaii . . . Honolulu . . . Pearl Harbor." And — an error, as it happened — "Manila . . . the Philippines."

The program was resumed. Her hands were shaking as she turned the dial. She went out on the sidewalk. The town lay safe and peaceful in the clear sunlight. As the crowd debouched from the auditorium, she walked rapidly down the street passing the word along. The people stared at her without speaking; it was not until they reached home and turned on their own radios — now a jumble of excited comments — that they understood and believed. And as the homing travelers returned, each with his own experience of a word passed at a filling station, a buzz on some distant little-town Main Street, a radio turned on in the car, they too fell upon their radios and felt realization.

The first reaction was surprisingly uniform — "Those dirty little Jap skunks at Washington!" For Prairie *had* been watching events in the Pacific with more tensity than it had been willing to admit. The isolationism and the pacifism had been an escape mechanism; underneath all along it had known the facts it would not face. Now these facts were dominant.

At the same instant came personal realization of the community's scattered sons in training camps or on duty in the far reaches of the Pacific; even of the boys growing into happy youth at home. It was this thought that kept the town awake that night. In a good many homes the radio was left on all night. A few families did not go to bed at all. One woman, a widow whose son was believed to be in the Philippines, spent her dark vigil making cookies, finding steadiness in the familiar household task.

Every person in the community listened when the President addressed Congress the next morning. A radio was fitted up in every room in the school, and when the chaplain's prayer came in even the littlest children bowed their heads, vaguely moved by a solemn sense of destiny. Prairie was in the war, man, woman, and child.

The tension lasted about three days; then the community settled down to its task. The passing months have revealed the dimensions of this task, and Prairie's strength and weakness in carrying it through. There is a striking difference in the reaction to this and a similar situation in 1917–18; for the pioneer generation that met every previous crisis in the community's history has passed into the background, and a new generation, the product of more complex forces, is at the helm.

There is an almost complete absence of demonstration. Nobody observing the cheerful crowd at public gatherings would suspect that its strongest ties had been wrenched by the hand of war. And Prairie has not been spared its tragedy. Two home-town boys were on Bataan . . . at Corregidor . . . in a Japanese prison . . . one finally reported dead, the other — one hopes — still living. Others have been in peril on Guadalcanal, on Atlantic

convoy, on Pacific submarine, in Tunisia, Sicily, Italy . . . But
even their parents show no outward grief; only rarely a close friend
stumbles upon some secret depth.

There is a strange absence of hate. Part of this is Christian —
"They've been taught wrong. We're partly to blame; we could've
sent more missionaries. And we're not perfect ourselves; we've got
some black spots on our own history. Besides, there are some good
people there — Kagawa, Niemüller, no doubt thousands of others."
More of it is the product of a civilized consciousness — education,
imagination, intelligence. When enemy cities are bombed — "It
seems awful, though." If there is talk of reprisals — "This is getting
to be a *mean* war; I was hoping we could avoid such things." When
there are public attempts to stir up blood lust, "I was sorry to hear
that broadcast last night. We have had enough of hating." If it is
necessary, as some experts assert, to hate the enemy, Prairie falls
completely short.

There is entire freedom from intolerance, from attempts to enforce conformity. There is no hysteria, no "traitor" baiting, no spy
hunting, no fear. Red Cross drives, stamp sales, bond drives, rub-
ber drives, scrap drives — all are conducted on a voluntary basis.
The immediate results are far less imposing than the community
totals in the emotion-charged, slacker-hating atmosphere of the
First World War: for example, a Red Cross quota of $2,200 and a
subscription of $3,003 in the spring of '17, a quota of $600 and a
subscription of $500 in the spring of '43; a subscription of $40,000
to the Fourth War Loan in the fall of '18, of $12,840 to the Third
War Loan in the fall of '43, although at the last date through inflated live stock prices and the shortage of consumer goods deposits in the bank had piled up to $400,000. But perhaps this more
rational method will prove more profitable in permanent values,
will preserve the sanity that may be sorely needed in post-war
years. The American spirit can hardly risk a resurgence of the mass
emotionalism that produced the Klan.

This time Prairie has no open or covert enemy sympathizer, no
radical opponent of the war. There are in fact no radicals; the opposition party is composed of conservative Democrats and even
more conservative Republicans. As for the people of German de-
scent, they are indistinguishable from their fellow Americans.

The Czechs do have a secret reaction, of which Prairie catches
only obscure glimpses. There was the time in the fall of '38 when a

high school class was discussing the dismemberment of Czecho-Slovakia. Suddenly fourteen-year-old Ludvik Kubicek spoke out in his husky but careful English — "My grandmother keeps a picture of Hitler in her bedroom, and she scratches his eyes with pins." And after the Nazi hordes surged into the doomed republic the following spring, there was the story of Frank Babek's nephew in the Old Country, who managed somehow to steal a plane and fly to France, only to disappear a year later when France fell; and there were hints of gatherings in the Bohemian Hall to meet the brother of President Beneš. But if the Americanism of Prairie's Czechs is reinforced by hidden loyalties, that is so much gain.

Thus Prairie unites to support the war. And again as in 1917–18 there is the strong community affection for its sons in service. Always there is a group in front of the drug store window, where the photographs of smiling boys in uniform are crowded together without regard to official rank or community standing. A special outgrowth of this spirit is the Lions' *Service News.*

During this war the community has been able to keep its good school superintendent, who is friend and father confessor to all his former graduates. When his boys entered the service, it was as natural to write to him as to their parents. He answered every one faithfully, tapping out the letters on his own typewriter. But the task was reaching proportions beyond his time and strength. A friend suggested a regular mimeographed message to every man from the community, and the Lions' Club agreed to raise money for the postage. The commercial teacher and her class took over the mechanical work, leaving the superintendent the correspondence and the actual writing. The druggist furnished the addresses. The result is a three- to six-page letter issued regularly every two weeks. The first number, August 3, 1942, was sent to 124 Prairie men; the anniversary number a year later went to 237 men — and women.

The recipients vary in rank from Colonel Claude Abbott, who has remained in the army since the First World War, down to the newest private. Along with the sons and daughters of present residents are those whose parents have moved away, but all have lived in the community long enough to be interested in its message. And it goes to remote islands, to battle fronts, to tropical jungles, to regions locked in ice and snow; it is known that at least one number reached the lonely boy counting the dreary days in a Japanese prison. It carries home town news — football, the band, the wheat harvest — but mainly it is a clearing house for the service men's (and women's) messages to each other and to the community.

Their letters show a pattern surprisingly uniform. Prairie's boys are bored by drills and marching, though it is apparent that their physical condition is superb. They are happy in technical training — radio, Diesel engines, flying, airplane mechanics, even gunnery. Most of all, they are enraptured by the planes — "I'm just a grease monkey, learning to be a specialist on the heavy bombers, and boy they are as sweet as any guy's home town girl," "We have a new type of plane here, and are they honeys," "It gives me a thrill to think I'll be a radio operator on one of these big babies." They work ardently for promotion, and the great increase of commissioned officers over the number in the First World War is eloquent of Prairie's educational progress in twenty-four years.

They show more reserve than their predecessors in speaking of patriotic ideals. Under stress of battle they write briefly, tersely, but with unashamed religious faith — "A couple of times I thought it was my number He was calling, but it all comes in a day's work." Above all is their appreciation for the little paper, and an overmastering love for the little town — "I've seen lots of country, but I wouldn't trade Prairie for all of it," "We're doing our best to finish the job, for the quicker we get it done, the quicker we'll be back home." They are fighting not for abstractions, but specifically and concretely for their community; as one wrote from the Pacific, "If all the other boys from Prairie let the paper affect them as it does me, then it's a bad day for the Japs. We know that Our People are behind us to the limit, and that's what counts."

And in this enterprise the people *are* behind them to the limit; they support the paper with a unanimity not shown since the first years of pioneering. And at least among the more serious minded there is a clearly defined purpose of making the community worthy of its defenders.

This new seriousness is most apparent in the high school. While Prairie reads of juvenile delinquency of appalling proportions in some parts of the country, it has the steadiest young generation in its history. Paradoxically the injustice that has thrust upon their immature shoulders the burden of a bungled society has brought them a happy sense of creative opportunity.

Some of this new-found independence expresses itself in early marriages. Four of the twenty-one members of the Class of '43 were married before graduation; several of the others had announced their engagement. Only the future will reveal the permanence of these ties formed on the eve of parting, but certainly they have grown out of associations reaching back through all the life of the community.

This graduation of '43 meant immediate separation, with the girls leaving for war work in the cities before the end of the week, and every boy awaiting the call to military service after harvest. Facing this insistent future, the young class prophet rejected the usual humorous forecasting of individual careers, and tried seriously, if boyishly, to distinguish some form and substance through the murk ahead.

"We prophesy strength," he said, "for each of our members: strength of duty, of mind, of loyalty, and of character. Duty to our country will always come first, and we shall never shirk that duty. We cannot, of course, prophesy total world peace in the near future or at any other time, but we are very certain that our class will live to see many great inventions for the benefit of mankind, new advancements in medicine and science, and also a greater and more lasting brotherhood among men. We firmly believe that the world shall eventually become a better place, and that all the degrading influences of our civilization shall at last be erased and all men shall once again be free."

Prairie's adults can see more clearly the suffering and disillusionment that lie along the road. No eighteen-year-old would ever have been drafted if they had had their way. Taking older men from family and settled place does not seem half so shocking to them as this mass sacrifice of their youth. But it has proved a convenient way to raise a quota; the boys step in blithely, while the men, mindful of personal interests, draw back and seek exemption.

In lesser sacrifices also the adults have proved less willing than the youth. There is a sense of personal outrage over any shortage of consumer goods. When rationing is imminent, they rush to the stores to buy and hoard; when it comes, they are bitterly resentful, not at some admitted mismanagement, but at the fact of rationing itself. "We might just as well be under Hitler, when the Government tells us what we can eat," they complain. Some of this of course comes from general human selfishness. More comes from the restless years that they have lived without restraint, expressing themselves in immorality and lawlessness, or in individual initiative and creative energy.

There are very general evasions — trading of coupons, fraudulent representations to the ration board. But even so, the people have done their share in increasing the food supply, for they have worked more effectively at gardening and canning than ever before in their history.

Prairie knew — or soon learned — that Japan had captured its automobile tires; but the people drove as before, free from spacial limitations as the winds that swept across the plain. The very thought of mileage restrictions brought a defiant — "Believe me, I'm goin' to drive my car while I can." But when gasoline rationing came — frankly to force the saving of tires — they submitted with less grumbling than might have been expected. Incidentally the young people adjusted themselves quickly and cheerfully to a social life in town, and discovered an exciting pleasure in horseback riding. The weekly allowance furnishes plenty of latitude for business and pleasure in the community, but reduces the radius of longer trips.

Agricultural operations have been carried on with perplexing material shortages and labor shortages. But thanks to the speed of power machinery and the slender strength of young high school students working through vacations and Saturdays, the land has all been planted and the crops have all been garnered. The farmers still have many hours to stand in friendly conversation on the street.

The year 1942 set a high record for agricultural production. Unforgettable sights of the wheat harvest were a little boy of eight or nine standing at the steering wheel of a tractor as he hauled a loaded trailer down to the elevator, because his father's truck tires were worn out, and a slender girl swinging a scoop with practiced rhythm as she shoveled truck-load after truck-load into a vacant building on Main Street. The alfalfa was cut five times that year, the fall furnished abundant wheat pasture, and fat cattle, sheep, and hogs were hauled to the stock yards from every farm.

In the dry spring of '43 the "green bugs" destroyed the barley and oats and damaged the wheat; and a severe summer drought cut short the alfalfa and sorghum crops. This meant less than ten bushels of wheat to the acre — though 77,000 bushels is still stored in the Farmers' Elevator — and a serious feed shortage. The farmers rejoiced when they learned that because of shipments abroad

and the manufacture of industrial alcohol, there would be no acreage limitation for the wheat planting of '43 — "Now we'll show
what this land can do," they exulted — but the continued drought
through the normal time for sowing has made the next year's crop
highly problematical.

The farmers are prosperous, though not receiving the huge incomes of the First World War. The most striking difference has
come from a surplus rather than a shortage of wheat: a price *held
down* by Government action to two dollars a bushel in 1917–18, a
price *held up* by Government action to $1.20 plus benefit payments
for the harvest of '43. Other prices, as in the First World War, have
been artificially checked at a level calculated to stimulate production but to protect the consumer, though the system as before is
tempered by political expediency. Hog prices have been higher
than at any time since 1920, cattle have surpassed the former figure, butterfat has reached 49 cents a pound, chickens 25 cents, eggs
38 cents a dozen. Poultry raising has been especially active, on the
farms for market, in the town for family food; the hatchery turned
out 110,000 chicks for the community in the spring of '43.

A land boom such as brought such disastrous results after the
First World War has not yet appeared. Only two or three farms
have changed hands, and at prices that have remained relatively
stable for many years except during the depression; one level, well-
improved quarter, for example, sold at auction for $12,000 in June
of '43.

Half a dozen farmers in the community have quit the farm —
one or two because of old age and the military induction of a son,
the remainder because of the lure of high wages in war plants.
The town has been disrupted far more than the rural area; probably one-fourth of the families have moved away to centers of war
industry, mainly to Oklahoma cities, but in some cases to the West
Coast. Most of the services that made living convenient are non-
existent; but essential farm services — the elevators, the lumber
yard, a produce market, repair work, tractor supplies — are still
available, and it is through its farms that the community makes its
contribution to war production.

The sight of its deserted houses and the scarcity of farm workers have deepened Prairie's ever-present hostility towards labor.
When the people hear of a strike anywhere in the United States,
they regard it as a personal affront, not to be mitigated by any

miracles of industrial production. The community to a man — and woman — is not only anti-strike, but anti-union, anti-closed shop, anti-wage, anti-labor. This feeling, unless balanced by the return of workers with industrial experience, will be a force to be reckoned with in any post-war reconstruction.

"These labor fellows are all racketeers," "The Government won't let us plant wheat," "How do they expect me to farm when they draft my hired man," "I can't buy a bathtub," and "I bet old Roosevelt'll get plenty of coffee" all entered into the election of 1942. Prairie expressed its anger — the vote was 155 to 46 in some cases — by voting for a Republican governor, a Republican Senator (a Democrat who had supported Willkie in 1940), a Republican Representative, and a Republican member of the legislature.

But the people have never relaxed their support of the war itself. They watch military movements with an hour-to-hour sense of imminence. They are calm in defeat — "It don't look so good," was the sole tight-lipped comment through the disastrous early months of '42 — sober, but tremendously uplifted by victory. They are alert to every event of world significance; apparently they understand at last that their own future is tied up intimately with the welfare of humanity. They are not infallible in forming judgments; and their dependence on favorite radio commentators is almost frightening in its implications. They are not even immune to the divination of witch doctors; they listen — with something less than complete acceptance, but they listen — to a radio preacher of a neighboring city who rants of the end of the world and the fulfilment of prophecy. Thus with unswerving loyalty, albeit with grumbling, with intelligent awareness, and some gullibility, they are attempting to formulate a policy that will guide them — and humanity — through the war and into a constructive peace.

The new society that will emerge is of course uncertain, and Prairie's future is more uncertain still. Probably few of the war workers will ever return. Even the young soldiers who think of the quiet little community with such homesick longing, will probably never find economic opportunities there. The war has probably hastened the decline of the town that was started by the use of the automobile and the growth of mechanized farming, and accelerated by the general depression and the collapse of the oil boom. But the fields still produce, and the world still eats, and the agriculture of Prairie has the elements of permanence.

Possibly the community is witnessing the close of a great cycle that has swung through all the centuries of American agriculture. The "gentleman farmer" living in town and driving his car out to his fields may be at once a reversion to the past and a portent of the future. Centuries ago his European peasant ancestors, like the American Indians, the African natives, the Asiatics, lived in agricultural villages and went out daily to tend their crops. It was a late — and possibly an adventitious — development that put the American farmer alone upon his land. Why not a new village of farmers, citizens of the world through schools and radio and space-consuming transportation, grouped together in friendly sociability, building directly upon the soil? For many years the history of Prairie has been shaping itself toward some such end. But whatever the future, a deal of life has been lived there. It was Plutarch who said:

"As for me, I live in a small town, where I am willing to continue, lest it grow smaller."

INDEX

Cherokee Strip, 4, 24, 40–9, 50–1, 56–7, 60–2, 64–5, 68, 73, 75, 78–9, 89–90, 144–5
China, 234–5
Chinch bugs, 60, 72
Chisholm Trail, 7
Choctaw Nation, 33, 87
Cholera infantum, 37
Christian Church, 32–5, 37, 41, 43, 57, 69, 83–4, 95, 151, 164–5, 168, 231; see also Churches
Christmas, 37, 105, 149, 199–202
Churches: organization of, 32–6, 69, 104–5; finance, 33–5, 37, 56, 83–4, 149; "Strippers" in, 41, 56–7; buildings, 56–7, 66, 70, 74, 83–4, 95, 100, 104–5, 113, 117, 123, 151, 160; activities, 94, 149; influence of Ku Klux Klan, 164–5, 168–71; present condition, 231–2; see also Baptists, Catholics, Christian Church, "Come-outers," Evangelical Church, Methodists, Mormons, Religion, Sunday schools
Clark, John, 8, 18–19, 21, 27, 30–1, 43, 47, 116; family of, 33, 201; Mrs. Clark, 24, 33, 84
Cleveland, Grover, 14, 38, 41, 53, 55, 71
Climate, 104; see also Weather
Clothing, 18, 25, 28, 81
Coal mines, 33, 87, 131
Cobb, Chester, 173
Cobb, Jim, 10–11, 15, 21, 24–5, 31, 43, 45–6
Colby, "Dad," 3–4, 14, 26, 28–9, 31–4, 39, 43, 50, 57–8, 66, 74, 77, 116; "Mother" Colby, 6, 43, 52
Colby, Frank, see Colby, "Dad"
Cole, Jonathan, 70–1, 74, 80, 89, 125, 134–5
Colorado, 86, 134, 180
Combines, 176, 179, 192–3, 212
"Come-outers," 36
Commercial Club, 98–102, 132, 179–80; see also Chamber of Commerce
Communism, 232
Confederate veterans, 70–1, 139–40
Congressional delegate, 16, 38, 71–5, 87–9, 103, 121
Conscription, 152, 154, 235, 241
Constitution of Oklahoma, 122, 125–6, 130
Constitutional convention, 121–2, 124

Co-operatives, see Farmers' Co-operatives
Corporation Commission, 130, 194
Cotton, 102, 127–8, 134–6
Councils of Defense, 153, 155–8, 173
County government, see Government, county
County seat, 14, 16, 28, 61, 68, 98, 101, 139, 180
Covered wagons, 4–5, 38, 43, 46–7, 67, 84, 86
Cowboys, 7–8, 24, 26, 42, 48–9, 88
Coyotes, 5, 46–7, 67, 71
Credit, 10, 25–6, 59, 63–4, 72; see also Bankruptcies, Banks, Mortgages
Crime, 48, 107, 132, 195; see also Outlaws, Thieving
Cross, Bill, 121
Cultural influences, 106, 143, 180, 195, 232; see also "Literaries," Schools
Czecho-Slovakia, 239
Czechs, 76, 105, 231, 238–9

Dairy products, 59–60, 91, 101–2, 133–4, 158, 175, 185–6, 193, 211–12, 243
Dalton gang, 8
Dancing, 23–4, 30, 35, 51–2, 56, 81
Decoration Day, 70–1, 124, 139–40, 195
Deer, 5, 9, 23, 46
Delegate to Congress, see Congressional delegate
Deming Investment Company, 63, 85
Democrats, 14–16, 20–1, 38, 52–3, 55, 62, 72–3, 88, 121–2, 125–6, 130, 151, 166, 171, 238, 244
Depressions: of 1893–6, 59–65, 72; money panic of 1907, 127, 137; of 1921–4, 163, 167, 178; of 1929–33, 195–214
Diphtheria, 38
Drought, see Weather
Drunkenness, 52, 94, 129, 132, 182, 194–5; see also Bootlegging, Prohibition, Saloons

Eaton, Perry, 24, 48, 53, 56, 66, 81, 103, 125, 179, 189
Education, 19, 167, 172; see also Schools
Eighteenth Amendment, 182–3, 225–6; see also Prohibition
Eighty-Niners, 23, 180, 230
Elections: of 1890, 13, 15–16, 20; of 1891, 20–1; of 1892, 38; of 1894, 53–

leges, 7, 50, 54; deeding land for public purposes, 17, 38; by speculators, 41, 43–4, 50–1, 85–6, 95–6; contests, 44, 65; filing on claims, 45, 47; final proof, 50, 54–5, 63, 85, 87, 89; commuting, 54, 85, 87; buying claims, 54, 64–5, 89–90; Free Homes, 72–5, 87–9; in "New Country," 86; in western Oklahoma, 86

Hoover, Herbert, 158–9, 213–14, 219, 233

Hopkins, "Brother," 32–5, 37, 41, 43, 47, 57, 84; "Sister" Hopkins, 57

Horses, viii, 8, 11–12, 27, 41–2, 45, 66, 79, 82, 133, 136, 139, 193, 242

Hoskins, Lew, 48

Hotels, 51, 54, 57

Houses, 4, 6, 8, 14, 17–18, 38–41, 55, 80; see also Buildings

Hughes, Charles Evans, 151

Humor, 10–12, 19, 24–5, 37, 55, 77, 81, 157, 184

Hydrophobia, 113

Idaho, 86

Ideals of pioneers, 11–12, 23, 28–9, 35, 217

Illinois, 27, 85

Immigration, 54, 85–6, 103–4, 135, 147

Incorporation of Prairie City, 98–9

Indian Territory, 7, 120–21, 124–25

Indiana, 13–14, 105

Indians, 8, 40, 44, 120–1, 124, 128, 190

Industrial Legion, 38, 56, 71–2, 81, 215

"Infidel," the community, 31–2

Influenza, 160–1

Insanity, 10, 48, 109–14, 132

Interest rates, 63, 89, 122, 177

Iowa, 6, 85, 122

Irish, 18–19, 33, 36, 73, 105, 167

Isolationism, 150–1, 183, 234–5, 237, 244

Japan, 234–7

Japanese, 134, 238

Jenkins, Old Bareheaded, 19, 24, 81

Jews, 166, 169, 234

Jezek, Anton, 76, 105, 231

Kansas, 4–5, 7, 13–15, 18, 20, 27, 29, 40, 44, 53, 61, 63, 67–8, 73, 87, 100–1, 124, 131, 152, 208

Kansas City, 102, 115

Kennedy, Matt, 52

Kentucky, 13, 104, 108

King, Mrs. Rufus, 81, 201

Kingfisher, 50, 55, 72

Kingman, C. T., 52, 57, 59, 62, 74, 82

Koch, Albert, 157, 160

Koch, Hermann, 44, 76, 85, 89, 98, 115, 134, 160; Mrs. Koch, 76, 160

Ku Klux Klan, 163–72, 178, 183, 213–14, 238

Labor, 10, 27, 33–4, 40, 51, 60, 75, 79, 82, 95–6, 134–5, 152, 163–4, 166, 175, 193–4, 210–11, 215–16, 229, 243–44; see also Unemployment, Work relief

Labor unions, 38, 164, 166, 243–4

Land: size of farms, 20, 64–5, 78–9, 103, 176, 229–30; tenancy, 20, 65, 79, 103, 136, 176–7, 193, 229; sales, 50, 54, 64–5, 85–6, 89, 103–4, 135–6, 176, 193, 212, 243; prices, 50, 64–5, 86, 92, 103, 136, 176, 178, 212, 243; oil leases and royalties, 99–100, 151, 178, 184–9, 191–2, 196, 212; owned by pioneers, 230; see also Homesteading, Mortgages, School land

Land-offices, 45, 50, 55, 65

Land openings, see "New Country," Runs

Lawton, 126

Legislature, territorial: First, 13–14, 16–17, 20; Second, 38; Third, 71; Fourth, 75

Le Rossignol, Antoine, 41, 43, 47, 50–1, 76–7, 87, 92

Lester, Charles, 14, 29, 72, 75, 122, 124

Leutze, Jacob, 154, 157

Lindsey, Dr. C. D., 41, 43–4, 47, 50–3, 85, 89, 92–3, 95–6, 98–9, 115, 125

Lions' Service News, viii, 239–40

"Literaries," 18, 24–5, 56, 81

Live stock, 5, 9, 11–12, 25, 38, 40, 59, 79, 101–2, 133–4, 136, 139, 158, 175, 178, 193, 211–12, 234, 242–3

Livery stables, 91, 137

Lockwood, Helen, 109–13

Lockwood, Martha, 110–12, 114

Lockwood, Paul, 36, 69, 110, 112–14

Lockwood, Thomas, 17, 21, 27, 29, 36, 69, 75, 107, 109–14; Mrs. Lockwood, 25, 29, 31, 36, 69–70, 109–14

Lockwood, Tiny, 109–14

Lockwood, Virgil, 109–13